Using
GRAMMAR
to
IMPROVE
WRITING

SARAH TANTILLO

Using
GRAMMAR
— to —
IMPROVE
WRITING

RECIPES FOR *ACTION*

With Illustrations by
Sandy Gingras

ISBN: 978-1-54393-258-4 (print)
ISBN: 978-1-54393-259-1 (ebook)

Printed in the United States of America

First edition

ACKNOWLEDGMENTS xi

ABOUT THE AUTHOR.. xiii

Introduction: What Problems This Book Attempts to Solve, and How... xv

PART ONE: GUIDING PRINCIPLES OF EFFECTIVE GRAMMAR
AND WRITING INSTRUCTION 1

    CHAPTER 1: What should we STOP doing?................................ 3

    CHAPTER 2: How can we teach grammar more effectively and
    integrate it with writing more systematically? 11

        HOW TO CARRY SOUP.. 12

        PRINCIPLE #1: TREAT STUDENTS LIKE DETECTIVES. 17

        PRINCIPLE #2: EXPLAIN *WHY* THIS LESSON MATTERS......... 18

        PRINCIPLE #3: ASK, "WHAT DO YOU *LIKE* ABOUT THAT
        SENTENCE?" 21

        PRINCIPLE #4: GIVE FASTER FEEDBACK. 27

        PRINCIPLE #5: CELEBRATE SUCCESS...................................... 33

        PRINCIPLE #6: PROVIDE ORAL SUPPORT. 34

        PRINCIPLE #7: MODEL, MODEL, MODEL. 37

HOW TO FIT EVERYTHING IN 38

CHAPTER 3: How can we help students who are not on grade level? 43

FIGURE OUT WHERE THEY ARE. 43

IT'S OK—AND NECESSARY—TO GO BACKWARDS BEFORE YOU GO FORWARDS. 48

START SMALL. 50

KEEP TRACK OF PROGRESS. 50

MAKE SURE EVERYONE IS READING GRADE-LEVEL TEXTS. 51

CHAPTER 4: Which other factors affect how well we write? 53

THE MOST IMPORTANT WRITING STANDARD 53

GENRE, AUDIENCE, AND TONE... 58

ARGUMENT VS. EVIDENCE, STEPS 1-3 REVISITED 62

THE CHALLENGE OF CONCLUDING... 74

COMBATTING LEARNED HELPLESSNESS 75

PART TWO: WHAT SHOULD WE TEACH, GRADE BY GRADE, IN K-12 ELA? 85

CHAPTER 5: Grades K-2 Writing and Language Instruction 87

K-2 WRITING STANDARDS WITH INSTRUCTIONAL GUIDANCE 87

K-2 LANGUAGE STANDARDS... 93

K LANGUAGE STANDARDS: A DEEPER DIVE 95

GRADE 1 LANGUAGE STANDARDS: A DEEPER DIVE 101

GRADE 2 LANGUAGE STANDARDS: A DEEPER DIVE 114

CHAPTER 6: Grades 3-5 Writing and Language Instruction 125

GRADES 3-5 WRITING STANDARDS WITH INSTRUCTIONAL
GUIDANCE 125

GRADES 3-5 LANGUAGE STANDARDS 135

GRADE 3 LANGUAGE STANDARDS: A DEEPER DIVE 139

GRADE 4 LANGUAGE STANDARDS: A DEEPER DIVE 155

GRADE 5 LANGUAGE STANDARDS: A DEEPER DIVE 169

CHAPTER 7: Grades 6-8 Writing and Language Instruction 183

GRADES 6-8 WRITING STANDARDS WITH INSTRUCTIONAL
GUIDANCE 183

GRADES 6-8 LANGUAGE STANDARDS 194

GRADE 6 LANGUAGE STANDARDS: A DEEPER DIVE 196

GRADE 7 LANGUAGE STANDARDS: A DEEPER DIVE 204

GRADE 8 LANGUAGE STANDARDS: A DEEPER DIVE 209

CHAPTER 8: Grades 9-12 Writing and Language Instruction 217

GRADES 9-12 WRITING STANDARDS WITH INSTRUCTIONAL
GUIDANCE 217

GRADES 9-12 LANGUAGE STANDARDS 226

GRADES 9-10 LANGUAGE STANDARDS: A DEEPER DIVE 228

GRADES 11-12 LANGUAGE STANDARDS: A DEEPER DIVE 237

PART THREE: ADDITIONAL RESOURCES 243

CHAPTER 9: Recommended Reading 245

FOUNDATIONAL TEXTS...245

OTHER GRAMMAR BOOKS OF INTEREST 246

WHERE TO FIND MENTOR TEXTS FOR STUDENTS...............247

CHAPTER 10: Appendix..249

K-12 SELECTED LANGUAGE CCS TRACKER   249

SAMPLE OVERVIEWS OF WEEKLY ELA ROUTINES 262

SAMPLE WEEK OF LESSON PLANS: POETRY ANALYSIS AND PARAGRAPH WRITING 267

BONUS CONTENT AND HOW TO ACCESS IT   284

HOW TO USE THE LITERACY COOKBOOK WEBSITE   285

ACKNOWLEDGMENTS

Like my other two books, this one is based on extensive work in the field with passionate, committed educators who wrestle daily with the thorny problem of how best to teach and support the students we all care so deeply about. I cannot name all of my teaching partners here (the list is too long), but I must give special shout-outs to a few.

First, I bow with gratitude to John Norton and Susan Curtis at MiddleWeb SmartBrief for inviting me to write periodically for their helpful blog (https://www.middleweb.com/); those opportunities planted many seeds for this project.

Multiple cheers for Bianca Licata and Allison Paludi: I'm so appreciative of their willingness to try out new ideas—testing the partner feedback protocol, drafting the "Clarify, Elaborate, Praise" Chart (see Chapter 2), and adapting my reading-for-a-purpose ideas (see Chapter 4). Thanks, also, to Jessica Harrell, who contributed several ideas on how to combat learned helplessness (see Chapter 4), and Allison Miller, who provided definitive help with the title. And Mary Ann Reilly's book recommendations (see Chapter 9) are priceless.

For their timely, wise, essential, thought-provoking feedback that measurably strengthened this text, I thank Steve Chiger, Rahshene Davis-Bowie, Jonathan Dec, Christine Gallucci, Anibal Garcia, Doug Lemov, and Katy Wischow.

Once again, I am tickled and honored to include illustrations by my dear friend Sandy Gingras, whose own writing projects continue to inspire me (see https://www.sandygingras.com/).

Last but definitely not least, many thanks to my family and friends for their persistent encouragement and support.

ABOUT THE AUTHOR

S arah Tantillo is the author of *The Literacy Cookbook: A Practical Guide to Effective Reading, Writing, Speaking, and Listening Instruction* (Jossey-Bass, 2012) and *Literacy and the Common Core: Recipes for Action* (Jossey-Bass, 2014) and creator of The Literacy Cookbook Website (http://www.literacycookbook.com). She consults with schools (especially urban schools) seeking to improve student achievement. She taught high school English and humanities in both suburban and urban New Jersey public schools for fourteen years, including seven years at the high-performing North Star Academy Charter School of Newark, New Jersey, where she chaired the Humanities Department and her students achieved a 100 percent passing rate on the High School Proficiency Assessment for Language Arts and Literacy. In addition to teaching, she founded the New Jersey Charter School Resource Center and the New Jersey Charter Public Schools Association. She led the Resource Center from 1996 to 1999 and the Association from 1999 to 2003. Since 2007, she has coached K–12 schools on literacy instruction, curriculum development, data-driven instruction, school culture-building, and strategic planning. She currently writes two blogs, The Literacy Cookbook (http://theliteracycookbook.wordpress.com/) and Only Good Books (http://onlygoodbooks.wordpress.com/). Tantillo earned her B.A. from Princeton University, her M.Ed. from Harvard University, an M.A. from Johns Hopkins University, and her Ed.D. from Rutgers University.

Introduction:

What Problems This Book Attempts to Solve, and How

M any students do not write clearly. I have known this for a long time. We all have.

In my two previous books, I've tried to address this problem by focusing on the role that reading plays in writing because people need to read well in order to write well. *The Literacy Cookbook* shows—among other things—how to use what we know about the comprehension process and vocabulary needs in order to strengthen students' reading and writing skills.[1] Also among other things, *Literacy and the Common Core* zooms in on close reading strategies and explains how to teach argument and evidence in ways that improve students' writing.[2]

While both books chip away at the problem, it's become apparent to me that struggles with grammar are still holding students back. And although there is no shortage of grammar books out there, I haven't found one that integrates grammar and writing instruction, aligned with the Common Core State Standards,[3] as systematically as I would like.

---

1 Sarah Tantillo, *The Literacy Cookbook: A Practical Guide to Effective Reading, Writing, Speaking, and Listening Instruction* (San Francisco: Jossey-Bass, 2012).

2 Sarah Tantillo, *Literacy and the Common Core: Recipes for Action* (San Francisco: Jossey-Bass, 2014).

3 For all references to the Common Core Standards in this book, here is the citation: National Governors Association Center for Best Practices, Council of Chief State School Officers, Common Core State Standards, English Language Arts Standards. Publisher: National Governors Association Center for Best Practices, Council of Chief State School Officers, Washington, DC. Copyright 2010. For more information, visit http://www.corestandards.org/ELA-Literacy.

So I decided to write my own.

Grammar instruction to date has suffered as a result of several key factors. For one, many teachers did not receive effective grammar instruction themselves, so they are uncomfortable with teaching it. It seems outdated and old-fashioned, like riding a horse and buggy to go visit someone in the next town because you don't have a car or a phone. When elders talk about how they used to "diagram sentences," it sounds dry, dull, and quaint. No one wants to go back to those olden times.

Uncertain of the rules and how to present them in an organized and purposeful way, some teachers barely touch on grammar or skip it altogether. Others rely heavily on textbooks that present rules in isolation with repeated drilling as the primary mode of instruction. While students might be able to complete the drills, they often fail to apply the rules in their own writing. This reinforces the impression that teaching grammar seems pointless. Also problematic is that many materials available to support grammar instruction are not helpful—or worse, they actually undermine students' understanding of grammar, syntax, and writing.

How we frame grammar instruction matters. If you view it as "fixing incorrect sentences," you teach it that way. If you view it as "building strong, compelling sentences," you take a different approach. This book explains a new way to teach grammar—systematically and purposefully—in order to strengthen student writing. It offers detailed guidance on which grammar standards to teach when and how to use grammatical forms to capture ideas. This new approach will enable students to write more efficiently and effectively.

In short, though pitched as a grammar instructional manual, this is secretly a book about how to teach students how to write clearly. It should be useful not only to K-12 educators but also to college writing instructors and writers interested in strengthening their practice.

HOW TO USE THIS BOOK

The book is divided into three parts, titled "Basic Ingredients," "Entrées," and "Desserts." Each chapter ends with a "Doggie Bag" of questions to take away and reflect on. These questions will help you review the material and ensure that you're on track to apply what you've learned. You might want to preview these questions before you read each chapter because they can also provide a useful guide to key points.

Where should you start? Although you can certainly dive in any-where, I would strongly encourage you to review Part One's Basic Ingredients, which address fundamental concepts underlying effective grammar instruction. Chapter 1 issues caveats on what *not* to do, Chapter 2 explains essential strategies for integrating grammar and writing instruc-tion, Chapter 3 discusses how to support students who are not on grade level, and Chapter 4 addresses other factors that influence how well we write.

The Entrées in Part Two target the Common Core Language Standards—specifically those regarding the conventions of standard English (i.e., grammar and syntax)—and address this question: "What should we teach, grade by grade, in K-12 ELA?" Each chapter focuses on an important grade band (K-2, 3-5, 6-8, and 9-12) and includes the following:

- The trajectory of selected relevant Writing Standards (e.g., re: writ-ing types) with guidance on how to teach them and

- Language Standards pertaining to conventions with guidance on how to teach them, including sample mini-lessons with pitches that connect the grammar points to reading and writing (with "GENRE ALERT" tags: *If you're teaching THIS writing genre, focus on this grammar standard)*, plus suggestions/examples for how to efficiently assess/diagnose them.

I have clustered the grade levels (K-2, 3-5, 6-8, and 9-12) because my philosophy is that while you should know the standards for the grade you are teaching, you also should be aware of where students are coming from and where they are going. Also, in the Common Core State Standards, the reading bands cut across grade levels. Note: In order to make each grade-level section as comprehensive as possible, I have included all of the information you need, regardless of whether or not it repeats something discussed in a previous grade level. So if you prefer to read only about the grades you teach, you won't miss anything (except all the other grades).

The Desserts in Part Three provide sweet resources, including recommended reading and the K-12 Selected Language CCS Tracker, which will enable you to identify where your students actually are so that you can target their needs and push them forward. Part Three also includes sample overviews of weekly ELA routines and a sample week of lesson plans to illustrate "how to fit everything in." And it explains how to access free bonus content and your free 30-day trial to The Literacy Cookbook (TLC) Website, www.literacycookbook.com, which includes all of the files referenced in this book plus hundreds and hundreds more.

The complete meal, as it were, should enable you to fortify your students with knowledge of grammatical forms that will transform their writing.

ONE LAST THING: THE LITERACY COOKBOOK BLOG

If you would like to keep tabs on my latest thinking on topics related to literacy instruction and the Common Core, in addition to reading this book and using the resources on the TLC Website, please consider following The Literacy Cookbook Blog, which is free and can be found at http://theliteracycookbook.wordpress.com/. Many of the ideas in this book appeared in earlier form in the TLC Blog.

Let's dig in!

Part One:
Guiding Principles of Effective Grammar and Writing Instruction

If you've read either *The Literacy Cookbook* or *Literacy and the Common Core* (or, ideally, both), you already know that the Basic Ingredients deal with the fundamentals of the book. In this case, we're talking about the fundamentals of effective grammar and writing instruction. In this section, we first tackle what *not* to do, then explore essential strategies for integrating grammar and writing instruction, identify ways to support students who are not on grade level, and finally, consider other factors that influence how well we write.

chapter
ONE

What should we STOP doing?

If you ask most people to define "grammar," they will probably rattle off a list of items such as parts of speech, punctuation, capitalization, subject-verb agreement, syntax, sentence structure, and maybe "gerunds, but I can never remember what they are." The sad truth is that most people view grammar as disconnected from writing. One could even argue that the Common Core State Standards have reinforced this distinction by listing grammar standards separately from writing standards.

So it should be no surprise that for decades (or longer), teachers have tended to address grammar in isolation, as in, "Today is Tuesday, so we're doing prepositions. Turn to page 57 in your grammar book."[4] Which is not exactly a motivational approach.

Here's another non-surprise: When grammar is taught this way, students do not apply grammar rules in their own writing. In fact, considerable research has shown that teaching grammar in isolation does not improve student writing.[5]

And yet, unsure how else to proceed, many teachers have continued to take this approach.

This book is about choosing a different approach—a different set of recipes.

It's a truism that when you want to make a change, you must first acknowledge there is a problem. We have now done that.

The next thing you must do is *stop doing things that don't work.* I've identified four key things to stop doing immediately. Note: You might think something on this list "worked" when you were a student. Keep in mind that some people can learn things no matter how they are taught. Considerable research shows that these four items do not help most students learn how to apply grammar rules in their writing.

Number one: Stop launching lessons where you make students copy down the rules or definitions for grammatical terms first. I've seen many teachers start grammar lessons this way; possibly they believe they are building students' background knowledge before discussing how to use whatever grammar concept they want to introduce. But this approach does not work—because **telling is not teaching.** Students are not empty vessels that we pour knowledge into. Taking notes without processing the information does not lead to learning. And if you explain a rule or definition first, you've killed any suspense or motivation to learn more. So even a few minutes later when you show some examples of the concept, students are like, "Meh." They are not invested because you have not inspired their curiosity. There is no mystery, nothing to figure out. They don't see what's

---

4 Some ideas from this chapter were previously raised in my MiddleWeb blog "What We Can Do When Kids Don't Write Clearly," Nov. 3, 2015, found at https://www.middleweb.com/26076/what-we-can-do-when-kids-dont-write-clearly/.

5 Constance Weaver, *Teaching Grammar in Context* (Portsmouth, NH: Boynton/Cook, 1996), 9-10.

in it for them. It's just another rule, which they might or might not want to follow. Just to be clear: **I'm *not* saying we should *never* mention rules or definitions, only that we shouldn't *lead* with them.** In the next chapter, we'll talk about how to flip the script in a way that's more effective.

Number two on the hit list is the "Daily Oral Language" (DOL) approach, in which teachers provide sentences riddled with random errors and students are supposed to correct them. Reading specialist Mark Pennington enumerates sixteen reasons why DOL doesn't work, and I agree with each one. He points out that DOL is proofreading, not sentence construction; that it tries to teach writing without actually having students write; that it uses bad writing models to teach good writing; and that it doesn't teach the *whys* and *hows* of grammar and mechanics.[6] Requiring students to fix grammatically incorrect sentences might be a form of assessment, but it is not instructive. Students who know the relevant grammar rules will do fine; the ones who don't will not learn the rules. We must teach before we assess.

Even worse, some teachers implement this weak approach incorrectly. I cannot overstate the horror I've felt while watching students copy down incorrect sentences first—*practicing the wrong thing!*—and then struggling to keep up as the class went over the corrections; those students were actually *damaged* because all they walked away with was a list of ungrammatical sentences.

One day as I was explaining the problems with DOL to a group of teachers, one woman raised her hand and said, "Wait. I'm the Grammar Queen. Let me tell you what I do." I listened. She explained that if she were teaching, say, misplaced modifiers, she would give students a sentence with a misplaced modifier and ask them to correct it, to see if they could.

My response was twofold. First, if you want to use grammatically incorrect sentences for diagnostic purposes, that's OK as long as the sentences manifest only the *one* error that you're trying to diagnose. DOL sentences typically contain four or more errors, all arbitrarily strewn

---

6 "Why Daily Oral Language (D.O.L.) Doesn't Work," Mark Pennington, Pennington Publishing Blog, Aug. 29, 2009, found at http://penningtonpublishing.com/blog/grammar_mechanics/why-daily-oral-language-d-o-l-doesnt-work/.

throughout the sentence like dirty socks. And second, it would be better if you gave students *two* sentences instead—one with a misplaced modifier and one without—and asked students to explain what was different about the two sentences, identify which one was incorrect, and explain how they would fix it. Students sometimes offer the correct answer ("*I think you need a comma there?*") without knowing what they're talking about. We must push them to *explain* their ideas to demonstrate understanding.

Number three: Stop drilling. Again, just because students can "circle the abstract nouns in the sentences on page 45," it doesn't mean their writing will include such nouns. In these types of activities, students often guess. The other day, I sat in the back of a classroom where a boy identified "Brazil" as an abstract noun. The teacher said, "Try again," and he offered, "Concrete?"—clearly uncertain even though it was the only other option. There is no way such exercises will translate into effective writing. So stop. Please stop.

Last, but definitely not least: Let's stop over-editing student work. Many English teachers spend hours and hours marking up students' papers (I personally lost years of my life to this grueling exercise), and when they hand those papers back, the students simply glance at the grade and do nothing with the feedback. The result is that the teachers become highly skilled at copy editing and their students' writing does not improve. So here's some good news: You don't have to lose entire weekends to paper grading anymore. Instead, you must decide this: *What do you want students to do with your feedback?* If they are not going to use it to revise, then notes are not really necessary—and even if students are going to revise, those notes don't have to be *extensive*. Over-editing is also pointless because editing marks alone can't teach grammar rules; at best, they remind students of rules they already knew.

As we'll discuss in Chapter 2, your feedback should be timely and strategic—in short: targeted. Consider using the following "Essay Writing Rubric," which includes space for brief, targeted remarks and a separate section for "Self-Improvement Goals" that students can set in each subsequent paper, using your comments as a guide. You can weight the skills you've taught more heavily, and you don't have to assess all aspects of the rubric every time.

Essay Writing Rubric:[7]

NAME:		ASSIGNMENT:
WRITING STANDARDS	**PTS.**	**COMMENTS**
INTRODUCTION: • ENGAGING HOOK • 1-2 SUPPORTING STATEMENTS • THESIS/MAIN ARGUMENT • THESIS SUPPORT STATEMENT		
TOPIC SENTENCES: • TRANSITION from previous paragraph • Provide ARGUMENT for the paragraph that answers "HOW?" and "WHY?" in response to the thesis		
EVIDENCE: • Use ACCURATE information and detailed support to prove thesis and topic sentences, including: • CONTEXT surrounding quote (who, what, where when, why?) • QUOTE/PARAPHRASE • EXPLANATION of quote and how it illustrates/proves the point		

---

7 This "Essay Writing Rubric" is on the TLC "Using Grammar to Improve Writing" page found at https://www.literacycookbook.com/page.php?id=161. It can also be found, along with many other writing rubrics, on the TLC "Writing Rubrics" page at https://www.literacycookbook.com/page.php?id=87.

CONCLUSION: • Draw logical, thoughtful conclusions and/or make reasonable predictions. • ENGLISH: Usually answers, "What is the author's ultimate message?"		
PROPER MLA CITATION FORMAT: • PARENTHETICAL CITATIONS in proper format		
LENGTH requirement: _____paragraphs/pages.		
OVERALL PERSUASION/COHERENCE/ DEPTH OF ANALYSIS: • Build convincing paragraphs and an overall argument that flows clearly. • Make thoughtful, logical, and substantial inferences throughout the paper. • Anticipate potential counter-arguments. • Find meaningful connections.		
GRAMMAR: • USE STANDARD ENGLISH (S/V agreemt, present tense, pron/ant agreemt). • PUNCTUATE PROPERLY. • STRUCTURE SENTENCES EFFECTIVELY.		
EFFECTIVE USE OF SOPHISTICATED VOCABULARY:		
SUBTOTAL	**/100**	
SELF-IMPROVEMENT GOALS:		
	/20	

At this point, you might be asking: *If we're not going to improve student writing, why teach grammar at all?* Some teachers ask this rhetorically and use it as an excuse to opt out of teaching grammar altogether. Which is unfortunate. Because when you write, you need to know enough grammar to be dangerous (or interesting, or clear, or compelling). Knowing none is not a solution.

So let's look at what you *should* do.

- How did the ideas in this chapter challenge, change, or confirm what you previously believed about grammar instruction?*

- Which resources and ideas from this chapter will you share with colleagues? Why?

*See footnote[8]

8 I want to give a shout-out to Kylene Beers and Robert E. Probst in Reading Nonfiction: Notice & Note Stances, Signposts, and Strategies (Portsmouth, NH: Heinemann, 2016) for pointing out the value of this question—along with two others I also love: "What surprised you?" and "What did the author think you already knew?"

chapter
TWO

How can we teach grammar more effectively and integrate it with writing more systematically?

When I was growing up, my grandmother used to cook the most delicious meat sauce with spaghetti. Every time I visited, I'd pester her for the recipe and she'd always say, "I'll give it to you when you get married!" This went on for years. Then one day I happened to arrive early, and caught her pouring a jar of Prego into the pot. So I didn't have to get married.

What is the point of this story? Sometimes the best dishes are prepared with pre-made ingredients. And that analogy holds true for the sentences and paragraphs we write. Let me explain.

HOW TO CARRY SOUP

The central premise underlying this book is that **we use our understanding of grammar and grammatical forms to generate writing; so, the more deeply we understand grammar and grammatical forms, the more effectively we can write.** Much like my grandmother's use of the store-bought tomato sauce that formed the foundation of her famous meat sauce, these forms enable writers to carry content forward—almost like containers.

The problem for students is that until they learn these forms, they don't have the containers they need in order to show what they know. Imagine trying to carry soup without a container: That's what writing is like for many students. It looks like they only know carrots.

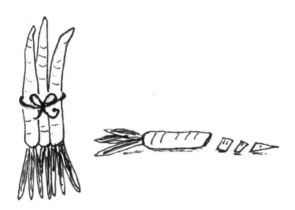

This is not a new idea. A number of writers have shed light on the importance of these forms. For example, in *They Say/I Say*, Gerald Graff and Cathy Birkenstein provide an array of templates to help students organize their thoughts, such as "According to X…" and "X disagrees when she writes…."[9] As the subtitle suggests—*The Moves That Matter in Academic Writing*—you need to know certain "moves" in order to acknowledge others' arguments and generate your own.[10] In *How to Write a Sentence and*

---

9 Gerald Graff and Cathy Birkenstein, *They Say/I Say: The Moves That Matter in Academic Writing* (New York: W.W. Norton, 2010, 2nd edition), 46.

10 Gerald Graff and Cathy Birkenstein, *They Say/I Say: The Moves That Matter in Academic Writing* (New York: W.W. Norton, 2010, 2nd edition).

How to Read One, Stanley Fish points to their book as a demonstration of the idea that "forms are the engines of creativity." He continues:

> "Our templates," say Graff and Birkenstein, "have a *generative quality* [italics mine], prompting students to make moves in their writing they might not otherwise make or even know they should make" or (I would add) even know they could make. "When we ask students to write sentences using the form 'at this point you probably object that'—they invariably come up with objections—content—that had never occurred to them and they would never have written on their own."[11]

As Graff and Birkenstein have demonstrated, such forms can actually help students generate ideas and language. Along these same lines, in *Image Grammar*, Harry Noden deploys the analogy of the writer as artist, painting with participles, absolutes, appositives, and so on.[12] Noden was to some degree following in the footsteps of Francis Christensen, whose *Notes Toward a New Rhetoric* in 1967 paved the way for others to look at sentences in chunks and use grammatical forms (such as participles, appositives, and absolutes) to expand them.[13]

Christensen himself gives credit to John Erskine, the originator of the Great Books courses, who in 1946 advanced this principle: "When you write, you make a point, not by subtracting as though you sharpened a pencil, but by adding." Erskine noted that nouns and verbs and main clauses "serve merely as the base on which meaning will rise....The modifier is the essential part of any sentence."[14] Christensen devotes much of his book to demonstrating how to unpack and expand sentences with modifiers.

---

11 Stanley Fish, *How to Write a Sentence and How to Read One* (New York: HarperCollins, 2011), 29-30. He is referring to Graff and Birkenstein's pages xx and xxi.

12 Harry Noden, *Image Grammar: Using Grammatical Structures to Teach Writing* (Portsmouth, NH: Heinemann, 1999).

13 Francis Christensen and Bonniejean Christensen, *Notes Toward a New Rhetoric: Nine Essays for Teachers* (n.p., 3rd ed., ed. Donald Stewart, 2007).

14 Christensen, 21-22, citing John Erskine in his essay "The Craft of Writing," found in *Twentieth Century English* (Philosophical Library, 1946).

Constance Weaver has also written about the challenges of grammar instruction and the value of teaching modifiers to help students write good sentences.[15] As she notes in *Grammar to Enrich and Enhance Writing*, there are several ways to teach grammatical constructions for writing:[16]

1) **Sentence imitating**, in which students follow the pattern used in a model: e.g., you write a two-word sentence; they write a two-word sentence.

2) **Sentence expanding**, in which students expand a sentence with a modifier that follows the pattern used in the model: e.g., you show them how an appositive works, and they add appositives to given sentences, like adding train cars to a toy train.

---

15 For example, see Constance Weaver, *Teaching Grammar in Context* (Portsmouth, NH: Boynton/ Cook, 1996) and *The Grammar Plan Book: A Guide to Smart Teaching* (Portsmouth, NH: Heinemann, 2007).

16 Constance Weaver and Jonathan Bush, *Grammar to Enrich and Enhance Writing* (Portsmouth, NH: Heinemann, 2008), 89. Note: The constructions are hers; the examples are mine.

3) **Sentence combining**, in which students combine two or more sentences to create a longer, more effective sentence: e.g., you model how to combine independent clauses, and they follow suit.

4) **Sentence restructuring**, in which students revise an existing sentence to make one or more parts subordinate to the main part, or rearrange the elements to best effect: e.g., you could show them how to add a relative clause such as "who loves flowers" to a given independent clause such as "Her daughter Margaret rearranged the flowers in the vase," resulting in: "Her daughter Margaret, who loves flowers, rearranged them in the vase."

In *Teach Like a Champion 2.0*, Doug Lemov proposes a technique called "**Art of the Sentence**," in which students are given either **sentence starters** (e.g., "Over time…" or "The author tries to convey the message that…" or "Although the main character appears to…") or **sentence parameters** (e.g., "Using the word *ambiguous*…" or "Write a sentence about the Jersey Shore that includes the words *tourism* and *erosion*") to prompt students to craft thoughtful sentences about complex ideas.[17] This

---

17 Doug Lemov, *Teach Like a Champion 2.0: 62 Techniques That Put Students on the Path to College* (San Francisco: Jossey-Bass, 2015). For a detailed description of "Art of the Sentence," see 285-289.

technique, to some degree, could incorporate all four of the approaches that Weaver discusses.

Significant research has shown that sentence combining has produced positive results—and in *The Teacher's Guide to Effective Sentence Writing*, Bruce Saddler focuses his entire book on that approach and provides useful guidance and practical tools to implement it.[18] While this approach can be helpful, research has also found that sentence combining alone is *not sufficient* to improve writing.[19]

More recently, in *The Writing Revolution*, Judith Hochman and Natalie Wexler explain how to teach with the Hochman Method, which "breaks the writing process down into manageable chunks and then has students practice the chunks they need, repeatedly, while also learning content."[20] For example, they note that if you want students to make their sentences more informative and varied, you can't just tell them to do that; you have to teach them "specific ways of creating more complex sentences—for example, by using appositives." And again, you won't simply tell them what an "appositive" is. They explain:

Instead, you'll show them examples of appositives and then have them underline appositives in sentences you provide. For example, you might give them "George Washington, the first president of the United States, is often called the father of our country." In that sentence, they would underline "the first president of the United States." Then you'll give them a list of nouns—related to the content they've been studying—along with a list of appositives, and ask them to make the appropriate matches. After that, students will add appositives to sentences you provide or construct sentences around appositives you give them. After a while, you'll ask your

---

18 Bruce Saddler, *The Teacher's Guide to Effective Sentence Writing* (New York: The Guilford Press, 2012).

19 Constance Weaver, *Teaching Grammar in Context* (Portsmouth, NH: Boynton/Cook, 1996), 134-135.

20 Judith C. Hochman and Natalie Wexler, *The Writing Revolution: A Guide to Advancing Thinking Through Writing in All Subjects and Grades* (San Francisco: Jossey-Bass, 2017), 7.

students to create their own sentences using appositives—and eventually, they'll simply do that spontaneously.[21]

What Hochman and the others recognize is this essential idea: **Good writers write one good sentence after another.**[22] It sounds really obvious when you say it, but if you spend enough time in classrooms, you will realize that most people don't frame writing instruction in this way. Teachers often assume students can write sentences, so they skip to things like paragraphs, "small moments," and essays. There is nothing wrong with these assignments. But we need to build up to them. Students might be able to write simple sentences, but can they write *complex* sentences? The inability to write complex sentences is one reason that their paragraphs can seem so repetitious and wooden—or as Doug Lemov puts it, like this: "I think X. I think Y. I think Z."[23]

Now let's look at the key principles that will guide us in designing effective lessons to help our students write better sentences.

PRINCIPLE #1: TREAT STUDENTS LIKE DETECTIVES.

As I noted in Chapter 1, having students copy down definitions or rules *before* they see the concept in action is ineffective. Students may not possess enough background knowledge to comprehend the definition or rules, and even if they do, mere exposure to definitions and rules does not make them stick. The act of copying something down does not teach you the information. As Brown et al. note in *Make It Stick*, "When you're asked to struggle with solving a problem before being shown how to solve it, the

---

21 Judith C. Hochman and Natalie Wexler, *The Writing Revolution: A Guide to Advancing Thinking Through Writing in All Subjects and Grades* (San Francisco: Jossey-Bass, 2017), 7.

22 Some ideas from this chapter were previously raised in my MiddleWeb blog "What We Can Do When Kids Don't Write Clearly," Nov. 3, 2015, found at https://www.middleweb.com/26076/what-we-can-do-when-kids-dont-write-clearly/.

23 Doug Lemov, *Teach Like a Champion 2.0: 62 Techniques That Put Students on the Path to College* (San Francisco: Jossey-Bass, 2015), 285.

subsequent solution is better learned and more durably remembered."[24] In other words, one must *wrestle* with information in order to own it.

For this reason, we should teach grammar and grammatical forms *inferentially*. **Think of your students as detectives.** Your job is to provide clues and let them figure things out. They should analyze given forms (especially looking for patterns), explain how the forms work, and apply this knowledge in their own writing. For example, to teach how pronouns work, you could start by posting a few simple pairs of sentences on the board:

	COLUMN A	COLUMN B
1.	I like John.	I like him.
2.	I saw Shana at the game.	I saw her at the game.
3.	I met Christine and Rochelle for dinner.	I met them for dinner.
4.	I like basketball.	I like it.

Then, ask students to discuss with a partner what they notice about the sentence pairs. While some will undoubtedly remark that every sentence begins with "I," others will notice the pattern and grasp that "him" is representing John, "her" is Shana, and so on. In this way, they can derive the definition of "pronoun" as "a word that stands in for a noun." Once students can explain *how* pronouns work (at least in this preliminary way), we'll need to turn to the next step: *why* they matter.

PRINCIPLE #2: EXPLAIN *WHY* THIS LESSON MATTERS.

On the heels of figuring something out about pronouns, students might be excited for a moment, but that won't last. Pretty quickly they will wonder why they should care.

---

24 Peter C. Brown, Henry L. Roedigger III, and Mark A. McDaniel, *Make It Stick: The Science of Successful Learning* (Cambridge, MA: The Belknap Press of Harvard University Press, 2014), 86.

Every lesson needs a pitch or rationale, and grammar lessons are no exception. To arrive at a persuasive pitch, it helps to start with a lesson objective that is RPM: rigorous, purposeful, and measurable. A detailed discussion of RPM objectives appears in *Literacy and the Common Core.*[25] Here's a quick overview:

How to Create RPM Objectives*

Example: Students will be able to identify personal pronouns and explain how they work in order to use pronouns in their own writing.

- **Rigorous:** Use Bloom's Taxonomy to push for higher levels of rigor. Check out this Website on Bloom's Taxonomy: https://cft.vanderbilt.edu/guides-sub-pages/blooms-taxonomy/
- **Purposeful:** Use the key phrase "in order to." Students need to know why they're doing this work, and so do you. The phrase "in order to" forces you to clarify the purpose for the lesson.
- **Measurable:** Your objectives should imply the use of assessment. As the word suggests, they should be "able to be measured." For example, "Students will draw inferences from Chapter Six of *The Kite Runner* in order to determine key traits of the main characters" implies that students will record those character traits in some fashion—possibly on a graphic organizer.** Or perhaps they will write paragraphs or essays analyzing the main characters. In any case, you can explain to students why they are going to draw these inferences so that they will do so with, again, a greater sense of purpose. PS: Doing something "in order to pass a quiz" is rarely motivating, so it's better to stay away from explicitly stating such assessments in your objectives.

*See footnote [26] / **See footnote [27]

Once you've written your objective, you'll need to decide **how to frame the pitch.** Here are some options:

1. **Springboard from your RPM objective to clarify WHY we're doing what we're doing TODAY** ("because by the end of class today,

---

25 Sarah Tantillo, *Literacy and the Common Core: Recipes for Action* (San Francisco: Jossey-Bass, 2014), 76-82. The review table that follows is slightly modified from the original.

26 Sarah Tantillo, *Literacy and the Common Core: Recipes for Action* (San Francisco: Jossey-Bass, 2014), 77-78. This review table is slightly modified from the original.

27 Khaled Hosseini, *The Kite Runner* (New York: Riverhead Books, 2003).

you will be able to _____"). *After this pronoun lesson, you will be able to write your own sentences using pronouns.*

2. **Explain how having this skill/information will make their lives easier** ("being able to/knowing _____ will make your life easier because _____"). *Good writers use pronouns to avoid repeating themselves. Imagine how silly it would sound if I wrote an entire paragraph about dinner with Christine and Rochelle and never used "they" or "them"! "Christine and Rochelle ordered lasagna. Christine and Rochelle liked the garlic bread. Christine and Rochelle talked about their jobs...."*

3. **Point to FUTURE USES of the skill(s)/information IN CLASS** ("because by the end of this unit/this week, we will use this skill/information to _____"). *We're going to move from writing sentences with pronouns to writing stories with pronouns! We're also going to learn about other types of pronouns and how they work!*

4. **Point to FUTURE USES... IN COLLEGE, CAREER, AND LIFE** ("because when you're in college/at work, you will want to be able to _____"). *Knowing this information about pronouns will help you become a stronger writer, something you'll need to be in college, in whatever job you have, and in life.* [OK, maybe this one is a bit melodramatic. Perhaps not the best frame for pronoun acquisition.]

5. **Remind students that once they master this skill/information, NO ONE CAN TAKE IT AWAY FROM THEM.** *This is true.* [Also a bit dramatic.]

Note: Making a pitch at the beginning of a lesson is necessary but not sufficient. It's best to remind students *throughout the lesson* why you're doing what you're doing to increase engagement and motivation.

When it comes to grammar concepts, it helps to tie them to the *genre* of writing you're working on if you can. For example, you might say, "Since we're writing narratives, it's important for us to remember how to format dialogue properly." In Part Two, we'll identify genre-related opportunities as we comb through the grammar standards.

PRINCIPLE #3: ASK, "WHAT DO YOU *LIKE* ABOUT THAT SENTENCE?"

One of my favorite quotes is the advice Henry James offered to a novice writer: "Try to be one of the people on whom nothing is lost!"[28] To a writer, this suggests the importance of paying close attention to the details of your life. To a reader, I think it means you should read like a writer, analyzing the text to see "how it's done" so you can emulate what you appreciate about the writing. And this is where grammatical forms come in.

We can learn a lot about grammatical forms when we analyze text. Let me demonstrate with this paragraph:[29]

> It's true. The inside of a typical fifth-grader's desk is difficult to keep organized and clean. There is never enough room for all of the textbooks, workbooks, independent reading books, binders, and notebooks, much less the pens, pencils, and erasers. Plus, because students are normally not permitted to leave their seats during class, it is tempting to use the desk as a personal trash can. Crumpled paper, used tissues, bent paper clips, and loose pencil shavings need a place to go, and the desk makes a convenient hiding spot.

Find the Topic Sentence

I like to use this paragraph to teach "Argument vs. Evidence Step 3" (see Chapter 4). The initial goal of our analysis is to *locate the topic sentence* in this body paragraph (ostensibly from an essay on how challenging it is to be a fifth-grader). But I also bake in some teachable moments. As you will see, we pay microscopic attention to every sentence. And at the end of this

---

28 Henry James, "The Art of Fiction" (published in *Longman's Magazine* 4 [September 1884], and reprinted in *Partial Portraits* [Macmillan, 1888]); found at https://public.wsu.edu/~campbelld/amlit/artfiction.html.

29 This paragraph and a different version of its explanation originally appeared in Sarah Tantillo, *The Literacy Cookbook: A Practical Guide to Effective Reading, Writing, Speaking, and Listening Instruction* (San Francisco: Jossey-Bass, 2012), 40-41.

section, you'll find a bonus recipe that explains how to move from this paragraph analysis into an essay-writing lesson cycle.

A student volunteer reads one sentence at a time as we pick the paragraph apart. Here's the script I typically follow:

"We're going to use what we've learned about *how to tell if something is an argument or not* to determine which sentence seems like the argument of the paragraph; that's our topic sentence. Usually the topic sentence appears in the first two or three sentences. Very, very rarely, it might be the last sentence. But we're going to look at the beginning and see what we can figure out."

After the volunteer reads, *"It's true,"* I feign perplexity. "It's true? What's true? I don't even know what the writer is talking about. Wait. Actually, I do know something. This is a TRANSITIONAL SENTENCE. Remember how I told you that this is a body paragraph in an essay about how it's challenging to be a fifth-grader? This sentence is referring back to the previous body paragraph." We mark "TRANS" next to that sentence.

After the volunteer reads the next sentence (*"The inside of a typical fifth-grader's desk is difficult to keep organized and clean"*), I ask students to turn to their partners and discuss whether they think this sentence is an argument or not, and if so, which of our three "argument rules" it follows:

> **ARGUMENTS...**
>
> 1: Use arguable/debatable words.
> 2: Use cause/effect language.
> 3: Raise "Why" or "How" questions.

I cold-call to see if students have noticed that the sentence uses arguable or debatable words ("typical," "difficult," "organized," and "clean")— "also known as ADJECTIVES," I remind them; also, the sentence raises "Why" or "How" questions ("Why/How is it difficult for a fifth-grader to keep his desk clean?").

Before the volunteer reads the next sentence, I cue the class: "If that *is* the topic sentence, then the rest of this paragraph should support that argument. Let's read the next sentence and see."

Teachable Moments

After we read "*There is never enough room for all of the textbooks, workbooks, independent reading books, binders, and notebooks, much less the pens, pencils, and erasers*," I ask students for a thumbs-up if they believe this sentence supports the previous sentence or a thumbs-down if not. Then I pause to get students to pay closer attention to the word choice. "Why didn't the writer simply say, 'There is never enough room for all of their *stuff*, period'? Tell your neighbor what you think about this."

Cold-calling should elicit that "stuff" is too vague and the details make the situation easier to visualize. Occasionally someone will also notice that the overstuffed-ness of the sentence: The *form* enacts the meaning; the sentence is as overstuffed as the desk. As I like to tell them, I know the writer. That was what she was aiming for.

As the volunteer resumes reading, "*Plus--*" I abruptly interject: "'Plus': an unusual transition! Much better than 'first, second, thirr-rrdzzzzz'" (here I feign falling asleep from boredom). Then we read the whole sentence:"*Plus, because students are normally not permitted to leave their seats during class, it is tempting to use the desk as a personal trash can.*"

Here's another teachable moment. Far too many humans have been told to "never start a sentence with 'Because,'" and I find this tragic. In my experience (fourteen years teaching high school English, and more than eleven consulting in schools), students who are told to never start a sentence with "because," tend to suffer from what I call "The Because Problem." Let me explain. If I said, "I like pizza because it has cheese on it," what could you infer about me? I like cheese, yes. But what if I said, "Pizza has cheese on it because I like it"? That would be wrong. Pizza has cheese on it *because that's the recipe for pizza.* But a lot of students contort their writing in this manner—like some kind of twisted pretzel—because they don't know how to use "because" properly. See the box below for a quick way to address this problem.

"Demonstrated Grammar"

Here's a quick way—in the middle of this lesson—to teach students how to start a sentence with "because" properly. I ask for a volunteer to stand up next to me. Let's pretend his name is James.

"James," I tell the class, "is a complete sentence, an independent clause. Look at him: He's independent; he can stand by himself. James, your sentence is, 'I drink lots of them.' Please say that."

James repeats the sentence.

"See? He's still standing, solid. He's a complete sentence, an independent clause. Now watch what happens when I come around, Miss *Dependent* Clause!" I stand on one foot and lean toward James, saying, "Because I like chocolate milkshakes, comma" and tap James's shoulder to indicate he should say his sentence.

"I drink lots of them," he says. I balance my weight by resting my hand on his shoulder.

"See what just happened? I'm Miss Dependent Clause, and when I attach myself to James, we can stand together, solid. But now watch what happens if he steps away from me."

James steps away, and I repeat, "Because I like chocolate milkshakes," but this time I almost fall down. "I'm a *dependent* clause. I can't stand alone. I need James, Mr. Complete Sentence, Mr. *Independent* Clause, to help me stand up." And, scene.

I call this Demonstrated Grammar.

"What Do You *Like* About That Sentence?"

As we prepare to read the last sentence, I announce, "I swear I'm not fishing for compliments, but after we read this sentence I want you to answer this question: 'What do you *like* about this sentence?' And let me also note: There is not one right answer to this question."

The volunteer reads: "*Crumpled paper, used tissues, bent paper clips, and loose pencil shavings need a place to go, and the desk makes a convenient hiding spot.*" I invite students to confer with their partners and try to identify at least three things they like about that sentence. I'm hoping they will notice how the adjectives transform the nouns ("because paper isn't trash until it's crumpled…"), the objects are personified, "convenient" is a strong vocabulary word, and the conclusion is punchy (not "This shows how difficult blahblahblah…").

Asking, "What do you *like* about that sentence?" could be game-changing. Think about what this question implies: 1) Sentences have structures that writers create purposefully, which we can analyze and admire; 2) Sentences can be written well or poorly; 3) If you figure out "what works" in that sentence, you could imitate it and write your own good sentences.

In order to be able to ask that question, though, we need great texts to analyze. Not all texts are created equal. Some are dry, repetitious, formulaic, dull (*I'm looking at you, most content-area textbooks!*). Others are lucid and compelling. Or, poignant. Or, they percolate with wit. They make us think and feel; they take us to a particular locale and a specific, memorable instance. We can feel the writer's pulse. Captivating models can change how students feel about reading (eliciting, "Hey, this is funny!" or, "That's so true!") and in turn, how they feel about writing. If we want students to think of themselves as writers, the message must be inviting—as in, "Look: you could write like *this!*"

In sum, asking, "What do you *like* about that sentence?" suggests that individual sentences are important and worth crafting carefully. Here are some final tips:

- Ask this question with student writing as well as professional texts.

- Remind students that there is "not one right answer to this question" so that they won't freeze up in fear that they are missing something but will instead open themselves to the possibilities.

- Model your own answers to the question so that students get a sense of ways in which it could be answered.

- Make sure there *is* something to admire about the sentence you're analyzing.

BONUS RECIPE: How to Move from Paragraph Analysis into Essay Writing*

1. After analyzing this "desk" paragraph, if you'd like to move into an essay-writing lesson cycle, here is a recipe for that.

2. DIRECTIONS: "The original paragraph was a body paragraph from an essay on how challenging it is to be a fifth-grader [or sixth-grader, or seventh-grader]. So now we're going to reconstruct that essay."

3. BRAINSTORM: Students brainstorm 10-12 places where they store things besides a desk (e.g., backpack, bedroom closet, locker).

4. FILTER: Remind them that "good writers don't just brainstorm and pick the first shiny object; they filter." Direct students to star the three items on the list that they think they could say the most interesting things about (not the *most* things, the most *interesting* things). Then direct students to select ONE of those three to write about.

5. USE THE MODEL: Students replace "desk" in the original topic sentence with their selected item ("The inside of a typical fifth-grader's _____ is difficult to keep organized and clean.") and write the rest of the paragraph on their own. While they might imitate the original paragraph in some ways—and that's fine—remind them that they must pick appropriate details: "We don't store exactly the same things in our bedroom closet as in our desk at school." Actively monitor and support students as they draft.

6. SHOW CALL:** Using your document camera, share a few exemplars. Celebrate success. Provide constructive feedback.

---

7. REPEAT the process for the next body paragraph, except this time the brainstorming is on "reasons why it's challenging to be a fifth-grader" (e.g., more homework, more responsibilities at home, etc.). Filter again. This time, students draft their own topic sentences. Monitor their efforts and Show Call to share some exemplary topic sentences. Then let them finish the paragraphs and Show Call again.

8. DISCUSS THE PURPOSES OF AN INTRODUCTION: At this point, students have three body paragraphs: mine, ours, and theirs. Now they need an introduction. Ask them what the introduction needs to accomplish. They should be able to surface the ideas of hooking the reader and stating the thesis. The hook should be appropriate for the topic. For example, "I always thought growing up would be easy. But I was wrong," is better than "Have you ever been a fifth-grader?" Let students draft, then share a few of their examples.

9. DISCUSS WHAT A CONCLUSION SHOULD AND SHOULD NOT DO: For decades, many teachers taught this approach to writing: "Tell 'em what you're gonna tell 'em, tell 'em, then tell 'em what you told 'em." Ugh. Ugh, ugh, ugh. So repetitious and boring. Your readers are not dumb; you don't need to tell them the same thing three times. The conclusion should be insightful and punchy. It could be one sentence. For example, "I hope sixth grade is easier." Drop the mic and walk away.

*See footnote[30] / ** See footnote[31]

PRINCIPLE #4: GIVE FASTER FEEDBACK.

As I noted in Chapter 1, over-editing student work is not effective. Various factors influence students' responsiveness to comments on their writing: 1) whether or not they can revise the work, 2) whether or not they understand the comments and how to act upon them; and 3) how long it's been since

---

30 A slightly different version of this recipe appeared in Sarah Tantillo, *Literacy and the Common Core: Recipes for Action* (San Francisco: Jossey-Bass, 2014), 139-140.

31 Doug Lemov, *Teach Like a Champion 2.0: 62 Techniques That Put Students on the Path to College* (San Francisco: Jossey-Bass, 2015). For a detailed description of "Show Call," see 290-299.

they wrote the piece. Waiting two weeks to give extensive editing/revision comments that students cannot act upon is a recipe for indifference.

RECIPE FOR INDIFFERENCE

1 c. over-editing
½ c. impossible suggestions
¼ c. HUH? inciting comments
1 tbsp. no clues about how to fix anything
Stir slowly, wait two weeks, then
sprinkle with wishful thinking.
Bon Appetit!

For this reason, feedback must be *timely and strategic*. And it's easier to give quick feedback if students are working in manageable bites. If you wait until they've written an entire essay, it's too late. Drafting in chunks means they won't go too far afield before you redirect them. Nothing contributes to student disaffection with writing more than being told after they have written an entire essay that they need to rewrite the whole thing.

Feedback can be provided in several ways: 1) through teacher-led mini-lessons, 2) through teacher-student conferences, or 3) through a partner feedback protocol.

Mini-Lessons

One of my favorite techniques for revising/editing mini-lessons is what Doug Lemov calls "Show Call": The teacher selects student writing to share with the class by projecting it with a document camera and asks the class for input on what is effective and what can be improved.[32] What I particularly love about this technique is that it builds accountability for written work. When students know that their writing might be shared with the whole class—whether for praise or constructive feedback or ideally both—they tend to pay more attention to the quality of their work. Norming the class to expect this approach establishes the expectation that good writing can always be improved.

---

32 Doug Lemov, *Teach Like a Champion 2.0: 62 Techniques That Put Students on the Path to College* (San Francisco: Jossey-Bass, 2015). For a detailed description of "Show Call," see 290-299.

Whether you select student work while actively monitoring[33] the class or while sorting through drafts afterwards, Show Call enables you to provide targeted feedback on points that benefit more than one student. PS: Make sure you seal the deal at the end of the mini-lesson. My friend Katy Wischow, a writing consultant who observes classes frequently, notes, "A lot of teachers are on board with using student writing in lessons, but beyond asking for input, they're not sure what to do next – so it kind of fizzles out, into a 'Well, there you go' sort of an ending."[34] Instead of "Well, there you go," give students explicit directions, such as "Look at your own work now and ask yourself the same questions we just asked about these examples. Then do what you need to do."

Writing Conferences

By contrast, writing conferences obviously have a more limited audience. But your feedback should still be targeted. One reason teachers hesitate to confer with students is that they worry about how much time conferences take. **Here are some ways to save time:**

- Before you launch conferences, **tell the class what you plan to focus on** (e.g., "I'm just looking at your first body paragraph to see how effectively you've provided context and explanation for your evidence!").

- **Direct students to star or underline what you want to look at** (e.g., "Please underline the topic sentence in your first body paragraph!") before they meet with you.

- **Call three students up to meet with you at the same time.** Give them quick feedback one by one, noting, "Stay here and work on that; I'll come back to you in a few minutes." This approach—much like when you're in the Post Office and the clerk tells you to step aside but

---

33 I prefer the term "active monitoring" over Paul Bambrick-Santoyo's "aggressive monitoring," which to me sounds a bit hostile (See Paul Bambrick-Santoyo, *Get Better Faster: A 90-Day Plan for Coaching New Teachers* [San Francisco: Jossey-Bass, 2016], 43).

34 Katy Wischow, Email to the author, February 18, 2018.

stay at the counter to finish taping your package so you won't have to wait in line again—has several benefits. First, it offers *accountability with support*: Students begin working on revisions avidly, knowing you will circle back; and it eases their anxiety to know that if they have any questions, you're right there to help. Second, it enables you to *capitalize on students' inherent nosiness*: While waiting for their turn, they can "academically eavesdrop" and learn from the feedback that their peers receive. Third, it offers *flexibility*: If several students require the same coaching, you can spontaneously conduct a small-group mini-lesson instead.

Here are some additional points to consider:

- **Remember to start your comments with at least one bit of specific praise** (even if you have to say something hedgy like, "I like what you're trying to do here") and maintain an upbeat, appreciative tone to open their ears to whatever else you might need to say. When students become defensive, you may lose precious time trying to convince them to listen. And an instructional compliment is powerful in and of itself, not just to forestall defensiveness. Naming a specific positive thing that students are doing means they will repeat it (and they might have just done it by accident, so now they know it's a real thing!).

- **Try to frame your feedback in the form of questions instead of judgmental statements:** "Can you clarify what you meant here?" will be received more easily than "This part confused me," or "I don't understand this sentence."

- **When a student's writing is garbled, it helps to ask, "What were you *trying* to say here? Just tell me."** Often students can explain their ideas more effectively orally, and then you can say, "OK, that sounds good. Let's write that down."

- **You may want to ask students read their own work aloud** so you can praise them as they go and so they can catch their own errors, especially punctuation problems. You can prompt them with this:

"When you read this part, see if you *pause*, or if you *stop*. Then we can decide what to do."

- **Avoid specific corrections such as "You need a semi-colon here" because that kind of advice doesn't *teach* students anything.** Instead, provide grammatical context and ask a question to see if students can figure out how to make their own corrections. For example: *"You have two independent clauses—two complete sentences—separated only by a comma. So right now it's a run-on. What do you need to do to make this work?"* If the student appears stumped, offer options: *"You could add a conjunction after the comma, you could replace the comma with a semi-colon (if you think the sentences are closely related), or you could break this into two separate sentences. Which do you want to do?"*

Partner Feedback Protocol

Along these same lines, when it comes to *peer* feedback, be careful. Instead of "peer editing," which is often a recipe for the blind leading the blind ("I think you need a comma there, but I'm not really sure"), **students should take turns reading aloud their essays or narratives while their partners read along and pause to tap the desk twice** (with two fingers or a pencil, to avoid cacophony) **any time they have a question or a specific sentence or phrase to praise.**[35] The writers should pause to listen and make notes, but not respond orally because we don't want students to negotiate over the revisions (they might never get through the essay!); the writers will consult their notes and revise later.

This simple feedback can be powerful. Authentic praise is useful and motivating. The questions can be either a request for **clarification** ("Could you please clarify that?" or something more precise such as "Could you please clarify what you meant by 'Scout should have realized that'?") or a request for **elaboration** ("Could you please elaborate on that?" or "Could

---

35 This section draws from my MiddleWeb blog post "Shared Reading Needs to Have a Clear Purpose," Jan. 8, 2018, found at https://www.middleweb.com/36699/shared-reading-needs-to-have-a-clear-purpose/.

you say more about why you think Ponyboy did that?"). Questions along these two lines—as opposed to statements such as "That's confusing," which can raise defensive hackles—show that the reader is genuinely interested. More importantly, they also invite the writer *to explain*. Which is what good writers do. Relentlessly.

A couple of bonus notes:

- It's crucial to role-play this partner feedback protocol. Then invite students to share what they think could be challenging about using this approach. Do some preemptive troubleshooting.

- After students practice a few times, ask them to evaluate their feedback: "What went well? What do you need to work on?" Some of your strongest students might struggle because they are so eager to offer advice. And although it's tempting to answer the questions immediately, the writers should limit themselves to taking notes.

- See the chart below, designed by several teachers at Great Oaks Legacy Charter School in Newark to support middle school students using this protocol.[36]

---

36 Shout-outs to teachers Bianca Licata and Allison Paludi for this chart, which I have modified slightly.

Clarify	Elaborate	Praise
Could you please clarify that?	Could you please elaborate on that?	I really liked it when you wrote…
Who/what is this specifically about?	Where did this term come from?	I like the way you described…
Where is this taking place?	Why is this situation/event important?	I appreciate your perspective about…
Why is this taking place? How is this taking place?	How does this definition connect to your claim?	I would like to _____ the way you did because it ……
What exactly is happening here? Can you explain the definition of this term?	How does this evidence support your topic sentence?	It was helpful for me when you wrote _____.
What do you mean by…?	How does this reason connect to your overall thesis statement?	_____ helped me better understand your thesis statement.

PRINCIPLE #5: CELEBRATE SUCCESS.

It should probably go without saying, but one way to motivate students is to celebrate their success. Again, Show Call is a great technique for doing this, which is why it appears so frequently (as you will see) in the instructional guidance in Part Two.[37]

Students particularly love it when you project their work and ask, "What do you *like* about that sentence?" One teacher I know likes to review

---

37 Doug Lemov, *Teach Like a Champion 2.0: 62 Techniques That Put Students on the Path to College* (San Francisco: Jossey-Bass, 2015). For a detailed description of "Show Call," see 290-299.

the previous day's Exit Ticket (an explicit assessment of the objective)[38] with this question, featuring the best student exemplar(s) from the day before. This approach has inspired students to pay closer attention to the quality of their Exit Ticket writing in hopes that their work will be featured the next day.

PRINCIPLE #6: PROVIDE ORAL SUPPORT.

No one emerges from the womb knowing how to speak or write coherently. Depending on your home and school environment, you may or may not be surrounded by people who speak standard English. We learn to speak by imitating what we hear, and we tend to write the way we speak. Students who have been immersed in nonstandard English or who are English Language Learners (ELLs) will need to learn how to **code-switch**—i.e., how to switch from the informal language they might use with friends/family to the formal language required in school/work).

Please note that merely correcting students—ala "It's 'He does,' not 'He do'"—does not work. They do not retain the information (for the same reason that copying notes doesn't stick: telling isn't teaching), and at a certain point, they may feel so badgered by your relentless correcting that they shut down and stop talking. ELL students often struggle with a lack of confidence in speaking to begin with, painfully aware that they do not possess all of the vocabulary they need to say what they want to.

As Wheeler and Swords note, African American vernacular English (AAVE) is a form of English with its own system of rules, so framing it as "bad" or "wrong" can be confusing and demeaning to students. Moreover, such framing suggests that their loved ones who speak this way are doing something wrong. That's why it has to be presented as *different*, not less than.

---

38 Doug Lemov, *Teach Like a Champion 2.0: 62 Techniques That Put Students on the Path to College* (San Francisco: Jossey-Bass, 2015). For a detailed description of "Exit Ticket," see 190-193.

However, it is informal, and students must learn to distinguish between formal and informal language in order to use the appropriate language depending on what context they find themselves in.[39]

Research has shown that while the "correctionist" approach doesn't work, a technique called "contrastive analysis" does. Hanni Taylor found that leading students in explicit discovery by contrasting the patterns of AAVE and standard English showed a 59.3 percent decrease in African American vernacular features in their college writing after 11 weeks.[40] Taylor observed that students had been neither aware of their dialect nor of "grammatical black English features that interfere in their writing."[41]

To use "contrastive analysis" with third-graders, Wheeler and Swords took a few key steps. First, they introduced the notion of distinguishing between "formal" and "informal" codes with the analogy of dress codes. Students easily described the difference between what they were required to wear at school versus what they preferred to wear on the weekends.[42] Once they absorbed that distinction, they could readily apply it to speaking situations; for example, they recognized that "Yes, sir" and "Excuse me" are formal while "Yo, wa's up?" and "He ain' nobody" are informal. To reinforce this concept, Swords then devised a simple two-column chart with formal and informal plural patterns and invited students to compare and contrast the sentences in each column, as follows:[43]

---

39 Rebecca S. Wheeler and Rachel Swords, "Codeswitching: Tools of Language and Culture Transform the Dialectally Diverse Classroom," *Language Arts* 81, no. 6 (July 2004).

40 Hanni U. Taylor, *Standard English, Black English, and Bidialectalism: A Controversy* (New York: Peter Lang, 1991).

41 Hanni U. Taylor, p. 150, cited in Rebecca S. Wheeler and Rachel Swords, "Codeswitching: Tools of Language and Culture Transform the Dialectally Diverse Classroom," *Language Arts* 81, no. 6 (July 2004), 474.

42 Rebecca S. Wheeler and Rachel Swords, "Codeswitching: Tools of Language and Culture Transform the Dialectally Diverse Classroom," *Language Arts* 81, no. 6 (July 2004), 475.

43 Rebecca S. Wheeler and Rachel Swords, "Codeswitching: Tools of Language and Culture Transform the Dialectally Diverse Classroom," *Language Arts* 81, no. 6 (July 2004), 476.

Formal	Informal
I have two dogs.	I have two dog.
Taylor likes cats.	Taylor likes cat.
All the boys…	All the boy…

Swords then led students in a discussion in which they inferred the ways you could show "more than one"—not just that a noun ends with "-s" but also that number words and other words in the sentence or paragraph can provide clues.

By repeating this contrastive analysis technique with other grammar points (such as patterns for showing possession), Swords found that her students became increasingly adept at inferring the rules and applying them to create their own examples. And when she read *Flossie and the Fox*[44] with her students, they were able to notice that Flossie speaks in the patterns of AAVE while the fox speaks in standard English patterns.[45]

Once your students have accumulated a base of knowledge about such patterns, you can develop a checklist or "shopping list" so that students can self-edit papers by combing through them for informal patterns that need to be switched.[46]

Also relevant to code-switching is what Kristen Turner refers to as "digitalk"—when students write informally, the way they do while texting on their phones.[47] (Though not technically "oral," it is based on students' perceptions of speech.) Turner draws on Wheeler and Swords's work to suggest methods for making secondary students more aware of their use of texting language in school writing and less formal contexts. For example,

---

44 Patricia C. McKissack with Rachel Isadora (illustrator), *Flossie and the Fox* (New York: Penguin, 1986).

45 Rebecca S. Wheeler and Rachel Swords, "Codeswitching: Tools of Language and Culture Transform the Dialectally Diverse Classroom," *Language Arts* 81, no. 6 (July 2004), 476-477.

46 Constance Weaver and Jonathan Bush, *Grammar to Enrich and Enhance Writing* (Portsmouth, NH: Heinemann, 2008), 147; Figure 9-1 is modified from Wheeler and Swords (2006). *Code-Switching: Teaching Standard English in Urban Classrooms* (Urbana, IL: NCTE).

47 Kristen H. Turner, "Digitalk: A New Literacy for a Digital Generation," *Phi Delta Kappan* 92 (2010): 41-46. Print.

teachers can invite students to brainstorm an array of different speaking situations (e.g., in a classroom with a teacher, in the lunchroom with a friend, or at home with a parent), then ask them to translate a teacher-created sentence into each of the different settings. For example, the teacher-created text "Hello. How is your day?" might become "Yo, what's up?" with a friend. And again, teachers can create a checklist so that students can self-edit their work to switch from informal language to formal.[48]

Beyond raising students' awareness about the need to code-switch in different contexts, it's important to use class discussions as an opportunity to build students' working knowledge of grammar. As I noted in *The Literacy Cookbook*, the Number One way you can improve learning in your school is to strengthen students' speaking and listening skills and habits (See *TLC* Chapter 4 for more than a dozen tips on how to train students to speak and listen more effectively).[49] Training students how to use academic language and holding them accountable for that will translate directly into more fluent writing.

PRINCIPLE #7: MODEL, MODEL, MODEL.

It is a sad truth, but many teachers *assign and assess* writing instead of *teaching* it. Every year, from grade level to grade level, we assume the teachers before us taught our students how to write. And every year, we're surprised when they struggle. Probably the most common problem is that we neglect to model what we expect. If you want students to write an effective sentence, paragraph, or essay, you must begin by showing them what one looks like.

Here's how I think of it: The first time my elementary school gym teacher taught us how to shoot a layup, he didn't simply shoot a layup and walk away, saying, "Save yourselves!" He showed us how to hop and lift the ball and drive our knee up and flick the ball so it would hit that

---

48 Kristen H. Turner, "Flipping the Switch: Code-Switching from Text Speak to Standard English," *English Journal* 98.5 (2009): 60-65.

49 Sarah Tantillo, *The Literacy Cookbook: A Practical Guide to Effective Reading, Writing, Speaking, and Listening Instruction* (San Francisco: Jossey-Bass, 2012), 115-142.

box on the backboard. As we took turns trying to imitate him, he gave us immediate, specific feedback. He wasn't evaluating us. He was coaching us towards success.

What would it look like if writing teachers saw themselves more as writing *coaches*? In *Mechanically Inclined*, Jeff Anderson recommends a "mentor text" approach, which involves showing students models of sentence structures they can imitate.[50] For example, you might begin with a two-word sentence—subject-verb, as in, "She laughed."—and have students write their own quickly, on a white board, holding it up for instant feedback. Then you could build a longer sentence—say, a three-word sentence that includes a word that describes the verb, also known as an adverb. As in, "She laughed loudly." In the process of comparing examples with classmates, students would derive the understanding that adverbs are often formed by adding "-ly" to an adjective. In this way, we can teach parts of speech organically and authentically. It's a win-win cycle: As students practice applying the rules in their own writing, they build their knowledge of grammar rules and strengthen their writing.

And one last thing: *Implicit* instruction is just as important as explicit. Modeling proper grammar and strong vocabulary both orally and in writing—on all handouts and posted materials—is crucial.

HOW TO FIT EVERYTHING IN

A friend who read an early draft of this book observed that his 11th and 12th graders are "far too shaky" on the K-2 standards and wondered how often he should teach grammar in order to help them catch up. Indeed, "How can I fit everything in?" is a question every teacher asks. I wish there were one simple answer. In the Appendix, I've provided "Sample Overviews of Weekly ELA Routines" and a "Sample Week of Lesson Plans: Poetry Analysis and Paragraph Writing"[51] in an attempt to illustrate how it might

---

50 Jeff Anderson, *Mechanically Inclined: Building Grammar, Usage, and Style into Writer's Workshop* (Portland, ME: Stenhouse Publishers, 2005), 65-67.

51 The "Sample Week of Lesson Plans: Poetry Analysis and Paragraph Writing" can also be downloaded from the TLC "Using Grammar to Improve Writing" page found at https://www.literacycookbook.com/page.php?id=161.

look to integrate vocabulary building, close reading, a couple of targeted grammar standards, and writing with revision in one week of instruction.

My strong recommendation for ELA teachers is to target at least one grammar standard per week—or two, if possible. Some standards lend themselves to being combined, and many can be included as "teachable moments." For example, when you teach how to capitalize titles (L 3.2.A), it makes sense to also teach which titles to underline/italicize and which to put in quotation marks (L 5.2.D); you don't have to wait until students are in 5th grade to teach that. In Part Two, I point out such opportunities.

The good news is that the Language Standards are highly iterative. For example, pronouns are introduced in kindergarten, then reappear in various forms in grades 1, 2, 3, and so on. In the guidance for each grade, I note how previous grades address related grammatical forms. And the "K-12 Selected Language CCS Tracker" in the Appendix[52] enables you to quickly scan for such progressions.

In order to accomplish our goals, it helps to do what works. As I noted in Chapter 1, research has shown that teaching grammar in isolation does not work. This is why the guidance in Part Two stresses that **students should demonstrate their grasp of grammatical concepts in their own writing, first in sentences then in paragraphs.** And, to make their practice meaningful, authentic, and efficient, students should write about **a current text or topic they are studying.** There is no reason to write about arbitrary/random topics (such as those typically found in grammar textbooks).

And how you frame the work matters. Maybe instead of "wrestling," students should "dance, run, or play" with the content that they are excited about—the novel you are reading in class, or the lab experiment they just did. Writing should not be drudgery!

---

52 The "K-12 Selected Language CCS Tracker" can also be downloaded from the TLC "Using Grammar to Improve Writing" page found at https://www.literacycookbook.com/page.php?id=161. Additional standards-related resources are available on the TLC "Standards" page found at https://www.literacycookbook.com/page.php?id=138.

"dancing with content"

One way to save time—to fit everything in—is to not waste it. **How you practice** what you are trying to learn will determine how effectively and efficiently you build those skills. The advice in this book is based largely on what cognitive scientists call **deliberate practice**, an approach to skill development that is characterized by the following traits (which I'll explain in the context of this book):[53]

- It develops skills that other people (i.e., experts such as published authors) have already figured out how to do, and it **requires coaching** by someone (i.e., a trained teacher) who knows how to help others develop those skills. And this coach/teacher must provide **timely feedback** so the students can quickly modify and improve their work (see "Principle #4: Give Faster Feedback" earlier in this chapter).

- It requires students to try things that are **just outside their comfort zone**, so they have to keep pushing themselves—for example, to learn how to use new grammatical forms, to combine forms, and to write increasingly complex sentences and longer texts.

- It sets **specific—not general—goals**. So students must "try to master how to weave subordinate conjunctions into their writing" as

---

53 Anders Ericsson and Robert Pool, *Peak: Secrets from the New Science of Expertise* (Boston: Houghton Mifflin Harcourt, 2016), 99-100. I've paraphrased their characterization of deliberate practice and incorporated examples that explain how my book reflects this approach.

opposed to vaguely "becoming better at writing" or even "writing more clearly."

- It requires **focused attention**. Whether you're evaluating text to answer "What do you *like* about that sentence?" or attempting to craft a compelling sentence of your own, you must pay close attention to detail.

- It produces and depends on **mental representations**. Students need to see and imitate models that use grammatical forms effectively. Grasping the models will enable them to apply these forms in their own writing. My belief is that taking the approach of deliberate practice (which undergirds the standard-by-standard guidance in Part Two) will set students up for greater writing success. But I also I want to make two additional points.

Number one: **Frequency** of deliberate writing practice (that applies grammatical forms) matters. Try to include a second opportunity to write every week. An efficient, effective way to do this is by using the "Read-Write-Discuss-Revise cycle," in which students read, write a quick response to an open-ended question, discuss their ideas with the whole class, then take time to revise their writing as a result of having learned something from that discussion.[54]

It might not be feasible to complete an entire essay or story every week. But you should try to include a Revision Day at least once every two weeks (though weekly would be better). Whether students need to revise an essay, narrative, or paragraph, the Revision Day should feature a whole-class mini-lesson followed by time for students to work independently, engage in the partner feedback protocol, and participate in writing conferences.

Secondly and finally for now: How often you introduce grammar concepts and have students practice them will depend on how far behind students are. My observations in the field indicate that many students in

---

54 Doug Lemov, Colleen Driggs, and Erica Woolway; *Reading Reconsidered: A Practical Guide to Rigorous Literacy Instruction* (San Francisco: Jossey-Bass, 2016), 172-174.

grades 4-12 are operating at a 2ⁿᵈ grade level when it comes to the Language Standards. My hope is that teachers will begin using this book as a guide from kindergarten forward, and in time, fewer students will have to play catch-up. Then, when they come to 12th grade, they'll actually be on the 12th grade level. But in the meantime, we will have to modify what we do. The next chapter looks at what to do when students are not on grade level.

- Of the seven principles discussed in this chapter, which ones changed, challenged, or confirmed what you previously believed?
- Which principle(s) do you think you need to pay more attention to? Why?
- Which resources and ideas from this chapter will you share with colleagues? Why?

chapter
THREE

How can we help students who are not on grade level?

The title of this chapter is a question I hear every day. No matter what grade(s) or subject(s) you teach, students will inevitably come to you with gaps. I have written about how to bridge reading gaps in *Literacy and the Common Core*.[55] Here are some things you can do related to grammar and writing gaps:

FIGURE OUT WHERE THEY ARE.

In any given class, for any particular skill, some students will be on grade level, some will be above, and some will be below. No matter what the mix

---

55 Sarah Tantillo, *Literacy and the Common Core: Recipes for Action* (San Francisco: Jossey-Bass, 2014), 45-55.

is, you need to know where every single student is. How do you figure this out? There is not one right answer. In fact, it will help to collect multiple data points to divine the clearest picture.

While this book focuses on writing and grammar skills, keep in mind that one must read well in order to write well. In fact, the writing standards also assess the reading standards: Beginning in grade 4, Writing Standard #9 requires students to "Draw evidence from literary or informational texts to support analysis, reflection, and research." Specifically, Writing Standard 4.9A states: "Apply grade 4 Reading standards to literature" and 4.9B states: "Apply grade 4 Reading standards to informational texts." So you should determine students' reading levels—probably even before you assess their writing.

Reading level assessments vary in cost, time-consumption, and utility. Here are some questions to answer when selecting a tool or program:

- How much can you afford to spend on the program and materials/technology?
- How much staff training will be required?
- How much staff time will be required to administer the assessment(s)?
- How much class time will be required?
- How subjective/objective is the assessment? Note: If teachers' Student Growth Plan results (and performance reviews) are dependent on their students' reading level improvements, they should not personally administer all of the assessments; an adaptive computer-based tool would be preferable or at least more objective.
- How frequently will you conduct assessments?
- How easily will you be able to translate the results into useful reports to drive instruction?

Once you've established a mechanism for ascertaining reading levels, look at student writing. A simple brief writing assessment—even just a paragraph—could be quite revealing of their grammar strengths and weaknesses.

Consider also paragraph responses (timed or untimed) based on the class's current reading. Depending on what grade level you teach and how much students know about the Argument vs. Evidence Steps (see Chapter 4), you might want to guide their writing by providing a text-based topic sentence for them to respond to. Here's an example of the directions and a model paragraph:[56]

---

56 This "Sample Paragraph Responses for *When I Was Puerto Rican*" can be found on the TLC "Using Grammar to Improve Writing" page found at https://www.literacycookbook.com/page.php?id=161. Additional paragraph response models for various texts can be found on the following TLC Website pages: "Analyzing Literature" (https://www.literacycookbook.com/page.php?id=2), "MS English Lessons & Units" (https://www.literacycookbook.com/page.php?id=42), and "HS English Lessons & Units" (https://www.literacycookbook.com/page.php?id=41).

Name_____ Date_____**CHAPTER 1**

<u>When I Was Puerto Rican</u>: "*Jibara*" questions (30 pts. project)

DIRECTIONS: For EACH TOPIC SENTENCE given, write a paragraph proving it, citing at least two direct quotes from the chapter. Each paragraph must be 7-10 sentences long (including the topic sentence). Be sure to cite the page numbers properly. See the model. Attach looseleaf if needed. Be sure to read the whole chapter before writing a paragraph.

<u>**EXAMPLE:**</u>

In the beginning of the story, Kenny's mother makes it clear that she does not respect his friend Harry. When Harry shows up to invite Kenny to his party, Kenny's mother is "furious" that Harry is in her house (82). She follows Kenny into his room to tell him why he should not be hanging around with such "*basura*" (82). She says that Harry acts like "the devil, tempting innocent barrio girls and boys with free drugs and easy living until they [are] hooked" (82). She goes on and on about how Harry's behavior is wrong. She says that people who follow Harry "pay the price" (82). She is clearly worried about how Kenny's friends will influence him.

Negi does not always obey her mother, and on several occasions her disobedience leads to negative consequences.

Here is a simple checklist for scoring paragraph responses.[57] (Note: I typically require students who score 7 or lower to rewrite their paragraphs until they've mastered the work. I provide mini-lessons and writing conferences to support their revision efforts.)

---

57 The "Paragraph Response Scoring Checklist" can be found on the TLC "Using Grammar to Improve Writing" page at https://www.literacycookbook.com/page.php?id=161. This and other writing rubrics can also be found on the TLC "Writing Rubrics" page at https://www.literacycookbook.com/page.php?id=87.

PARAGRAPH RESPONSE Scoring Checklist
NAME_____
___/2: Clarity ___/2: Context (for both quotes) ___/2: Evidence (2 quotes, either verbatim or paraphrased) ___/2: Explanation (for both quotes) ___/2: Length (7-10 sentences incl. the topic sentence) ___/10=TOTAL

Another useful data collection tool is Cloze reading passages (text with blanks they must fill in); although Cloze reading assessments typically focus on reading comprehension and vocabulary knowledge, they can also be customized to shed light on students' working knowledge of grammar. Below is an example for assessing personal pronoun usage.

Cloze Reading Passage: Personal Pronouns
Directions: Read the following paragraph and insert the appropriate personal pronouns in the blanks where needed. Today was an unusual, marvelous day. Although _____ was February 21st and should have been freezing out, _____ was 76 degrees and sunny. My dear friend Cecilia, an 80-year-old woman whom _____ have known for decades, came to my house for a visit. She had recently received some bad news from the doctor, and _____ told me about that. I made lunch for us, a simple salad with cold chicken, and _____ both drank hot lemon ginger tea. After lunch, _____ took a walk to the beach and marveled at the deliciousness of the salty air. When _____ returned to my house, _____ sat on the benches on my back deck, soaking in the sunlight. Then _____ both had the same idea at the same time. "Let's look at the clouds," she said. _____ both lay back on the benches and looked up at the sky. _____ was so peaceful to watch the clouds and birds moving overhead. We weren't in any hurry. _____ took our time, grateful for our friendship and this glorious day.

Last but definitely not least, you can create simple grammar diagnostic tools to quickly determine whether or not students are familiar with specific rules. In Part Two, we'll see examples of those.

IT'S OK–AND NECESSARY–TO GO BACKWARDS BEFORE YOU GO FORWARDS.

Understandably, it's a little unsettling when students come to you several grades below where they should be and you are expected to help them meet your grade's standards. It can be tempting to plow ahead with your grade's standards and disregard what students might have missed. But that would be a mistake. As I noted in *Literacy and the Common Core*, the standards are organized like a ladder: You can't really skip a rung.[58] And when it comes to grammar, the knowledge base is particularly cumulative: Students can't hop over the fundamental concepts in the standards for grades 3, 4, and 5, and simply start working on grade 6.

So yes, you have to go backwards. You need to figure out what students know and don't know. You don't have to reteach *every single standard*. As you will see, many skills are repeated throughout the grades. But you do need to fill in the gaps. Trajectory analysis charts (like the excerpt below) can help you identify those gaps.[59]

---

58 Sarah Tantillo, *Literacy and the Common Core: Recipes for Action* (San Francisco: Jossey-Bass, 2014), 163-166.

59 The complete files of "Trajectory Analysis Charts for Language Standards" and "Trajectory Analysis Charts for Writing Standards" are on the TLC "Using Grammar to Improve Writing" page found at https://www.literacycookbook.com/page.php?id=161. Additional standards-related resources are available on the TLC "Standards" page found at https://www.literacycookbook.com/page.php?id=138.

	STANDARD
L K.1	A) Print many upper- and lowercase letters. B) Use frequently occurring nouns and verbs. C) Form regular plural nouns orally by adding /s/ or /es/ (e.g., dog, dogs; wish, wishes). D) Understand and use question words (interrogatives) (e.g., who, what, where, when, why, how). E) Use the most frequently occurring prepositions (e.g., to, from, in, out, on, off, for, of, by, with). F) Produce and expand complete sentences in shared language activities.
L 1.1	A) Print all upper- and lowercase letters. B) Use common, proper, and possessive nouns. C) Use singular and plural nouns with matching verbs in basic sentences (e.g., He hops; We hop). D) Use personal, possessive, and indefinite pronouns (e.g., I, me, my; they, them, their; anyone, everything). E) Use verbs to convey a sense of past, present, and future (e.g., Yesterday I walked home; Today I walk home; Tomorrow I will walk home). F) Use frequently occurring adjectives. G) Use frequently occurring conjunctions (e.g., and, but, or, so, because). H) Use determiners (e.g., articles, demonstratives). I) Use frequently occurring prepositions (e.g., during, beyond, toward). J) Produce and expand complete simple and compound declarative, interrogative, imperative, and exclamatory sentences in response to prompts.
L 2.1	A) Use collective nouns (e.g., group). B) Form and use frequently occurring irregular plural nouns (e.g., feet, children, teeth, mice, fish). C) Use reflexive pronouns (e.g., myself, ourselves). D) Form and use the past tense of frequently occurring irregular verbs (e.g., sat, hid, told). E) Use adjectives and adverbs, and choose between them depending on what is to be modified. F) Produce, expand, and rearrange complete simple and compound sentences (e.g., The boy watched the movie; The little boy watched the movie; The action movie was watched by the little boy).

L 3.1	A) Explain the function of nouns, pronouns, verbs, adjectives, and adverbs in general and their functions in particular sentences. B) Form and use regular and irregular plural nouns. C) Use abstract nouns (e.g., childhood). D) Form and use regular and irregular verbs. E) Form and use the simple (e.g., I walked; I walk; I will walk) verb tenses. F) Ensure subject-verb and pronoun-antecedent agreement. G) Form and use comparative and superlative adjectives and adverbs, and choose between them depending on what is to be modified. H) Use coordinating and subordinating conjunctions. I) Produce simple, compound, and complex sentences.

See Chapter 4 for more thoughts on how to use trajectory analysis charts to strengthen instruction (and see the TLC Website for the actual charts).[60] And in Part Two, we'll explore how to use the trajectory of the Language Standards to teach them systematically.

START SMALL.

No matter how pressured-for-time you might feel, don't try to master three standards in one day. Because you won't.

KEEP TRACK OF PROGRESS.

In the interest of efficiency, don't waste time teaching standards that students have already mastered. In order to monitor skills they are learning, create a system that enables you to track progress on particular skills/ standards. It could be as simple as a spreadsheet with a list of skills/standards and three or four columns noting how you have addressed them (and when): *introduced, practiced, practiced again, assessed.* See the TLC Website to download the "K-12 ELA Common Core Standards Tracker"

---

60 The complete files of "Trajectory Analysis Charts for Language Standards" and "Trajectory Analysis Charts for Writing Standards" are on the TLC "Using Grammar to Improve Writing" page found at https://www.literacycookbook.com/page.php?id=161. Additional standards-related resources are available on the TLC "Standards" page found at https://www.literacycookbook.com/page.php?id=138.

and the "K-12 Selected Language CCS Tracker."[61] (Note: The "K-12 Selected Language CCS Tracker" also appears in the Appendix.)

Also, consider giving students a personal tracker to remind them of what they have mastered and what they still need to master. Invite students—especially middle and high school students—to self-assess on which skills/standards they believe they've mastered, then give them a diagnostic to see if they actually have mastered those skills/standards. It's important for students to own their progress. If they don't know their own strengths and weaknesses, how can they take steps to improve?

MAKE SURE EVERYONE IS READING GRADE-LEVEL TEXTS.

One day I was sitting with a group of ELA teachers whose school leaders had brought me in because they were concerned about their students' standardized test results. Trying to figure out what was going on, I asked the teachers to share their biggest challenges. After several in a row said, "Our students are not reading on grade level," I asked them what books their students were reading in class. It turned out that students were only required to read in small groups "at their own level." They were not reading grade-level texts as a class. So, most students never read or practiced analyzing grade-level texts *at all*. Not ever.

Bingo. It sounds kind of obvious when you say it this way, but: *If students never read anything on grade level, how will they develop the capacity to read on grade level?* Just to be clear, we can't merely place grade-level texts in front of students; we have to provide supports. Whole-class instruction with rigorous, complex texts enables us to support struggling readers and strengthen their close-reading analytical skills. This doesn't mean you can't use guided reading groups; in fact, such groups can be beneficial. So can encouraging students to engage in a high volume of independent reading. (PS, see *Literacy and the Common Core* for guidance on how to run an

---

61 The "K-12 ELA Common Core Standards Tracker" and "K-12 Selected Language CCS Tracker" are on the TLC "Using Grammar to Improve Writing" page found at https://www.literacycookbook.com/page.php?id=161. These and other standards-related resources are also available on the TLC "Standards" page found at https://www.literacycookbook.com/page.php?id=138.

effective independent reading program in your class or school.[62]) But what you *can't* do is limit students to what they can already do. You need to push them. With support.

PS: This story had a happy ending: The teachers revised their curriculum.

- What are the key steps to supporting students who are not on grade level?
- How do you measure student reading levels at your school?
- How did the ideas in this chapter challenge, change, or confirm what you previously believed about supporting students who are not on grade level?
- Which resources and ideas from this chapter will you share with colleagues? Why?

---

62 Sarah Tantillo, *Literacy and the Common Core: Recipes for Action* (San Francisco: Jossey-Bass, 2014), 15-41 and 184-232.

chapter
FOUR

Which other factors affect how well we write?

As I noted in Chapter 2, we use our understanding of grammar and grammatical forms to generate writing, so the more deeply we understand grammar and grammatical forms, the more effectively we can write. However, other factors also influence how well we write. This chapter addresses several.

THE MOST IMPORTANT WRITING STANDARD[63]

Ironically—because one must read well in order to write well—I would argue that *the most important writing standard is actually a* reading *standard.*

---

63 This section draws heavily from my MiddleWeb blog post "The Gr-2 ELA Standard You May Need to Teach," Oct. 6, 2015, found at https://www.middleweb.com/25459/

Maybe we're not supposed to have favorites when it comes to the Common Core Standards, but I do. I fell in love with Reading Informational Text (RIT)[64] Standard #2.1 one day when a group of third-grade teachers told me that their students had just bombed a test on RIT Standard #3.1 and so they were going to "reteach it."

"Hang on," I said, because usually what people mean when they say "I'm going to reteach it" is *I'm going to try the same approach again—possibly louder—and hope for the best.*

We looked at the third-grade version of the standard:

RIT 3.1	Ask and answer questions to demonstrate understanding of a text, referring explicitly to the text as the basis for the answers.

Then I asked them: "Can your students do the second-grade version of this standard?" We looked at it:

RIT 2.1	Ask and answer such questions as who, what, where, when, why, and how to demonstrate understanding of key details in a text.

They said, "Um, no."

I asked, "What about the first-grade version? Can they do that?" We looked again:

RIT 1.1	Ask and answer questions about key details in a text.

"Yes," they said. "They can do that."

We sat down and created a simple tool for the second-grade standard, and this "5Ws and H Organizer Model" (which follows)[65] enabled

---

the-gr-2-ela-standard-you-may-need-to-teach/.

64 Note: For Reading Standard #1, the Reading Informational Text and Reading Literature Standards are identical.

65 The "5Ws and H Organizer Model" is on the TLC "Using Grammar to Improve Writing" page found at https://www.literacycookbook.com/page.php?id=161. This and other analytic tools are available on the TLC "Analyzing Literature" page found at https://www.literacycookbook.com/page.php?id=2. Examples in the model are based on *How the Grinch Stole Christmas!* by Dr. Seuss (New York: Random House, 1957).

them to teach their students how to ask and answer these questions in one sitting. Since then, I have used this tool with students in other grades, as well, because it turns out that many middle and high school students need it, too.

5Ws and H Organizer Model		
	Question	**Answer**
Who (name)	*Who asks the Grinch why he is stealing her family's tree?*	Cindy-Lou Who asks the Grinch, "Santa Claus, why are you taking our Christmas tree? WHY?"
What (thing)	*What does the Grinch expect to hear after he steals everything from the residents of Who-ville?*	The Grinch expects to hear the residents of Who-ville crying on Christmas morning.
When (time)	*When does the Grinch realize that he has not stopped Christmas from coming?*	The Grinch realizes he has not stopped Christmas from coming when he hears the residents of Who-ville singing happily on Christmas morning.
Where (place)	*Where does the Grinch live?*	The Grinch lives just north of Who-ville in a cave.
Why (because)	*Why does the Grinch hate Christmas?*	No one is really sure why the Grinch hates Christmas, but it's possible that "his heart was two sizes too small." Maybe he hates Christmas because he does not have any family or friends to celebrate with.
How (by___)	*How does the Grinch attempt to ruin Christmas for the residents of Who-ville?*	The Grinch attempts to ruin Christmas for the residents of Who-ville by stealing their food, trees, and gifts.

The beauty of RIT #2.1 is that it is one of the few standards that students can master more or less in one sitting. The information they need to know is very specific and concrete, and they can see it modeled and practice it immediately; you can tell very quickly if they are "getting it" or not.

The other reason I love this standard is that it is essential to effective reading and writing. We need to be able to ask and answer "How" and "Why" questions in order to infer and explain. Students who cannot ask and answer "How" and "Why" questions will struggle with comprehension, and they will struggle to explain ideas, both orally and in writing. **If you have students whose writing is very list-oriented with unexplained evidence, it could mean that they have not mastered this standard.**

In *The Writing Revolution*, Hochman and Wexler illustrate how students can use the 5Ws and H questions to expand their sentences.[66] Students begin with "a kernel sentence" such as "Jane ran," then ask whichever questions seem most appropriate—in this case, *when, where,* and *why* (since we already know *who* and *what*). Students take notes on their responses ("7 a.m., park, to get into shape"), then write the complete sentence incorporating those notes ("At seven in the morning, Jane ran in the park because she wanted to get in shape."). Hochman and Wexler advise that students should always begin sentences with the answer to *when* because it gives them practice with a construction that is common in writing but not in speech.[67]

As the authors point out, this approach to sentence expansion has numerous benefits:

- Enables students to anticipate what a reader needs to know and to provide that information
- Checks comprehension
- Teaches note-taking strategies…

---

66 Judith C. Hochman and Natalie Wexler, *The Writing Revolution: A Guide to Advancing Thinking Through Writing in All Subjects and Grades* (San Francisco: Jossey-Bass, 2017), 55-63.

67 Judith C. Hochman and Natalie Wexler, *The Writing Revolution: A Guide to Advancing Thinking Through Writing in All Subjects and Grades* (San Francisco: Jossey-Bass, 2017), 57-58.

- Enables students to craft written language structures
- Develops the ability to summarize.[68]

Bottom line: RIT #2.1 is a high-leverage standard, one that—once your students master it—can have a dramatic impact on their reading and writing growth.

A Few Additional Thoughts on Trajectory Analysis

Again, notice how we viewed the Common Core Standards as a ladder and targeted instruction to help students climb by directly teaching them the specific skills they needed. No matter what grade or subject you teach, you can use this approach to figure out where your students are. One day while analyzing the trajectory of RIT #1 from K-12, a 7th-grade teacher remarked: "I have a class of 25 students. I know ten are on the 5th-grade level for this standard, ten are on the 6th-grade level, and five are on grade-level." She realized she could use this knowledge to differentiate instruction.

Identifying what grade level students are on for any given standard, however, is just the beginning. Most standards involve mastery of at least a half-dozen skills. For example, RIT #6.1, "Cite textual evidence to support analysis of what the text says explicitly as well as inferences drawn from the text," requires students to do the following:

- Paraphrase
- Ask questions about text
- Draw inferences
- Distinguish between argument and evidence
- Identify evidence relevant to particular arguments
- Build arguments with relevant evidence and explanation, and
- Cite sources properly.

---

68 Judith C. Hochman and Natalie Wexler, *The Writing Revolution: A Guide to Advancing Thinking Through Writing in All Subjects and Grades* (San Francisco: Jossey-Bass, 2017), 56.

Students might be able to do some of those skills. Our job is to determine which skills they need help with in order to master the whole standard.

GENRE, AUDIENCE, AND TONE[69]

Another reading-writing connection we must attend to involves genre, audience, and tone—probably best in that order. "Genre" signals the author's purpose broadly—for instance, a play is meant to entertain, while an op-ed piece is meant to persuade. "Audience" narrows the field: *Who will want to read or see this play? Is it for adults or children? Is it for lovers of comedy or tragedy?* "Tone" answers some of these questions; the writer chooses words that suggest attitude and a more pointed purpose. For example, it's hard to imagine how Hamlet's "To be, or not to be" soliloquy would fit in a comedy.

Readers use their background knowledge about these features to ascertain what messages the writer is trying to convey. Conversely, writers must harness these features to ensure their messages are clearly sent.

In order to help students grasp how these features work, we need to begin by training students to annotate text *as purposefully as possible*.

I think we can all agree that annotating texts helps students comprehend them more deeply.[70] But not all forms of annotating are helpful. *How* you annotate matters. It's a problem when students cover their texts with so many notes that it seems to have taken them an hour to read one page. And while it's great that students can annotate with generic strategies such as underlining topic sentences and starring supporting details, the truth is that **they need to learn how to analyze texts more effectively and efficiently.** It's not efficient to notice *everything*. If you notice *everything*, that might be a sign that you can't figure out what is *most important*.

How can we teach students to determine what is most important?

---

69 Most of this section is drawn from my MiddleWeb blog post "Teaching Students to Set a Purpose for Reading," Apr. 23, 2017, found at https://www.middleweb.com/34655/teaching-students-to-set-a-purpose-for-reading/

70 I made the case for annotation in *The Literacy Cookbook: A Practical Guide to Effective Reading, Writing, Speaking, and Listening Instruction* (San Francisco: Jossey-Bass, 2012), 64-68.

Students must learn to set a purpose for reading. Too often, teachers set the purpose (with assignments such as "Read Chapter 7 and answer these three questions" or "Read this article and write a summary") and students do not actually learn how to set a purpose on their own. Some might not even realize that they can.

Again, a helpful first step is to identify the *genre* of the text. If you're reading a book review, the most obvious guiding question is "Why should we read this book?" Students would then take notes on that, not on every single thing that might be interesting about the text. After discussing the notion of genre, I would invite students to infer how they would approach different genres. For example: "Here's an editorial from the *New York Times*. What should our purpose be?" And don't forget this follow-up: "How could you tell?" Once students recognize the clues and characteristics of different genres, they can not only identify the genre but also explain its purpose (in this case, to persuade) and our purpose for reading it (to recognize the writer's arguments and evaluate his/her support for those arguments).

When I was in high school, our chemistry teacher gave us an amazing assignment at the end of the year; he called it "Unknowns." We received samples of different-colored chemicals/compounds and had to run experiments to figure out what each "unknown" consisted of. This assessment required us to demonstrate lab skills and content knowledge about the properties of elements we'd studied all year. English teachers could take a similar approach with random texts: Students would use clues to identify the genre and decide what purpose(s) they would set for reading.

Beyond using genre to set purpose, students can use other clues, as well. **When it comes to nonfiction/informational texts,** it helps to look at the title of the text (no matter what size that text is—book, chapter, article, sub-section) and ask questions about that title. These questions—preferably "How" and "Why" questions—should guide our reading. For example, an article titled "Lifting School Cell Phone Bans" would suggest questions such as "Why should schools lift their cell phone bans?" and "Why do schools ban cell phones in the first place?" Presumably these questions would be answered in the text.

Two teachers I've worked with, Alison Paludi and Bianca Licata, adapted my advice on reading for a purpose[71] and created this mini-lesson on close reading of nonfiction:

Close Reading of Nonfiction: MINI-LESSON

1. **Read the title and turn it into a question** (typically a HOW/WHY question). *By the end of close-reading, you may find more than one answer to the question.*

2. **Read the introduction** (or first 2-3 paragraphs, if they are short) and underline important words/phrases/sentences that could help you understand what the article is about.

3. Based on the first couple of paragraphs, **determine the genre of the text and the author's purpose for writing it.** *Why would someone write this? What's so important about it?*

4. AS YOU READ, annotate for key details that help support or develop the main idea, to **figure out the main argument.**

5. AS YOU READ, **determine the structure and role of each paragraph** and annotate. *How does this paragraph support the main idea? What role does the paragraph play in the development of the text? How does the author present the information in this paragraph?*

6. Once you get to the end of the text, consider how the author wraps up the text and annotate. ***What do we, as readers, get from the article? What was the answer to your original question (from the title)?***

When it comes to fiction/narratives, we can of course analyze text for a variety of purposes. For instance, we might ask students to focus on character development or the use of symbolism to convey meaning. But often when reading novels, we want students to read a chapter and figure out what's important *on their own.*

I've actually designed an organizer for this called—wait for it—the "What's Important Organizer."[72]

---

71 Sarah Tantillo, "Teaching Students How to Set a Purpose for Reading," *The Literacy Cookbook Blog*, April 30, 2017, found at https://theliteracycookbook.wordpress.com/2017/04/30/teaching-students-how-to-set-a-purpose-for-reading/

72 Sarah Tantillo, *The Literacy Cookbook: A Practical Guide to Effective Reading, Writing, Speaking, and Listening Instruction* (San Francisco: Jossey-Bass, 2012), 48-49. The "What Is Important Organizer" and "What Is Important Organizer Model-*Animal Farm* Ch 2" can be found on the TLC "Using Grammar to Improve Writing" page found at https://www.literacycookbook.com/page.

NAME_____DATE_____

DIRECTIONS: Use COMPLETE SENTENCES to answer all five questions. You may either PARAPHRASE or PROVIDE QUOTES to support your assertions, but either way, you MUST GIVE PAGE NUMBERS to indicate where the evidence can be found. Refer to the model to ensure that you are doing this properly. Give AT LEAST TWO PIECES OF EVIDENCE PER QUESTION.

1. **DECISIONS WITH PURPOSE: What major decisions do the characters make, and why?**

2. **CONFLICTS/OBSTACLES/CHALLENGES: What conflicts, obstacles, or challenges do the characters face, and how do they deal with them?**

3. **LESSONS/INSIGHTS/MESSAGES: What lessons do any of the characters learn? What do WE learn?**

4. **CAUSES AND EFFECTS: What events/actions have major effects on characters? How do the characters react?**

5. **PATTERNS: What patterns from either this passage or the rest of the book do you notice in this passage?**

In addition to training students in what to look for when reading *any* narrative, this organizer supports them in the practice of summarizing. Perhaps more importantly, it reminds them that there are specific things you should look for when reading a narrative (whether it's a story or a chapter) in order to grasp its most fundamental ideas.

Once students have learned that they don't have to underline *everything*, you can turn their attention to writing strategies that accomplish

---

php?id=161. These and other analytic tools are also available on the TLC "Analyzing Literature" page found at https://www.literacycookbook.com/page.php?id=2.

what they've noticed as readers. With heightened awareness about genre, audience, and tone, they can—again—note *what they like about particular sentences* and reflect on how those sentences serve the writer's purposes. Then, with your guidance, they can imitate the techniques they admire.

ARGUMENT VS. EVIDENCE, STEPS 1-3 REVISITED

As I established in *Literacy and the Common Core*, writers need to know the difference between "argument" and "evidence" in order to write their own arguments supported by evidence and explanation. In that book, I explained six steps that could take students from asking "What's the difference between argument and evidence?" to writing a research paper from scratch.[73]

As a quick refresher, here are the six steps:

1. Given a list of statements, distinguish the arguments from examples of evidence.

2. Given a list of statements, identify arguments and their relevant evidence.

3. Given arguments, support them with your own relevant evidence and explanation.

4. Given questions, answer them with arguments and relevant evidence and explanation.

5. Generate your own questions that warrant research and debate.

6. Generate your own questions, then research and build arguments supported with evidence and explanation.

In the past few years, I've gained some insights about those steps—including that I needed to add Step 2.5!—so in this space, I'm re-explaining Steps 1-3 with new lesson guidance and materials.

---

73 Sarah Tantillo, *Literacy and the Common Core: Recipes for Action* (San Francisco: Jossey-Bass, 2014), 131-145.

Step 1: Given a list of statements, distinguish the arguments from examples of evidence.

This step can be taught in one class period, though you might want to repeat it for review purposes (and also to catch up any students who were absent). Here's an overview of the lesson:

- <u>Objective</u>: SWBAT infer three rules for determining if a statement is an argument in order to distinguish arguments from facts/evidence.

- <u>Pitch</u>: *After today, you're going to be a better writer, guaranteed. Good writers write arguments and support them with relevant evidence and explanation. In order to do that, you first need to know the difference between "argument" and "evidence." Today we're going to learn THREE WAYS you can tell if something is an argument or not.*

To teach the difference, you provide several statements (ideally about a text or content you've been working on), and students must determine which are arguments and which are facts/evidence. There are three rules for determining if something is an argument or not, but don't tell them the rules up front because you want them to wrestle with the content and figure out the rules.

Here's an example based on *Stone Fox*,[74] a third-grade text:

***Argument vs. Evidence Step 1** (top half of handout)**
Which of these statements are arguments, and which are facts/evidence? ____1. Grandfather and Willy live on a potato farm. ____2. It was going to be difficult to find a horse. ____3. Because of Grandfather being in bed, Willy takes on a lot of responsibility. ____4. A ten-year-old boy cannot run a farm.

*See footnote[75]

---

74 John Reynolds Gardiner (illus. Marcia Sewall), *Stone Fox* (New York: HarperCollins, 2005).

75 The complete "Argument vs. Evidence Step 1-Stone Fox" is on the TLC "Using Grammar to Improve Writing" page found at https://www.literacycookbook.com/page.php?id=161. Also, all of

Discuss one statement at a time, surveying students each time: "Raise your hand if you think it's an argument; raise your hand if you think it's a fact or evidence." Then ask, "Why do you think that?" or "How did you know?" or "What specifically in the sentence gave you a clue?" Here is what students should figure out:

- Statement #1 is a straight-up fact. It's evidence. And **evidence doesn't require evidence in order to be understood fully.** Arguments do.

- Statement #2 is an argument. It includes **debatable/arguable language—also (in this case) known as an ADJECTIVE:** "difficult." Note: Adverbs can also function this way—as in, "She studied carefully." Not everyone would have the same definition for "carefully."

- Statement #3 is an argument. It includes **cause/effect language:** "Because." (PS, you might want to pause here to generate a list of "cause and effect words" for future reference.)

- Statement #4 is an argument. It **raises How/Why questions:** e.g., *Why can't a ten-year-old boy run a farm?*

Careful readers will notice that #2 also raises How/Why questions: e.g., *Why was it going to be difficult to find a horse?* Arguments often meet more than one of these three criteria, and that's OK.

Review the three criteria and invite students to work with a partner to create additional examples of each rule. For example, you might say, "Write an argument about Willy that uses debatable/arguable language." Then cold-call after partners have had a minute or two to come up with something. Providing the limitations of 1) following the first rule and 2) making the sentence "about Willy" ensures that students will use content from the text (Reviewing content: Yay!), and it is more efficient than having them compose a completely random sentence. Here's the rest of the handout:

Argument vs. Evidence Step 1 *(bottom half of handout)*

---

my Argument vs. Evidence materials are curated on the TLC "Argument vs. Evidence" page found at https://www.literacycookbook.com/page.php?id=159.

What are the rules for whether a statement is an ARGUMENT or not?

RULE #1)_____

EXAMPLE:_____

_____

RULE #2)_____

EXAMPLE:_____

_____

RULE #3)_____

EXAMPLE:_____

_____

Step 2: Given a list of statements, identify arguments and their relevant evidence.

This step can be introduced in one class period but should be repeated because students will need the practice. It's a great way to review content, so it can easily be baked into social studies or science lessons (as well as ELA, of course). In this model lesson, I extended the *Stone Fox* content forward. Here's an overview of the lesson:

- Objective: SWBAT identify arguments and their relevant evidence in order to build logical arguments with relevant facts/evidence.

- Pitch: *The other day, we learned THREE WAYS you can tell if something is an argument or not. But good writers don't just write arguments; they must also find relevant evidence to support their arguments. Today we're going to practice sorting arguments and evidence again, and then we're going to MATCH the evidence to the argument it supports.*

NOTE: Prior to the lesson, you need to prepare the following materials:

1) Create twelve sentences:

- Five arguments with five factual statements that support them,

- One argument with no support, and

- One factual statement that doesn't relate to any of the arguments.

2) Mix up the order of the sentences (so they are not obviously paired in sequence), number them, then copy the list and cut it into sentence strips.[76] Each pair of students will need an envelope with all twelve sentences. PS: The numbers make it easier to refer to the sentences during the class discussion, and they also facilitate clean-up when you want to collect the materials.

3) Create an answer key for yourself. Here's my sample answer key:[77]

---

76 For a sample list of sentences, see "Argument vs. Evidence Step 2 Statements-*Stone Fox*" on the TLC "Using Grammar to Improve Writing" page found at https://www.literacycookbook.com/page. php?id=161. Also, all of my Argument vs. Evidence materials are curated on the TLC "Argument vs. Evidence" page found at https://www.literacycookbook.com/page.php?id=159.

77 "Argument vs. Evidence Step 2 Answer Key-*Stone Fox*" is on the TLC "Using Grammar to Improve Writing" page found at https://www.literacycookbook.com/page.php?id=161. Also, all of my Argument vs. Evidence materials are curated on the TLC "Argument vs. Evidence" page found at https://www.literacycookbook.com/page.php?id=159.

Argument vs. Evidence Step 2 Answer Key-Stone Fox

Arguments with support:

1--Willy is a hard worker. (ARG)

7--The next day, Little Willy began to prepare for the harvest.

12--There was a lot of work to be done for the harvest.

3--The underground shed had to be cleaned and the plow had to be sharpened.

6--Willy and Grandfather are able to communicate.

11-Grandfather put his hand on the bed with his palm upward, which was a signal for yes.

8--It was easy to tell when it was winter in Wyoming.

2--There is snow on everything, the trees, the house and the roads.

9--Searchlight is protective of Willy.

4--She barked and snarled and jumped at the tax collector who was trying to get into the house.

Argument with no support:

5--Willy hates school.

Factual statement that does not relate to any of the arguments:

10--Searchlight has a white spot on her head.

Phase 1 of the lesson:

Direct pairs to sort their twelve sentences into two piles: arguments and evidence. Circulate and actively monitor so you can overhear any confusion. After a few minutes, call the class back and cold-call to solicit the arguments. Ask students to explain which of the three "argument rules" (from Step 1) their arguments manifest. Clear up any confusion. Remember, just because a statement is "true," that does not mean it's a fact.

Phase 2 of the lesson:

Tell pairs they are now going to match as many arguments as they can with one piece of relevant evidence. Remind them that not all arguments will necessarily have relevant evidence. Model one or two matches to make sure students understand what "relevant" means. Then let them go for it. Again, circulate and actively monitor their work. After a few minutes, call the class back and cold-call to solicit their matched arguments and evidence. Ask students to defend their matches, and ask if anyone disagrees with the responses. Try to step back as much as possible and let students hash things out.

Wrap-up:

You can invite students to reflect on this lesson in any number of ways. Any time I ask students to do something challenging—especially the first time they do it—I like to ask, "What was challenging about this activity?" This question serves several purposes: 1) It acknowledges that the task was difficult and tacitly praises them for sticking with it; 2) It invites students to reflect on what *they* perceived to be challenging, which gives the teacher more insight into what they might need more help with; and 3) It reminds them that they can handle challenging tasks and inspires them to keep persisting at such tasks.

At the end, students should put their twelve sentences back into their envelopes so that you can use this activity with your next class.

Step 2.5: Given arguments, select the *most relevant* evidence to support them.[78]

While working with teachers on how to help students write more effective paragraphs and essays, I found that although students could quickly master Steps 1 and 2, they needed more scaffolding to move from Step 2 to Step 3.

I realized there needed to be a "Step 2.5."

Step 3 gives students an argument and asks them to support it with relevant evidence and explanation. Breaking this down, it means they need to know what "relevant" means, how to select that evidence, and how and why to explain. It becomes more challenging to select relevant evidence

---

78 Most of this section is drawn from my MiddleWeb blog post "Help Student Writers Find the Best Evidence," Feb. 23, 2016, found at https://www.middleweb.com/28000/help-student-writers-find-the-best-evidence/.

when it appears not as a few isolated sentences but immersed somewhere in a complete text. You have to know what to look for and what to rule out.

Students have a tendency to look simply for words or phrases that seem related, and often their quest for evidence is too superficial, which causes them to select evidence that is not helpful.

As part of "Step 2.5," therefore, we're teaching students what to rule out, AKA ineffective evidence. "Ineffective" evidence manifests one of three problems: 1) It opposes the argument, 2) It's irrelevant, or 3) It's true but not as relevant.

A good pitch might be: *We've been talking about matching evidence with arguments. Today we're going to drill down on how to find the BEST evidence. If you can't find relevant evidence, your "evidence" might not prove your argument and might even disprove it. You could end up proving the opposite of what you intended.*

Here's a tool to teach this point, with the answers and explanation provided:

Argument vs. Evidence Step 2.5 Answer Key*

Directions: Put a star next to the evidence from the choices below that BEST supports the argument. For each choice, tell why you would or would not use it. THEN write a logical sentence that would follow from your choice, explaining how the evidence supports the argument.

ARGUMENT: Eating too much candy causes stomach aches.

EVIDENCE OPTIONS	Would you use this "evidence"? Why/Why not?
1. One time my brother ate 60 KitKats and nothing happened	NO. It opposes the argument.
2. I like Hershey kisses best.	NO. It's irrelevant.
3. My sister collected three bags of candy yesterday.	MAYBE: It's true but not totally relevant. I'd have to explain it.
4. Yesterday I ate 22 Snickers bars and threw up. *	YES. It clearly supports the argument.

Next logical sentence: <u>Obviously, I had overdosed on sugar, and my stomach could not hold so much "content."</u>

***

Here's a template for practice:

ARGUMENT: [Teacher provides this.]

EVIDENCE OPTIONS	Would you use this "evidence"? Why/Why not?
1. [Teacher provides these.]	[You should change the order, and in early practice, at least one option should oppose, one should be irrelevant, and one should be true but not totally relevant. In later practice, you can mix/double up the options so that students won't simply use process of elimination.]
2.	
3.	
4.	

Next logical sentence: [Student completes this.]

*See footnote[79]

As noted, this tool requires students to generate an explanation that follows logically from the "best" evidence they choose. Although one choice might be the strongest, we should remind students that sometimes "perfect" evidence is hard to find, and "good enough" or "maybe" evidence can work if you support it with sufficient explanation. For example, if I selected #3 above ("My sister collected three bags of candy yesterday"), I might write this follow-up sentence: "Unfortunately, she ate most of it in one sitting and paid the price after that."

Another way to present Step 2.5 is to use the analogy of the hashtag (#). Students familiar with Twitter know that a hashtag signifies a category

---

[79] "Argument vs. Evidence Step 2.5 Answer Key" is on the TLC "Using Grammar to Improve Writing" page found at https://www.literacycookbook.com/page.php?id=161. Also, all of my Argument vs. Evidence materials are curated on the TLC "Argument vs. Evidence" page found at https://www.literacycookbook.com/page.php?id=159.

full of examples (e.g., #NeverAgain). Similarly, writers look for patterns in a text then label or code their evidence—sorting it into categories. Then they sort through the evidence to find the strongest evidence to support their ideas and arguments. For example, if you were writing an essay on F. Scott Fitzgerald's use of symbolism in *The Great Gatsby*, you'd skim for images such as the green light, automobiles, the Valley of Ashes, or the eyes of Dr. Eckleburg and tag them (#symbol), then pull out the quotes (i.e., the text around the symbols, to establish the context in which they appear) and analyze how they convey meaning in the novel. You'd use this analysis to determine which of the examples were most useful to building your argument.

Step 3: Given arguments, support them with your own relevant evidence and explanation.[80]

When students are struggling to write clear, coherent essays or aren't explaining their evidence enough, often what it boils down to is this: They need help in writing stronger paragraphs. Whether you are preparing them for writing on standardized tests, trying to strengthen their fundamental writing skills, or looking for a more meaningful way to assess their reading comprehension, teaching students how to build clear, coherent paragraphs is a good use of everyone's time.

Step 3 is crucial because if you can't explain how your evidence supports your argument, readers will not be able to follow your "logic." Your paragraph will lack clarity and coherence.

One of the biggest challenges in Step 3 is that students do not explain their ideas well, if at all. They tend to shovel evidence into their paragraphs like coal into a stove. This is partly our fault because sometimes we give them directions that say, "Support your answer with evidence from the text" and forget to mention they should *explain* their evidence. It is also a function of how much or little exposure they've had to explanations; many

---

80 Most of this section is drawn from my MiddleWeb blog post "Teach Students to Write Strong Paragraphs," Apr. 12, 2016, found at https://www.middleweb.com/29202/teach-students-to-write-strong-paragraphs/.

children grow up in households where adults do not explain much. As I noted in *The Literacy Cookbook*, the "word gap" that Hart and Risley discovered (i.e., the finding that children from wealthier families heard over 1,500 more words *per hour* than children from the poorest families) is also an *explanation* gap—because exposure to fewer words means that one hears fewer examples of complex thinking: fewer sentences, fewer questions, and fewer explanations of ideas or arguments.[81]

So we need to explain why explanation is necessary. Conceptually, students can understand this idea if you provide an example they can relate to. I like to demonstrate with what I call the "Mean Mom" skit. A colleague plays my "Mean Mom," and the dialogue goes something like this:

> **Me:** Mom, can I go to the movies this weekend?
> **Mean Mom:** No.
> **Me:** But I did all of my chores this week!
> **Mean Mom:** So? You're supposed to do that.

Here I pause for a meta-moment, to point out that I've given her *facts* and she is not convinced. Let me try a different approach…

> **Me:** Doing my chores shows how responsible I am, and if you let me go to the movies, you know I will represent the family well; also, by doing my chores, I earned my allowance so I can pay for my own ticket!
> **Mean Mom:** Hmmn….
> **Me:** Plus, my friend Sally says if I'm allowed to go, her mom will pick me up and bring me home, so you can have a free night on Saturday!
> **Mean Mom:** What's Sally's mom's number?

I then review what happened: *When I offered facts, she was not convinced. When I* explained *the facts, I won her over.* It's important to add the caveat that just because you explain your ideas, it doesn't mean you will always get what you want. But you will have a much better chance of persuading your audience if you do.

---

81 Sarah Tantillo, *The Literacy Cookbook: A Practical Guide to Effective Reading, Writing, Speaking, and Listening Instruction* (San Francisco: Jossey-Bass, 2012), 12, citing Betty Hart & Todd R. Risley, *Meaningful Differences in the Everyday Experiences of Young American Children* (Baltimore: Paul H. Brookes. 2002, 3rd printing of original 1995 book).

This skit makes a great mnemonic device, by the way. Weeks later, if you walk past a student who is writing and say, "Oh, so you don't want to go to the movies this weekend?" that student will know what you mean: *You're not explaining enough.*

We then analyze my "desk" paragraph (see Chapter 2, "Principle #3: Ask 'What Do You *Like* About That Sentence?'" for a step-by-step description of the lesson), then move on to the "paragraph response" approach: Given topic sentences about whatever they're reading—a chapter from a novel, an article to build content knowledge, or something else—students must write the rest of the paragraph, including well-explained evidence. The topic sentence provides a lens through which to read the text and guides their annotation (see Chapter 3 for "Sample Paragraph Response Directions with Model" and "Paragraph Response Scoring Checklist").

An Argument for "Quote Lasagna"[82]

Although I've been a longtime proponent of teaching "quote sandwiches" to help students write effective paragraphs,[83] I've begun to notice that students who use this approach (context, quote/evidence, explanation) seem to overemphasize the "quote" part, often to the detriment of the explanation. They seem to believe that the evidence is the most important part, possibly because of the name "*quote* sandwich"—i.e., it's not "*explanation* sandwich." Either they skimp on the explanation or the explanation does not actually explain how the evidence supports their argument. As a result, their paragraphs feel disjointed.

While conducting writing conferences with students, I've found that when I ask them to simply explain their ideas, they can do so pretty easily. If I then ask them to explain how the evidence supports their ideas, sometimes they can and sometimes they can't. Some are clearly struggling with Argument vs. Evidence Step 2.5 ("Given arguments, select the *most*

---

82 This section originally appeared as a blog post called "An Argument for 'Quote Lasagna'" on *The Literacy Cookbook Blog* by Sarah Tantillo, March 3, 2018, found at https://theliteracycookbook.wordpress.com/2018/03/03/an-argument-for-quote-lasagna/.

83 For a detailed explanation of how to teach quote sandwiches, see Chapter 9 of *Literacy and the Common Core: Recipes for Action* (San Francisco: Jossey-Bass, 2014), 147-151.

relevant evidence to support them.")). As long as they find *something*, they think they can drop it in. After all, it's a *quote*, and that's what a quote sandwich needs, right?

So now I'd like to propose a new metaphor: "quote lasagna." As any lasagna fan knows, the recipe calls for *multiple layers* of pasta, sauce, meat, veggies, and various cheeses. While most chefs adhere to that general principle, there is not one correct way to make lasagna. The goal is to create something yummy by blending these ingredients, layer upon layer, in a way that makes sense (I think we can all agree that five layers of noodles without anything in between would be silly and not within the definition of "lasagna").

How does this idea translate to paragraph writing? **Effective paragraphs *blend* evidence and explanation.** As long as you provide enough context so that we know what you're talking about, there is not one right way to sequence what you want to say. Sometimes you need to explain *before* you provide details. Students who believe they are only allowed to provide evidence *first* might struggle to explain not because they've picked weak/irrelevant evidence but because they feel constricted by the "rule" that the evidence should be between the context and the explanation.

I think using the metaphor of layers and blended ingredients might free students to start with explanation if they need to. With a slightly less rigid structure, they might write more clearly and coherently.

THE CHALLENGE OF CONCLUDING

For many years—decades and perhaps centuries—people have taught essay writing with this adage: "Tell 'em what you're gonna tell 'em, tell 'em, then tell 'em what you told 'em." I cannot overstate how much this "advice" makes me want to put pins in my eyes. And I have spent years trying to undo the damage that it does to students who write this way. It might sound workmanlike and organized, but it is merely repetitious. There is no need to tell your reader the same thing three times.

Because this approach is so prevalent, it's very common to hear teachers advising students to "restate the claim" in a paragraph or "restate your thesis" in the conclusion. I think many people default to restating because it sounds "conclude-y." And they don't know what else to do.

The authors of the Common Core Standards offer little guidance on conclusions. "Provide a concluding statement or section related to the information or explanation presented" is about as committal as they get, and I can't say I blame them. There is not one correct way to write a conclusion. How you conclude depends on the genre, the tone, the audience, and ultimately, your intentions and what you have figured out by writing the piece.

My preference is to end with something punchy (See Chapter 2, "Principle #3: Ask, 'What Do You *Like* About That Sentence?'" for some examples). Provide an insight or raise a question, concern, or new (but related) idea.

Make us think.

COMBATTING LEARNED HELPLESSNESS[84]

It might seem odd to include "combatting learned helplessness" in a book on grammar and writing instruction. But research increasingly points to the influence of grit and persistence (or the lack thereof) on academic performance.[85] And when it comes to facing the challenges of grammar and writing, students absolutely need to be able to persist. Through draft after draft after draft.

Indeed, what is revision if not persistence?

For some time now, I've been thinking about the ways in which we either inculcate or prevent learned helplessness in students. Some practices help strengthen students' self-efficacy, motivation, and confidence, while others have the opposite effect. And the irony is that teachers might not even realize they are doing things that create this opposite effect.

---

84 This section draws heavily from my MiddleWeb blog post "17 Ideas to Help Combat Learned Helplessness," Dec. 18, 2016, found at https://www.middleweb. com/33614/17-ideas-to-help-combat-learned-helplessness/.

85 For example, see Angela Duckworth, *Grit: The Power of Passion and Perseverance* (New York: Scribner, 2016) and Paul Tough, *How Children Succeed: Grit, Curiosity, and the Hidden Power of Character* (New York: Houghton Mifflin Harcourt, 2012).

The positive practices fall into three categories: 1) Encourage Engagement and Accountability, 2) Provide Models for Clarity, and 3) Encourage Risk-taking. Below is a "Combatting Learned Helplessness Tool" that is useful for observations and self-reflection.[86] Each category zeroes in on problems, consequences, and solutions.

Combatting Learned Helplessness Tool
Encourage Engagement and Accountability

1. HOLD STUDENTS ACCOUNTABLE.		
IF…You assign class-work and go over it before holding students accountable for having completed it,	THEN…students realize they can wait till the timer rings, then copy the answers as you go over them. So they don't even try to do the work. They will sit quietly or chat with a neighbor, which is more fun.	SO, INSTEAD: Either circulate and assign credit (with a stamp or initial) as students work, collect it before reviewing, or provide and give credit for "notes from discussion" that students must complete in addition.
2. MAKE THE PITCH.		
IF…You fail to make a pitch for the lesson's objective,	THEN…students will wonder, *Why are we doing this?* Being told WHAT they are doing (i.e., the agenda) is not enough. Without knowing the purpose for the lesson, students feel like hostages, and while they might comply with your demands, they are less likely to feel motivated or personally invested in the work.	SO, INSTEAD: Share the objective (which is ideally "RPM"—rigorous, purposeful, and measurable[i]) and make a pitch that explains what's in it for them. And remind them of that purpose throughout the lesson (*"Let's not forget WHY we're looking for the most relevant evidence: so we can wow readers and convince them of our argument"*).
3. TEACH REVISION STRATEGIES.		

---

86 The "Combatting Learned Helplessness Tool" can be found on the TLC "Using Grammar to Improve Writing" page found at https://www.literacycookbook.com/page.php?id=161.

IF…You provide written feedback to students with many details about grammar, diction, organization, etc., in isolation,	THEN…students learn to depend on others to revise their work and can't recognize their own mistakes.	SO, INSTEAD: Teach revision strategies (i.e., outlining their own essays to ensure coherence, classifying fragments and complete sentences, fixing run-on sentences, checking for consistent verb tense, etc.) and build time for students to revise work—with your feedback on revisions.
4. USE TURN AND TALK[ii] AND COLD-CALLING.[iii]		
IF…You rarely use turn-and-talk and cold-calling,	THEN…students recognize that only peers who raise their hands will get called on, so they can sit back and wait for others to do the work. Also, quiet students who want to speak can become intimidated by those who tend to dominate the conversation.	SO, INSTEAD: Use purposeful turn-and-talk (and have students jot notes) with cold-calling to increase engagement and accountability for performance. Find a way to randomize cold-calling (i.e., use note cards with student names that you shuffle through), and other times, plan your cold-call (choose a few who are typically middle-of-the-road in understanding, one high, and one struggling student).
5. TREAT STUDENTS LIKE DETECTIVES.[iv]		
IF…You introduce new concepts or definitions by requiring students to copy down notes,	THEN…students will not necessarily grasp or retain this information because they have not had to wrestle with it. Copying down definitions does not teach students how the concept works or how to use it. Telling is not teaching.	SO, INSTEAD: When introducing NEW content, give clear examples of the phenomenon (e.g., two bold-faced examples of "metaphor," explained), then ask students to INFER from those examples what the phenomenon appears to be and how it seems to work. There is not one right answer.

6. INCLUDE INDEPENDENT WORK.		
IF…You do ALMOST ALL of the work as a class or in pairs,	**THEN…**students learn that they don't need to do the hard work since it's always done together and for them.	**SO, INSTEAD:** Plan and keep independent work time sacred in class with active monitoring and personal feedback.
7. LET THEM STRUGGLE A BIT.		
IF…You answer student questions immediately during independent work time,	**THEN…**students learn not to try or struggle on their own. They'll always wait for you to swoop in!	**SO, INSTEAD:** Set a timer as soon as 100% of students are actually WORKING and you have announced previously that you will address questions after 5 min of sustained work time. When the timer goes off, you can say, "Raise your hand if you need my attention," and write student names on the board. Students then return to work and you address questions in the order of the names on the board so students aren't sitting there waiting with their hands up.
8. TRAIN STUDENTS TO ASK QUESTIONS.		
IF…You ask all the questions,	**THEN…**students never learn to ask their own or invest themselves enough to wonder.	**SO, INSTEAD:** Create time for asking and answering questions about the text, problem, or content at hand. Invest students in seeking their own answers.[v]

Provide Models for Clarity

9. PROVIDE CLEAR MODELS.		

IF…You fail to model the work and/or you skip guided practice,	**THEN…**students will not work well independently. When students are unclear about what they are supposed to do, they do nothing. Or chat. Or do something else to get into trouble. Misbehavior is often the result of students feeling incompetent and acting out to distract from the fact that they don't know how to be successful at what you are asking them to do.	**SO, INSTEAD:** Provide a clear, instructive model of whatever skills or strategies you want students to use. And remember, "I Do" doesn't mean "I do everything while you sit silently and do nothing." You need to engage students and check for understanding during the modeling phase so that you can assess if students need more modeling, paired work, or independent work.
10. ANALYZE EXEMPLARS.		
IF…You don't provide students with model essays, sentences, or examples, BEFORE they need to complete a task,	**THEN…**they don't know what "good" looks like and will be uncertain about what to do.	**SO, INSTEAD:** Analyze an exemplar before you set students to work. Assess it together on a rubric or compare "good" and "great" so students can aim for "great" from the start.
11. INVITE STUDENTS TO USE GENERALIZABLE STRATEGIES.		
IF…You focus on the specific task/text/problem at hand without inviting students to apply a generalized skill/strategy,	**THEN…**they will miss the opportunity to access the tools in their toolbox. They might even forget that they possess relevant skills/strategies.	**SO, INSTEAD:** Teach and name STRATEGIES, then remind students to use them when faced with challenges. Not "What should we do here?" but "What strategy should we use *in a situation like this*?" Provide clear steps for strategies.
12. MODEL HAND-RAISING.		

IF...You ask questions during class discussions without modeling hand-raising,	THEN...students are likely to call out. While this might seem like a management problem, it can become an ENGAGEMENT problem because some students—esp. quieter ones—feel intimidated by those who tend to call out, so they share their ideas less often if calling out is the norm.	SO, INSTEAD: Model hand-raising to ensure that students raise their hands to answer. Ensure you call on multiple students—or better yet, let students know the expectation is to call on another student when they are done to continue the discussion without you driving it.
13. SET A PURPOSE FOR READING.		
IF... You assign reading without establishing a purpose for reading,	**THEN...**students don't know what they are supposed to look for or pay attention to. The default is NOTHING. So you can't blame them if they stare out the window and think about lunch.	**SO, INSTEAD:** Clarify why you are reading this particular bit of text and what they are supposed to do while reading. Either provide a question or ask them to generate their own questions about the text.[vi]
14. CLARIFY PARTNER WORK RULES.		
IF... You tell students to "read and work with a partner,"	**THEN...**you will see a lot of chatting and no reading. This is because students are unclear about their roles, so they wait for each other to take the lead, with the result that neither does. It's easier to chat.	**SO, INSTEAD:** Clarify the role that each partner will play in the work: e.g., "Partner A will read aloud while Partner B will raise and record How and Why questions about this page. On the next page, you will switch roles. Partner B will read, and Partner A will surface the questions and write them down." Choose the partners ahead of time so that you are purposeful in the groups with respect to ability/personality, etc.[vii]
15. MAKE STUDENTS PROVE YOUR ARGUMENTS.		

IF…You ask students to guess what word you're thinking of (which you think they should know),	THEN…students will call out random guesses until you give them enough hints to say the right word. Or they will say nothing because they don't know what you're talking about.	SO, INSTEAD: Stay away from guessing games like, "What word am I thinking of?" Tell them the word, tell them that you think it's important, and ask them why you think that. Focus less on recall questions and more on using information or clues to infer and explain.

Encourage Risk-taking

16. USE STOP AND JOT OR TURN AND TALK[viii] BEFORE COLD-CALLING.[ix]		
IF…You cold-call without using stop and jot or turn and talk first,	THEN…students feel put on the spot and are more inclined to opt out.	SO, INSTEAD: Give students a chance to think by writing something down and/or sharing with a partner before you cold-call.
17. REMIND STUDENTS "THERE IS MORE THAN ONE RIGHT ANSWER."		
IF…You ask open-ended questions without adding, "There is more than one right answer,"	THEN…students might believe there is ONE right answer, and they don't know it, so they will not take the risk of trying to answer.	SO, INSTEAD: Say, "There is not one right answer" more often to invite students to take more risks and participate without fear of being wrong.[x]
18. DON'T INCENTIVIZE THE EASY WAY OUT.		

IF... You ding students a point for every grammatical error in their writing,	THEN...students will avoid risking errors by writing simple/simplistic sentences instead of more complex ones that show critical thought.	SO, INSTEAD: Don't do that. Think about what kind of risk-taking you're rewarding, such as attempting to write complex sentences. Consider using a holistic score for grammar (e.g., "no errors, some errors, numerous errors").

[i]See footnote[87] / [ii]See footnote[88] / [iii]See footnote[89] / [iv]See footnote[90] / [v]See footnote[91] / [vi]See footnote[92] / [vii]See footnote[93] / [viii]See footnote[94] / [ix]See footnote[95] / [x]See footnote[96]

---

87 See Chapter 2, esp. "Principle #2: Explain Why This Lesson Matters," for an explanation of how to create RPM objectives.

88 Doug Lemov, *Teach Like a Champion 2.0: 62 Techniques That Put Students on the Path to College* (San Francisco: Jossey-Bass, 2015). For a detailed description of "Turn and Talk," see 324-335.

89 Doug Lemov, *Teach Like a Champion 2.0: 62 Techniques That Put Students on the Path to College* (San Francisco: Jossey-Bass, 2015). For a detailed description of "Cold Call," see 249-262.

90 See Chapter 2, esp. "Principle #1: Treat Students Like Detectives," for a more discussion of this idea.

91 For more guidance on training students to ask their own questions, see Sarah Tantillo, *Literacy and the Common Core: Recipes for Action* (San Francisco: Jossey-Bass, 2014), 115-127.

92 For more thoughts on teaching students how to set a purpose for reading, see Chapter 4, "Genre, Audience, and Tone."

93 For more guidance on shared reading, see my MiddleWeb blog post "Shared Reading Needs to Have a Clear Purpose," Jan. 8, 2018, found at https://www.middleweb.com/36699/shared-reading-needs-to-have-a-clear-purpose/.

94 Doug Lemov, *Teach Like a Champion 2.0: 62 Techniques That Put Students on the Path to College* (San Francisco: Jossey-Bass, 2015). For a detailed description of "Turn and Talk," see 324-335.

95 Doug Lemov, *Teach Like a Champion 2.0: 62 Techniques That Put Students on the Path to College* (San Francisco: Jossey-Bass, 2015). For a detailed description of "Cold Call," see 249-262.

96 For more thoughts on teaching students to embrace learning from mistakes, see Doug Lemov, *Teach Like a Champion 2.0: 62 Techniques That Put Students on the Path to College* (San Francisco: Jossey-Bass, 2015). For a detailed description of "Building a Culture of Error," see 64-72. See also Carol Dweck's explanation of fixed vs. growth mindset in *Mindset: The New Psychology of Success* (New York: Random House, 2006).

- What are several key factors that affect how well we write, and how do they affect our writing?

- How did the ideas in this chapter challenge, change, or confirm what you previously believed about writing instruction (or instruction in general)?

- Which resources and ideas from this chapter will you share with colleagues? Why?

Part Two:
What Should We Teach, Grade
by Grade, in K-12 ELA?

How can we apply the guiding principles of Part I systematically in K-12 ELA grammar and writing instruction? The following chapters target the Common Core Language Standards—specifically those regarding the conventions of standard English (i.e., grammar and syntax)—and each chapter includes the following:

- The trajectory of selected relevant Writing Standards (e.g., re: writing types) with guidance on how to teach them and

- Language Standards pertaining to conventions with guidance on how to teach them, including sample mini-lessons with pitches that connect the grammar points to reading and writing (with "GENRE ALERT" tags: *If you're teaching THIS writing genre, focus on this grammar standard*), plus suggestions/examples for how to efficiently assess/diagnose them.

I have clustered the grade levels (K-2, 3-5, 6-8, and 9-12) because my philosophy is that while you should know the standards for the grade you are teaching, you also should be aware of where students are coming from and where they are going. Also, in the Common Core Standards, the reading bands cut across grade levels. Note: In order to make each grade-level section as comprehensive as possible, I have included all of the information you need, regardless of whether or not it repeats something discussed in a previous grade level. So if you prefer to read only about the grades you teach, you won't miss anything (except all the other grades).

chapter
FIVE

Grades K-2 Writing and Language Instruction

K-2 WRITING STANDARDS WITH INSTRUCTIONAL GUIDANCE

We'll begin with a look at the trajectory of Writing Standards for K-2 so that we can see how the Language Standards fit in with them. Note: If you want to see all of the ELA Common Core Standards in one place, check out the "K-12 ELA Common Core Standards Tracker" on the TLC Website.[97]

---

97 The "K-12 ELA Common Core Standards Tracker" is on the TLC "Using Grammar to Improve Writing" page found at https://www.literacycookbook.com/page.php?id=161. This and other

	Writing Anchor Standard #1: *Write arguments to support claims in an analysis of substantive topics or texts, using valid reasoning and relevant and sufficient evidence.*
W K.1	Use a combination of drawing, dictating, and writing to compose opinion pieces in which they tell a reader the topic or the name of the book they are writing about and state an opinion or preference about the topic or book (e.g., My favorite book is . . .).
W 1.1	Write opinion pieces in which they introduce the topic or name the book they are writing about, state an opinion, supply a reason for the opinion, and provide some sense of closure.
W 2.1	Write opinion pieces in which they introduce the topic or book they are writing about, state an opinion, supply reasons that support the opinion, use linking words (e.g., because, and, also) to connect opinion and reasons, and provide a concluding statement or section.

With Writing Standard #1, K-2 students move from simply stating an opinion (orally and in writing) in kindergarten, to supporting their opinion with one reason (1st), to supporting it with more than one reason and using "linking words" (2nd). A few thoughts on instruction:

- Beginning in K, you can boost students' vocabulary by varying the word choice around how they state their opinions. Everything doesn't have to be "My favorite blahblahblah." Try, "I admire," or "I prefer," or "I respect," for example.

- Just because the grade 1 standard calls for "one reason" doesn't mean you should limit students to one reason. This is why I'm showing you the trajectory: so you can push them.

- The grade 2 reference to "because" and "also" brings to mind what Hochman and Wexler call "The Power of Basic Conjunctions: Because, But, So." They recommend giving students a sentence stem such as "Abraham Lincoln was a great president" and asking them to turn it into three complex sentences, using each conjunction in

standards-related resources can also be found on the TLC "Standards" page at https://www.literacy-cookbook.com/page.php?id=138.

turn: "Abraham Lincoln was a great president *because*...." "Abraham Lincoln was a great president, *but*...." "Abraham Lincoln was a great president, *so*...."[98] This approach compels students to wrestle with content more deeply.

- The standards provide little guidance on how to conclude, so you will need to show students examples of punchy concluding sentences to imitate.

	Writing Anchor Standard #2: *Write informative/explanatory texts to examine and convey complex ideas and information clearly and accurately through the effective selection, organization, and analysis of content.*
W K.2	Use a combination of drawing, dictating, and writing to compose informative/explanatory texts in which they name what they are writing about and supply some information about the topic.
W 1.2	Write informative/explanatory texts in which they name a topic, supply some facts about the topic, and provide some sense of closure.
W 2.2	Write informative/explanatory texts in which they introduce a topic, use facts and definitions to develop points, and provide a concluding statement or section.

Writing Standard #2 suggests that at the K-2 level, the writing is more descriptive and informative than explanatory. This standard should of course be taught in tandem with Reading Standard 2.1: *Ask and answer such questions as who, what, where, when, why, and how to demonstrate understanding of key details in a text.* And the writing doesn't have to be merely descriptive and informative. You can pull more interesting writing out of students by asking them "Why" or "How" questions about the topic *du jour*. Question-driven writing is more explanatory because you have to *explain how or why*; whereas topic-driven writing ("Jellyfish") tends to be very "listy"—as in, students list every fact they can find about jellyfish. If you instead ask students, "Why are some people afraid of jellyfish?" their writing will still surface (no pun intended) facts, but it will do so in the

---

98 Judith C. Hochman and Natalie Wexler, *The Writing Revolution: A Guide to Advancing Thinking Through Writing in All Subjects and Grades* (San Francisco: Jossey-Bass, 2017), 40-43.

service of an explanation. And again, Hochman and Wexler's "Because-But-So" approach will come in handy here.[99]

PS: If your state requires PARCC testing, Grade 2 teachers would benefit from training on the PARCC Research Simulation Task Writing so they are aware of those forthcoming Grade 3 expectations. For more information, see the TLC "PARCC Prep" page.[100]

	Writing Standard #3: *Write narratives to develop real or imagined experiences or events using effective technique, well-chosen details, and well-structured event sequences.*
W K.3	Use a combination of drawing, dictating, and writing to narrate a single event or several loosely linked events, tell about the events in the order in which they occurred, and provide a reaction to what happened.
W 1.3	Write narratives in which they recount two or more appropriately sequenced events, include some details regarding what happened, use temporal words to signal event order, and provide some sense of closure.
W 2.3	Write narratives in which they recount a well-elaborated event or short sequence of events, include details to describe actions, thoughts, and feelings, use temporal words to signal event order, and provide a sense of closure.

Although these words do not explicitly appear in the K-2 Writing Standards, students need to learn that narratives include a "beginning, middle, and end." Ideally, they would also learn that a story requires *conflict*—or else it is merely a listing of events. I've worked with many 3rd grade teachers who complain that their incoming students do not grasp these basic concepts. Many students seem to think that "I went to my grandmother's house and ate pie" is a story. For those who follow the Teachers College Writing Workshop approach,[101] starting with "a small moment" is

99 Judith C. Hochman and Natalie Wexler, *The Writing Revolution: A Guide to Advancing Thinking Through Writing in All Subjects and Grades* (San Francisco: Jossey-Bass, 2017), 40-43.

100 The TLC "PARCC Prep" page is found at https://www.literacycookbook.com/page.php?id=155.

101 For more information on the Teachers College Writing Workshop, see: https://readingandwritingproject.org

fine, but you need to move beyond that. And just to clarify, my friend Katy Wischow, a consultant for Teachers College, notes:

Actually, how we teach and use the term 'small moment' is that it *is* a story, but a small story—e.g., not an epic spanning decades as kids sometimes write. A story that takes place in a short time. In kindergarten, yes, kids are recounting events like eating pie. But they're also learning story structure through reading and oral storytelling, and so by grades 1 and 2 they're writing small moment stories.[102]

In my observation, not everyone implements Writing Workshop with fidelity, so this could be why we see so many pie-based/not-really-a-story stories in grades 1 and 2.

For a variety of resources to support reading and writing narratives, see the TLC "Analyzing Literature" and "Narrative Writing" pages.[103]

PS: If your state requires PARCC testing, Grade 2 teachers would benefit from training on the PARCC Narrative Writing Task to anticipate those forthcoming Grade 3 expectations. For more information on that task, see the TLC "PARCC Prep" page.[104]

Next we turn to Writing Standard #7 because there is no Writing Standard #4 for K-2, and Standard #5 speaks to process, and Standard #6 speaks to technology.

---

102 Katy Wischow, Email to the author, February 18, 2018.

103 The TLC "Analyzing Literature" page is found at https://www.literacycookbook.com/page.php?id=2. The TLC "Narrative Writing" page is found at https://www.literacycookbook.com/page.php?id=150.

104 For more information on PARCC testing preparation, see the TLC "PARCC Prep" page found at https://www.literacycookbook.com/page.php?id=155.

	Writing Anchor Standard #7: *Conduct short as well as more sustained research projects based on focused questions, demonstrating understanding of the subject under investigation.*
W K.7	Participate in shared research and writing projects (e.g., explore a number of books by a favorite author and express opinions about them).
W 1.7	Participate in shared research and writing projects (e.g., explore a number of "how-to" books on a given topic and use them to write a sequence of instructions).
W 2.7	Participate in shared research and writing projects (e.g., read a number of books on a single topic to produce a report; record science observations).

The wording of this standard is misleading: "Shared" implies "writing with a partner," which is not an effective way to write, especially if you are just learning how to write. Exactly how are teachers supposed to determine the level of participation of each partner in a collaborative writing project? I'm going to hope and assume the writers of these standards meant that students would *discuss* their texts and research findings with a partner or the class, but would then *write up their research on their own.*

Here are some additional thoughts on instruction:

- This standard presents an opportunity for students to examine patterns among related texts—whether they are related by author, approach, or topic. It will of course be important to *model how to identify patterns.* Discussions can address the sentence level—noting, for example, "I notice this author keeps repeating certain phrases" or "I notice this author uses humorous rhymes" and asking students how they feel about that. Or they can address the organizational/logistical level: "I notice these "how-to" books number the steps. Why do they do that? Why would it be a problem if they didn't?"

- As noted re: Writing Standard #2, research projects or reports should be *question-driven*, not merely topic-driven, to avoid "listy," plagiaristic writing.

- If students work together to collect evidence or examples to support their work, consider using a platform such as Google Docs so that they can work simultaneously on the same document. They can then pull from this shared research to write their own individual reports.

Note: Writing Standard #8 is about recalling information, which presumably students will do when writing their informational/explanatory texts. Writing Standards #9 and #10 do not apply to K-2 (they begin in 3rd grade).

K-2 LANGUAGE STANDARDS

In this section, we'll look at the K-2 trajectory of key Language Standards first, then go through the standards grade by grade (so: all K first, then all 1st, then all 2nd) so that we can dive more deeply into effective instructional practices. Note: If you want to track student progress on the K-12 Language Standards, check out the "K-12 Selected Language CCS Tracker" in the Appendix and on the TLC Website.[105]

	Language Anchor Standard #1: *Demonstrate command of the conventions of standard English grammar and usage when writing or speaking.*
L K.1	A) Print many upper- and lowercase letters.
	B) Use frequently occurring nouns and verbs.
	C) Form regular plural nouns orally by adding /s/
	or /es/ (e.g., dog, dogs; wish, wishes).
	D) Understand and use question words (interrogatives) (e.g., who, what, where, when, why, how).
	E) Use the most frequently occurring prepositions (e.g., to, from, in, out, on, off, for, of, by, with).
	F) Produce and expand complete sentences in shared language activities.

---

105 The "K-12 Selected Language CCS Tracker" can be downloaded from the TLC "Using Grammar to Improve Writing" page found at https://www.literacycookbook.com/page.php?id=161. Additional standards-related resources are available on the TLC "Standards" page found at https://www.literacy-cookbook.com/page.php?id=138.

L 1.1	A) Print all upper- and lowercase letters.
	B) Use common, proper, and possessive nouns.
	C) Use singular and plural nouns with matching verbs in basic sentences (e.g., He hops; We hop).
	D) Use personal, possessive, and indefinite pronouns (e.g., I, me, my; they, them, their; anyone, everything).
	E) Use verbs to convey a sense of past, present, and future (e.g., Yesterday I walked home; Today I walk home; Tomorrow I will walk home).
	F) Use frequently occurring adjectives.
	G) Use frequently occurring conjunctions (e.g., and, but, or, so, because).
	H) Use determiners (e.g., articles, demonstratives).
	I) Use frequently occurring prepositions (e.g., during, beyond, toward).
	J) Produce and expand complete simple and compound declarative, interrogative, imperative, and exclamatory sentences in response to prompts.
L 2.1	A) Use collective nouns (e.g., group).
	B) Form and use frequently occurring irregular plural nouns (e.g., feet, children, teeth, mice, fish).
	C) Use reflexive pronouns (e.g., myself, ourselves).
	D) Form and use the past tense of frequently occurring irregular verbs (e.g., sat, hid, told).
	E) Use adjectives and adverbs, and choose between them depending on what is to be modified.
	F) Produce, expand, and rearrange complete simple and compound sentences (e.g., The boy watched the movie; The little boy watched the movie; The action movie was watched by the little boy).

Next:

	Language Anchor Standard #2: *Demonstrate command of the conventions of standard English capitalization, punctuation, and spelling when writing.*
L K.2	A) Capitalize the first word in a sentence and the pronoun I.
	B) Recognize and name end punctuation.
	C) Write a letter or letters for most consonant and short-vowel sounds (phonemes).
	D) Spell simple words phonetically, drawing on knowledge of sound-letter relationships.

L 1.2	A) Capitalize dates and names of people.
	B) Use end punctuation for sentences.
	C) Use commas in dates and to separate single words in a series.
	D) Use conventional spelling for words with common spelling patterns and for frequently occurring irregular words.
	E) Spell untaught words phonetically, drawing on phonemic awareness and spelling conventions.
L 2.2	A) Capitalize holidays, product names, and geographic names.
	B) Use commas in greetings and closings of letters.
	C) Use an apostrophe to form contractions and frequently occurring possessives.
	D) Generalize learned spelling patterns when writing words (e.g., cage → badge; boy → boil).
	E) Consult reference materials, including beginning dictionaries, as needed to check and correct spellings.

Next:

	Language Anchor Standard #3: *Apply knowledge of language to understand how language functions in different contexts, to make effective choices for meaning or style, and to comprehend more fully when reading or listening.*
L K.3	**Begins in grade 2.**
L 1.3	**Begins in grade 2.**
L 2.3	Use knowledge of language and its conventions when writing, speaking, reading, or listening.
	A) Compare formal and informal uses of English.

(Note: Language Standards #4-6 deal primarily with vocabulary, so we will not analyze them here. For guidance on vocabulary instruction, see *The Literacy Cookbook*.[106])

K LANGUAGE STANDARDS: A DEEPER DIVE

In the next three sections, we'll dive more deeply into each grade's Language Standards and look at ways to teach and assess them more systematically, in conjunction with writing instruction. These are by no means the *only*

---

106 Sarah Tantillo, *The Literacy Cookbook: A Practical Guide to Effective Reading, Writing, Speaking, and Listening Instruction* (San Francisco: Jossey-Bass, 2012), 28-36. For online resources, see the TLC "Building Robust Vocabulary" page found at https://www.literacycookbook.com/page.php?id=4.

ways to teach these standards, just a few to illustrate how to connect grammar with writing and reading. We begin with kindergarten.

L K.1.A: Print many upper- and lowercase letters.

TEACHING THIS:

This book does not explain phonics instruction, but I recommend K-2 teachers use it to teach students how to read, which means that as they learn sounds attached to letters and phonemes, they also learn how to write them. That said, here are some additional tips:

- For a lesson on patterns, show "letter lines" (A-Z) of upper- and lowercase letters. Ask students to comment on what similarities and differences they notice (e.g., "B" is bigger than "b.").
- Discuss WHY we use capital letters when writing: 1) to show we are starting a new sentence, 2) to show respect for a name of a person, place, or thing (AKA proper nouns), and 3) to show we are shouting ("IS ANYBODY HOME???").
- Model writing the letters, reminding students about how they sound and words that begin with them.
- Point to examples of the letters in texts you read aloud.

ASSESSING THIS:

Dictated quizzes, especially with erasable white boards, can quickly capture which students are "getting it" and which need more support.

L K.1.B: Use frequently occurring nouns and verbs.

TEACHING THIS:

- This standard reminds me of when I first learned to speak French. We were taught to say and write things like, "The book is on the table. The pencil is on the desk. I need some paper. I write. I draw." In other words: basic, functional things that people could point to and comment on. In *Bringing Words to Life*, Beck, McKeown, and Kucan refer to these as "Tier 1" words.· These words are certainly important. But we should not forget that students' listening comprehension is higher than their reading comprehension, so let's also use Tier 2 words—more robust vocabulary—when speaking to the little ones. One day a kindergarten teacher came up to me about a week after I'd made this point in a workshop, and she said, "You'll never believe what happened. One of my students used the word 'continuum'! I asked him how he knew that word, and he looked at me and said, 'You used it last week.'"

*See footnote[107]

L K.1.C: Form regular plural nouns orally by adding /s/ or /es/ (e.g., dog, dogs; wish, wishes).[108]

- This book does not explain phonics instruction but recommends its use for this standard. That said, this standard provides an opportunity to discuss "formal vs. informal" language and code-switching. See Chapter 2—specifically "Principle #6: Provide Oral Support"—for suggestions on how to do this.

L K.1.D: Understand and use question words (interrogatives) (e.g., who, what, where, when, why, how).

---

107 Isabel L. Beck, Margaret G. McKeown, and Linda Kucan, *Bringing Words to Life: Robust Vocabulary Instruction* (New York: Guilford Press, 2002), 8.

108 The general rule, of course, is to add *–s* to form the plural of most nouns; add *–es* to singular nouns ending in *–s, -sh, -ch,* and *–x*. For more information on forming plural nouns, see Diana Hacker and Nancy Sommers, *Rules for Writers* (Boston: Bedford/St. Martin's, 2016, 8th edition), 346-347.

TEACHING THIS:

- This standard should be paired with *L K.2.B: Recognize and name end punctuation.*

- The most obvious way to introduce this standard is to ask questions orally and point to the written question words for visual support. You will definitely want an anchor chart for the 5Ws and H questions. See "The Most Important Writing Standard" in Chapter 4 for the "5Ws and H Organizer."

- In morning meetings, ask students questions about whatever topic you are discussing.

- You can kick things up a notch by teaching students how to play "Jeopardy"— responding to an "answer" with a question. For example:

  o "Answer: The Coolest Teacher on the Planet."

  o *"Question: Who is [Your Name Here]?"*

ASSESSING THIS:

- As noted above, to demonstrate understanding of how to use question words, students could play "Jeopardy": Given an answer (e.g., "in Newark"), students generate a logical question (e.g., "Where is this school located?" or "Where do we live?"). This is a good vehicle for reviewing content.

- Dictated quizzes, especially with erasable white boards, can quickly capture which students are "getting it" and which need more support.

L K.1.E: Use the most frequently occurring prepositions (e.g., to, from, in, out, on, off, for, of, by, with).

TEACHING THIS:

- You will need a soft object such as a squoosh ball or a small pillow—something that won't hurt anyone. Place the object in various locations and emphasize the phrases that capture its location: "The ball is *ON the desk*. The ball is *IN the closet*. I brought this ball *TO school* today *FOR you*." Invite students to generate their own sentences emphasizing the prepositional phrases.

- As always, reinforce oral language with visual support such as an anchor chart listing the prepositions you want them to use or a PowerPoint presentation that quizzes them.

ASSESSING THIS:

- First, read aloud sentences and invite students to identify the prepositional phrases (e.g., "to him"). You can engage the entire class in practice by doing this with a rapid-fire turn-and-talk approach. Don't forget to model this: "I'll say the sentence once, then Partner A will turn to Partner B and restate *only* the prepositional phrase to Partner B. For example, if I said, 'I gave the book to Joe,' Partner A would turn to Partner B and say, 'TO JOE.' Let's see a model pair try this…." Select a pair to demonstrate, then launch a whole-class attempt. Then cold-call and clarify if anyone was confused. Run a few rounds, then switch the partner roles.

- Students should move from identifying the phrases to imitating your sentences using prepositions, then writing their own.

- Cloze reading (text with blanks where, in this case, the prepositions belong) is another useful way to check for understanding.

L K.1.F: Produce and expand complete sentences in shared language activities.

TEACHING THIS:

- From Day One, students should be required to speak with complete sentences in every classroom. As I noted in *The Literacy Cookbook*, the oral practice of expressing complete thoughts translates into more penetrating reading and more coherent writing, plus it teaches other students (who hear these complete explanations) more in the process.*

- Whenever you're working explicitly on this standard—which you will probably do frequently—it's important to make students aware of what they are doing. Here's a sample pitch: *Class, whenever we speak or write, we always strive to use complete sentences. We do this because we want people to understand us. If I suddenly blurted out, "Dog!" you might imagine I saw a dog, but you couldn't be sure. Maybe I meant, "I want a dog!" Whereas, if I said, "I see a dog," you would know what I meant. "I see a dog" is a complete sentence, and that's helpful. But it might not be enough. It would be more helpful to be more specific. Like, I could say, "I see a big dog." Or, "I see a big dog on a leash." That way you would know it's OK; it's on a leash. Today we're going to work on building our complete sentences and expanding them to add more specific information….*

- After that pitch, you could tie your instruction to particular building blocks, such as nouns and verbs (L K.1.B), plural nouns (L K.1.C), question words (L K.1.D), or prepositions (L K.1.E).

- At the K level, students will need lots of practice in both speaking and writing complete sentences. Modeling is key. Also, don't forget to ask, "What do you *like* about that sentence?" Revisit "Principle #3: Ask, 'What Do You *Like* About That Sentence?'" in Chapter 2 for more ideas about this approach.

- PS: This is a great vehicle for reviewing content.

*See footnote[109]

L K.2.A: Capitalize the first word in a sentence and the pronoun I.

TEACHING THIS:

- This standard pairs well with *L K.1.A: Print many upper- and lowercase letters.*
- Remind students WHY we use capital letters when writing: 1) to show we are starting a new sentence, 2) to show respect for a name of a person, place, or thing (AKA proper nouns), and 3) to show we are shouting ("IS ANYBODY HOME???"). In this case, "I" is the person being respected.
- Write model sentences that include "I" and have students imitate these.

ASSESSING THIS:

- Dictated quizzes, especially with erasable white boards, can quickly capture which students are "getting it" and which need more support.
- With paper and pencil, you can also give students several words and ask them to use them in a sentence with proper capitalization and end punctuation.

L K.2.B: Recognize and name end punctuation.

TEACHING THIS:

- This standard should be paired with *L K.1.D: Understand and use question words (interrogatives) (e.g., who, what, where, when, why, how).*
- You might begin by inviting students to read two "sentences," noting, "I think something is wrong with one of them. Let's see if we can figure out what it is." For example: 1) "Olivia gets dressed." 2) "Olivia likes to go to the beach" (Hopefully they will notice that #2 is missing end punctuation and suggest adding a period, and you can move into your pitch.)
- Sample pitch: *As we work on writing complete sentences, one thing we need to pay close attention to is END PUNCTUATION. If you write a "sentence" without end punctuation, it's not actually over yet; it's not a complete sentence. If we don't end our sentences, readers will get confused [Give an example of a run-on here, to illustrate such confusion]. The kind of end punctuation we use depends on what we are trying to say. We have choices!*

---

109 Sarah Tantillo, *The Literacy Cookbook: A Practical Guide to Effective Reading, Writing, Speaking, and Listening Instruction* (San Francisco: Jossey-Bass, 2013), 116.

• Show students sample sentences with periods and exclamation points and read them with dramatic flair to demonstrate the difference. Then move into question marks.
ASSESSING THIS: • At the K level, you will begin with oral practice (students telling you which punctuation makes the most sense), then move into reading practice ("Read each sentence and add the appropriate end punctuation"), then move into more authentic writing practice ("Write three questions").

L K.2.C: Write a letter or letters for most consonant and short-vowel sounds (phonemes).

- This book does not explain phonics instruction but recommends its use for this standard.

L K.2.D: Spell simple words phonetically, drawing on knowledge of sound-letter relationships.

- This book does not explain phonics instruction but recommends its use for this standard.

L K.3: N/A: Begins in grade 2.

GRADE 1 LANGUAGE STANDARDS: A DEEPER DIVE

Next, we'll dive more deeply into the Grade 1 Language Standards and look at how to teach and assess them more systematically, in conjunction with writing instruction. Again, these are by no means the *only* ways to teach these standards, just a few to illustrate how to connect grammar with writing and reading.

L 1.1.A: Print all upper- and lowercase letters.

TEACHING THIS: *[This repeats L K.1.A.]*

This book does not explain phonics instruction, but I recommend K-2 teachers use it to teach students how to read, which means that as they learn sounds attached to letters and phonemes, they also learn how to write them. That said, here are some additional tips:

- For a lesson on patterns, show "letter lines" (A-Z) of upper- and lowercase letters. Ask students to comment on what similarities and differences they notice (e.g., "B" is bigger than "b.").
- Discuss WHY we use capital letters when writing: 1) to show we are starting a new sentence, 2) to show respect for a name of a person, place, or thing (AKA proper nouns), and 3) to show we are shouting ("IS ANYBODY HOME???").
- Model writing the letters, reminding students about how they sound and words that begin with them.
- Point to examples of the letters in texts you read aloud.

ASSESSING THIS:

Dictated quizzes, especially with erasable white boards, can quickly capture which students are "getting it" and which need more support.

L 1.1.B: Use common, proper, and possessive nouns.

TEACHING THIS:

- This standard should be paired with *L 1.2.A: Capitalize [dates and] names of people.*
- When it comes to introducing the differences among common, proper, and possessive nouns, you might begin by showing these three examples: dog, Snoopy, and Snoopy's. Then ask students to explain the differences among these three. Of course, you could also start smaller and simply compare "dog" to "Snoopy," then later move to "Snoopy" versus "Snoopy's."
- In your pitch, it makes sense to focus on the value of clarity. For example: *Why are we paying attention to the little differences between these two words [or among these three words]? Because good writers strive for clarity; they want to ensure that readers know what they are talking about, so they provide clues for the reader. We capitalize names like "Snoopy"—and in fact, we capitalize not just the names of people or animals but also the names of places (like "New Jersey") and things (like "the Democratic Party")—as a sign of respect. We're not just talking about any old dog; we're talking about Snoopy. And we add the "apostrophe –s" to show possession: Something belongs to Snoopy.*

- If you want to start with only common nouns, you might tell students that you need to make labels for every object in the classroom and need their assistance. Then take particular care to note why you are NOT capitalizing the labels for common nouns. Then you could label yourself, capitalizing your name, and delve into the pitch about proper nouns.

- After a preliminary introduction to SINGULAR possessive nouns, you should point out that PLURAL nouns can also be possessive. For example, "the children's favorite book" or "my two cats' food bowls." *Since the plural ends with –s (when it's regular), we only add the apostrophe.*

- Students should practice writing sentences that use these different types of nouns.

- Show students how to edit incorrect sentences by double-underlining the first letter for nouns that *should* be capitalized.

ASSESSING THIS:

- Give students sentences without nouns capitalized; they should double-underline the first letter of any word that should be capitalized. Also, either during the quiz or while going over it, they should also explain *why* that word should be capitalized, e.g., "Fido is the name of a particular dog, a proper noun, so it should be capitalized."

- As always, we want students to demonstrate their grasp of these grammatical concepts in their own writing, first in sentences then in paragraphs. Give them several words they must include in a paragraph about a text or topic they are studying, and tell them you will score the paragraph based on two things: 1) All sentences must be complete, and 2) Proper and possessive nouns should be written and punctuated correctly.

L 1.1.C: Use singular and plural nouns with matching verbs in basic sentences (e.g., He hops; We hop).

TEACHING THIS:

- This standard should be paired with *L 1.1.D: Use personal, possessive, and indefinite pronouns (e.g., I, me, my; they, them, their; anyone, everything).*
- Show students this information (or other regular verbs you prefer), and ask them what pattern(s) they notice:
  - o I talk.---------------I laugh.
  - o You talk.-----------You laugh.
  - o We talk.------------We laugh.
  - o They talk.----------They laugh.
  - o He/She/It talks.---He/She/It laughs.
- They should notice that only the 3rd person singular (He/She/It) verb ends with –s.
- Ask them to apply this rule with other verbs.
- Replace the pronouns with singular and plural nouns, and ask them to apply the rule again.
- This standard provides an opportunity to discuss "formal vs. informal" language and code-switching. See Chapter 2—specifically "Principle #6: Provide Oral Support"—for suggestions on how to do this.

ASSESSING THIS:

- Dictated quizzes, especially with erasable white boards, can quickly capture which students are "getting it" and which need more support.
- As always, we want students to demonstrate their grasp of these grammatical concepts in their own writing, first in sentences then in paragraphs. Give them several verbs they must include in a paragraph about a text or topic they are studying, and tell them you will score the paragraph based on two things: 1) All sentences must be complete, and 2) All verbs must agree with their subjects.
- Cloze reading (text with blanks where, in this case, the verbs belong) is another useful way to check for understanding.

L 1.1.D: Use personal, possessive, and indefinite pronouns (e.g., I, me, my; they, them, their; anyone, everything).

TEACHING THIS:

- This standard should be paired with *L 1.1.C: Use singular and plural nouns with matching verbs in basic sentences (e.g., He hops; We hop).*
- See Chapter 2, "Principle #1: Treat Students Like Detectives," for a description of how to introduce **personal pronouns.** See also Chapter 3 for "Cloze Reading Passage: Personal Pronouns."
- Following from that introduction, which includes the sentence "I met Christine and Rochelle for dinner," here's the pitch: *Good writers use pronouns to avoid repeating themselves. Imagine how silly it would sound if I wrote an entire paragraph about dinner with Christine and Rochelle and never used "they" or "them"! "Christine and Rochelle ordered lasagna. Christine and Rochelle liked the garlic bread. Christine and Rochelle talked about their jobs...."* Note: Based on this pitch, students should infer that pronouns should agree with their antecedents (i.e., "they" agrees with "Christine and Rochelle"), but you may need to emphasize this point if students seem confused.
- Use your current read-aloud text as the base from which to translate nouns into pronouns (e.g., replace "Olivia" with "she"). Invite students to help with this.
- Modeling and having students imitate sentences is the key. PS: Students don't need to know about your golf game. Use sentences from their current text(s) to reinforce content while simultaneously illustrating the grammar points you want to teach.
- A few technical points:
    - When you're ready to turn to **possessive pronouns** (*my, mine, your, yours, her, hers, his, its, our, ours, your, yours, their, theirs*), remember that some function as *adjectives* (e.g., *my* laptop).
    - Regarding **indefinite pronouns** (*anything, anyone, some*, etc.), most are always singular (*everyone, each*); some are always plural (*both, many*); and a few may be either. Most indefinite pronouns substitute for nouns, but some also function as adjectives (*All* campers must check in....).*

ASSESSING THIS:

- As always, we want students to demonstrate their grasp of these grammatical concepts in their own writing, first in sentences then in paragraphs. Give them several pronouns they must include in a paragraph about a text or topic they are studying, and tell them you will score the paragraph based on two things: 1) All sentences must be complete, and 2) All pronouns must be used properly.
- Cloze reading (text with blanks where, in this case, the pronouns belong) is another useful way to check for understanding.

*See footnote[110]

---

110 Diana Hacker and Nancy Sommers, *Rules for Writers* (Boston: Bedford/St. Martin's, 2016, 8th edition), 364. See this page for a list of indefinite pronouns.

L 1.1.E: Use verbs to convey a sense of past, present, and future (e.g., Yesterday I walked home; Today I walk home; Tomorrow I will walk home).

TEACHING THIS:
- This standard follows from *L 1.1.C: Use singular and plural nouns with matching verbs in basic sentences (e.g., He hops; We hop)*. Once students grasp basic sentence structure (subject + verb=sentence) and present tense, you can move into different tenses.

- **GENRE ALERT: Students will need to apply this standard when working on narrative writing (W 1.3).**

- Show students examples of different tenses. You can even use the exact words from this standard: *Yesterday I walked home; Today I walk home; Tomorrow I will walk home*. Invite them to explain how these sentences are different. Discuss the clues such as time-indicating words and different verb forms.

- Note that English is a challenging language with many exceptions to rules, so not all verbs are "regular." For example, even though we say, "I walked" and "I laughed," we don't say, "I runned" or "I haved." English contains numerous irregular verbs, and you simply have to learn them.

- Model writing a narrative paragraph in either past or future tense, inviting student input as you go. Be sure to point out transitions/signal words such as "then," "before," and "after." Remind students that transitions help readers steer through the text and follow what is going on; you can illustrate this by leaving out some transitions to show how confusing such writing can be.

- Let students imitate and practice sentences focused on different tenses, then move into paragraph writing.

ASSESSING THIS:
- As always, we want students to demonstrate their grasp of these grammatical concepts in their own writing, first in sentences then in paragraphs. For **past tense,** they could write a narrative paragraph about "what happened from when I entered school this morning till I arrived in this class" or some variation on that idea. For **future tense,** the topic could be "what I will do between leaving school and going to bed tonight." Tell them you will score the paragraph based on three things: 1) All sentences must be complete, 2) They should include transitions/signal words such as "then" and "after," and 3) All verbs must be written in the appropriate tense.

- Cloze reading (text with blanks where, in this case, the verbs or the transitions belong) is another useful way to check for understanding.

L 1.1.F: Use frequently occurring adjectives.

TEACHING THIS:

- **GENRE ALERT: Students should apply this standard when working on narrative writing (W 1.3).**

- Show students a few sentences (ideally about a text they're currently reading or a topic they're studying) in two columns: 1) Column 1 should be bare-bones statements with no adjectives; 2) Column 2 should be statements that include adjectives. Ask students to compare the sentences in Column 1 to those in Column 2: *What do you notice? What do you like about the sentences in Column 2?*

- The pitch: *Good writers—just like good artists—use a variety of tools to convey their messages to readers. One key tool is adjectives, which help us SEE what they are saying more clearly. It's easier to picture a cat if someone describes it beyond saying, "I have a cat." For example, I could say, "My cat Lulu has mostly gray and black fur, so her white paws look like fancy gloves or socks." And you would see that. If I added, "And she's fat—gigantic, really. She weighs 20 pounds!" that would give you an even clearer picture. And keep in mind that adjectives are not just about SEEING; they can address all five senses: sight, sound, smell, taste, touch. Starting today, we're going to pay more attention to how we use adjectives and sensory details in our writing....*

- Show students examples of sentences using adjectives to capture sensory details, and have them imitate these.

- Boost their vocabulary with lists of sensory-related adjectives.

- Then move into students generating their own adjective-laden sentences about a given text or topic. Note: Tying writing to the text or topic at hand is an effective way to review content. It also ensures that everyone has enough background knowledge to generate ideas. The direction "Write about whatever you want" can stymie students because some believe there is always a right answer and they don't know what it is, while others become so focused on impressing their peers that they cannot decide what to write about. With a common text or topic as the focus, students don't have to worry about any of that and can put their own creative spin on the material.

ASSESSING THIS:

- An early quiz might give students bare-bones sentences and ask them to insert adjectives to make them more compelling.

- As always, we want students to demonstrate their grasp of these grammatical concepts in their own writing, first in sentences then in paragraphs. Ask them to write a descriptive paragraph about a text or topic they are studying, and tell them you will score the paragraph based on two things: 1) All sentences must be complete, and 2) The paragraph must include at least THREE DIFFERENT KINDS of sensory details.

L 1.1.G: Use frequently occurring conjunctions (e.g., and, but, or, so, because).

TEACHING THIS:

- Show students a pair of sentences that could be logically combined with a conjunction—e.g., "I like peanut butter. I don't like jelly." Ask them, "If you had to combine these sentences and turn them into one sentence, how could you do it? There is not one right answer here, but I will ask you to explain your thinking. Talk to your neighbor." Students might come up with "Insert a semi-colon!" (There's always one in the crowd), but at some point they will realize that inserting a comma then "but" makes the most sense. Note that "but" is called a "conjunction" [specifically, **a coordinating conjunction**], and move into the pitch: *Today we're going to start paying more attention to conjunctions because they help us build bigger, stronger sentences. And they help us vary our sentence structures so that we're not always writing short, choppy sentences. With a conjunction, we can combine two simple sentences to form a "compound sentence." Let's look at some more short sentences that we can combine with conjunctions— and let's see if we can figure out what the other conjunctions are, besides "but."*

- Provide pairs of sentences and ask students to combine them logically. Note that a comma must precede the conjunction when two independent clauses are being combined. [Stunningly, this point is not addressed in the Common Core Standards until grade 4. See *L 4.2.C: Use a comma before a coordinating conjunction in a compound sentence.*]

- Note the useful mnemonic FANBOYS for coordinating conjunctions: *for, and, nor, but, or, yet, so.*

- Model other uses of conjunctions—phrases such as "this or that" and "bread and butter"—to remind students that conjunctions provide the glue to combine not only sentences but also words and phrases.

- After working through the coordinating conjunctions, introduce "because," **a subordinating conjunction**, and have students practice Hochman and Wexler's "Because, But, So" approach (described earlier in this chapter, in the "K-2 Writing Standards with Instructional Guidance" section).*

ASSESSING THIS:

- Ultimately, of course, you want students to practice using FANBOYS in their own writing.

- Also, per Hochman and Wexler, students should expand sentences with *because, but,* and *so.*

- Cloze reading (text with blanks where, in this case, the conjunctions belong) is another useful way to check for understanding.

*See footnote[111]

---

111 Judith C. Hochman and Natalie Wexler, *The Writing Revolution: A Guide to Advancing Thinking Through Writing in All Subjects and Grades* (San Francisco: Jossey-Bass, 2017), 40-43.

L 1.1.H: Use determiners (e.g., articles, demonstratives).

TEACHING THIS:
- This standard is a powerful reminder of how difficult it is to learn English. You might read the description and think, *OK, students need to know "A, an, the, this, that, these, those"*: What's the big deal? But if you consult a reference manual such as Hacker and Sommers's *Rules for Writers*, you will find NINE PAGES devoted to articles.[*] There are nuances to the use of articles that we never think about. For instance, the rule "Use *the* with most specific common nouns" is followed by SIX particular sub-rule situations:[**]

    1. The noun has been previously mentioned: e.g., "A rabbit ran in front of my car. Fortunately, THE rabbit was fast enough to avoid being hit."

    2. A phrase or clause following the noun restricts its identity: e.g., "THE strings in Christine's tennis racquet were not taut enough."

    3. A superlative adjective such as best or most intelligent makes the noun's identity specific: e.g., "She always wanted to talk to THE smartest man in the room."

    4. The noun describes a unique person, place, or thing: e.g., "He loved to swim in THE ocean."

    5. The context or situation makes the noun's identity clear: e.g., "I asked him to close THE window because I was freezing."

    6. The noun is singular and refers to a scientific class or category of items (most often animals, musical instruments, and inventions): e.g., "THE ice box was an early form of what we now call a refrigerator."

- All of this is to say: Do your homework. Buy *Rules for Writers* or some equally comprehensive manual (though that's my favorite) to review the minutiae of seemingly easy standards.[***] Then apply the seven principles I explained in Chapter 2. Start by showing examples of how articles and other determiners are used, let students derive the rules, and let them practice using these tools.

ASSESSING THIS:
- Students should practice using articles and demonstratives such as *a, an, the, this, that, these,* and *those* in their own writing.

- Cloze reading (text with blanks where, in this case, the articles and other determiners belong) is another useful way to check for understanding.

*See footnote[112] / **See footnote[113] / ***See footnote[114]

---

112 Diana Hacker and Nancy Sommers, *Rules for Writers* (Boston: Bedford/St. Martin's, 2016, 8th edition), 270-279.

113 Diana Hacker and Nancy Sommers, *Rules for Writers* (Boston: Bedford/St. Martin's, 2016, 8th edition), 272-274. Note: The explanations of the rules are theirs; the examples are mine.

114 Diana Hacker and Nancy Sommers, *Rules for Writers* (Boston: Bedford/St. Martin's, 2016, 8th edition).

L 1.1.I: Use frequently occurring prepositions (e.g., during, beyond, toward).

TEACHING THIS: *[This repeats L K.1.E.]*

- You will need a soft object such as a squoosh ball or a small pillow—something that won't hurt anyone. Place the object in various locations and emphasize the phrases that capture its location: "The ball is *ON the desk*. The ball is *IN the closet*. I brought this ball *TO school* today *FOR you*." Invite students to generate their own sentences emphasizing the prepositional phrases.

- As always, reinforce oral language with visual support such as an anchor chart listing the prepositions you want them to use or a PowerPoint presentation that quizzes them.

ASSESSING THIS:

- First, read aloud sentences and invite students to identify the prepositional phrases (e.g., "to him"). You can engage the entire class in practice by doing this with a rapid-fire turn-and-talk approach. Don't forget to model this: "I'll say the sentence once, then Partner A will turn to Partner B and restate *only* the prepositional phrase to Partner B. For example, if I said, 'I gave the book to Joe,' Partner A would turn to Partner B and say, 'TO JOE.' Let's see a model pair try this…." Select a pair to demonstrate, then launch a whole-class attempt. Then cold-call and clarify if anyone was confused. Run a few rounds, then switch the partner roles.

- Students should move from identifying the phrases to imitating your sentences using prepositions, then writing their own.

- Cloze reading (text with blanks where, in this case, the prepositions belong) is another useful way to check for understanding.

L 1.1.J: Produce and expand complete simple and compound declarative, interrogative, imperative, and exclamatory sentences in response to prompts.

TEACHING THIS:

- This standard should follow from *L 1.2.B: Use end punctuation for sentences.*
- After that mini-lesson on "why we NEED end punctuation," delve into different types of sentences. By this point, students should be familiar with simple and compound declarative sentences (assuming you have dealt with conjunctions: See *L 1.1.G: Use frequently occurring conjunctions.*), and they should have seen interrogative sentences in kindergarten (See *L K.1.D: Understand and use question words [interrogatives] [e.g., who, what, where, when, why, how]*). The two new types of sentences are **imperative** ("Turn off that TV.") and **exclamatory** ("Wow, that's loud!"); you can begin with either one.
- In either case, show students examples of the type of sentence you are introducing, and ask them to tell their neighbor what they notice, then share their ideas with the class. With imperatives, they should recognize that the sentences are requests or commands. With exclamatory sentences, they should notice the exclamation point: The purpose is to exclaim.
- Students should practice imitating the given sentences, then write their own. You could make this playful by providing scenarios for them to respond to. For example: *Imagine someone accidentally spilled milk on your desk. What POLITE imperative sentence might you say? What POLITE exclamatory sentence might you say?*

ASSESSING THIS:

- As always, we want students to demonstrate their grasp of these grammatical concepts in their own writing. Provide prompts/scenarios for them to respond to with a sentence or two.

L 1.2.A: Capitalize dates and names of people.

TEACHING THIS:

- The first half of this standard should be taught with *L 1.2.C: Use commas in dates [and to separate single words in a series].*
- You can address the first part of this standard every morning by modeling the correct format of the date—e.g., "Monday, January 8, 2018"—and reminding students that 1) we capitalize the NAMES OF DATES (days, months, and holidays) and 2) we need the commas to keep the information organized. For example, Monday and January are two different things. The comma between "8" and "2018" makes it easier to distinguish between the date and year.
- To teach the second part of this standard, see *L 1.1.B: Use common, proper, and possessive nouns.*

L 1.2.B: Use end punctuation for sentences.

TEACHING THIS: *[This repeats L K.2.B.]*

- This standard should precede *L 1.1.J: Produce and expand complete simple and compound declarative, interrogative, imperative, and exclamatory sentences in response to prompts.*

- Invite students to read two "sentences," noting, "I think something is wrong with one of them. Let's see if we can figure out what it is." For example: 1) "Olivia gets dressed." 2) "Olivia likes to go to the beach" (Hopefully they will notice that #2 is missing end punctuation and suggest adding a period, and you can move into your pitch.)

- Sample pitch: *As we work on writing complete sentences, one thing we need to pay close attention to is END PUNCTUATION. If you write a "sentence" without end punctuation, it's not actually over yet; it's not a complete sentence. And the kind of end punctuation we use depends on what we are trying to say. We have choices!*

- Show students sample sentences with periods and exclamation points and read them with dramatic flair to demonstrate the difference. Then move into question marks.

ASSESSING THIS:

- Initially, you will begin with oral practice (students telling you which punctuation makes the most sense), then move into reading practice ("Read each sentence and add the appropriate end punctuation"), then move into more authentic writing practice ("Write three questions about Frog or Toad"). Remember, working on skills is also a good time to review content and assess comprehension.

L 1.2.C: Use commas in dates and to separate single words in a series.

TEACHING THIS:

- To teach the first part of this standard, see *L 1.2.A: Capitalize dates [and names of people].*
- To teach the second part of this standard, show students a sentence with a list—e.g., "When I went on a picnic, I brought sandwiches, chips, and water." Ask them, "Why do you think I needed the comma between 'sandwiches' and 'chips'? Tell your neighbor what you think." Listen to what they say and steer them toward the notion that the comma separates items so that we can understand what the writer meant; otherwise we might think "sandwiches" was trying to describe "chips." As we know from studying and using adjectives, adjectives go directly before the nouns they describe (*"fast car*, not *fast, car"*) [See *L 1.1.F: Use frequently occurring adjectives.*]
- To practice, you could play "I'm Going on a Picnic, and I'm Bringing…" but require students to say, "Comma," after each item in the list: "I'm going on a picnic, and I'm bringing bread, comma, soda, comma, and cheese."

ASSESSING THIS:

- To assess the first part of this standard, see *L 1.2.A: Capitalize dates [and names of people].*
- Ask students to write a sentence about a current text or topic; the only requirement is that it must include a properly punctuated list.

L 1.2.D: Use conventional spelling for words with common spelling patterns and for frequently occurring irregular words.

- This book does not explain phonics instruction but recommends its use for this standard.

L 1.2.E: Spell untaught words phonetically, drawing on phonemic awareness and spelling conventions.

- This book does not explain phonics instruction but recommends its use for this standard.

L 1.3: N/A: Begins in grade 2.

GRADE 2 LANGUAGE STANDARDS: A DEEPER DIVE

Next, we'll dive more deeply into the Grade 2 Language Standards and look at how to teach and assess them more systematically, in conjunction with writing instruction. Again, these are by no means the *only* ways to teach these standards, just a few to illustrate how to connect grammar with writing and reading.

L 2.1.A: Use collective nouns (e.g., group).

TEACHING THIS:

- Remember that students were introduced to different types of nouns in 1ˢᵗ grade (*L 1.1.B: Use common, proper, and possessive nouns.*).
- Show students a list of collective nouns such as *committee, group, audience, class, family,* and *team* and ask them to discuss with a neighbor what they think these words have in common. Cold-calling should elicit that they are all words that describe a collection of people.
- The pitch: *Right, and for this reason they are called "collective nouns." But there is something a little unusual about them. I'm going to give you a few sentences using these words and see if you can figure out what is unusual.*
- Show them sentences such as:
  - o *The group is large, but I think it can fit in that classroom.*
  - o *When the rock star appeared on stage, the audience was thrilled.*
  - o *The committee gave its approval for the request.*
- If they are stumped, give them a hint: *Pay close attention to the verbs.*
- If they are still stumped, underline the nouns and circle the verbs. Then say, *If a collective noun represents a COLLECTION of people, that means it's more than one person. So wait: Why isn't the verb plural? Why don't we say, "The group are large"? This is the weird thing: Collective nouns are singular. Let's look at these examples….*
- Show students collective nouns for places, such as *range (of mountains), forest, suite, library*; and things (including living things), such as *basket, batch, deck (of cards), wad, swarm.*˙
- Brainstorm a more complete list of collective nouns for people, places, and things, and make this an anchor chart. Students should practice writing sentences using collective nouns.

ASSESSING THIS:

- As always, we want students to demonstrate their grasp of these grammatical concepts in their own writing, first in sentences then in paragraphs. List several collective nouns they must include in a paragraph about a text or topic they are studying, and tell them you will score the paragraph based on two things: 1) All sentences must be complete, and 2) Collective nouns should agree with their verbs.

- Cloze reading (text with blanks where, in this case, the proper verbs connected to collective nouns belong) is another useful way to check for understanding.

*See footnote[115]

L 2.1.B: Form and use frequently occurring irregular plural nouns (e.g., feet, children, teeth, mice, fish).

TEACHING THIS:

- This book does not explain phonics instruction but recommends its use for this standard. That said, this standard provides an opportunity to remind students of how we form *regular* plural nouns (See *L K.1.C: Form regular plural nouns orally by adding /s/ or /es/ [e.g., dog, dogs; wish, wishes]*) and to point out that English is a highly irregular language.

- PS: A quick Google search will produce a list of common irregular plural nouns.

ASSESSING THIS:

- As always, students need to practice writing with these forms.
- Be sure to review regular plural noun forms, as well. You can design quick quizzes in which students choose the correct form when the correct and incorrect forms are provided in context like this:
  - o The dog/dogs sat on the floor and ate their biscuits.
  - o For my birthday, I made three wishes/wishs.
  - o All of the childs/children in first grade like cupcakes.

  PS: Make sure students underline any context clues.

---

115 Jeff Anderson with Whitney La Rocca, *Patterns of Power: Inviting Young Writers into the Conventions of Language, Grades 1-5* (Portland, ME, Stenhouse Publishers, 2017), 117-118.

L 2.1.C: Use reflexive pronouns (e.g., myself, ourselves).

TEACHING THIS:

- Show students several sentences using reflexive pronouns (such as those that follow) and ask them to discuss with a neighbor first *Who is the subject?* Then *Who is the object?*
    - o I dressed myself.
    - o The chef accidentally cut herself.
- Cold-calling should elicit that the subject and object are the same person. This is one way to tell you need a reflexive pronoun as opposed to a personal pronoun: You wouldn't write, "I dressed me."
- Pitch: *Knowing how to use reflexive pronouns makes it easier for you to write more complex sentences. If you didn't know about reflexive pronouns, how could you buy yourself an ice cream cone? How would you say that—"I bought [Your Name Here] an ice cream cone"??? Which brings us to another important point:*
- Reflexive pronouns can also be indirect objects, as in "I made a cup of tea *for myself.*" In this case, the cup of tea is the object.
- Reflexive pronouns can also be used as **intensive pronouns**, as in "Bruce Springsteen *himself* sang at her brother's wedding.'"
- Caveat: Be careful not to replace personal pronouns with reflexive pronouns. "Sandy and myself went swimming" is incorrect. It should be "Sandy and I went swimming."
- Students should practice writing sentences about a current text or topic using reflexive and intensive pronouns.

ASSESSING THIS:

- Cloze reading (text with blanks where, in this case, the proper reflexive or intensive pronouns belong) is another useful way to check for understanding.

*See footnote[116]

L 2.1.D: Form and use the past tense of frequently occurring irregular verbs (e.g., sat, hid, told).

TEACHING THIS:

- This standard follows from *L 1.1.E: Use verbs to convey a sense of past, present, and future (e.g., Yesterday I walked home; Today I walk home; Tomorrow I will walk home).*

---

116 Diana Hacker and Nancy Sommers, *Rules for Writers* (Boston: Bedford/St. Martin's, 2016, 8th edition), 363-364.

- Again, we have another opportunity to remark upon how irregular the English language is! Start with the regular forms of past tense verbs—e.g., *talk*→ *talked* and *ask*→ *asked*—and show students examples of present tense verbs they know, such as *sit, hide,* and *tell.* Then simply ask them: *How would you talk about having done these things yesterday? Would you say, "I sitted"?* Elicit the proper past tense forms for these examples, then show them a vocabulary list of others they will need to learn (easily found online).

- Pitch: *Why do we need to learn these? Because good writers know these forms and use them fluently. And once you know them, no one can take them away from you.*

- Students should practice incorporating these forms into sentences.

ASSESSING THIS:

- As always, we want students to demonstrate their grasp of these grammatical concepts in their own writing, first in sentences then in paragraphs. Provide several present-tense verbs they must include in a paragraph about a text or topic they are studying, and tell them you will score the paragraph based on two things: 1) All sentences must be complete, and 2) These verbs must be used properly in the past tense.

- Cloze reading (text with blanks where, in this case, the proper past tense forms of the irregular verbs belong) is another useful way to check for understanding.

L 2.1.E: Use adjectives and adverbs, and choose between them depending on what is to be modified.

TEACHING THIS:

- This standard follows from *L 1.1.F: Use frequently occurring adjectives.* (It's a good idea to review the guidance there.)

- **GENRE ALERT: This standard is useful when working on narrative writing (W 2.3).**

- In order to teach this standard, it's important to know the rules:

  o Adjectives modify nouns or pronouns. They usually answer these questions: *Which one? What kind of? How many?*

  o Adverbs modify verbs, adjectives, or other adverbs. They usually answer: *When? Where? How? Why? Under what conditions? To what degree?**

  o Although many adverbs are formed by adding *–ly* to adjectives, not all are. Also, some adjectives end in *–ly* (*lovely, friendly*), and some adverbs don't (*always, here, there*).***

- More than likely, adverbs will come up when you are reviewing basic sentence structure. To be complete, a sentence must have a subject and a verb. As Jeff Anderson points out, you can teach this very simply by modeling how to write a two-word sentence: e.g., *She laughed.***** Students then write their own two-word sentences on their white boards and show you, then you extend this approach to "three-word sentences" by adding an adverb—e.g., *She laughed loudly.* Some people like to say that "adverbs *add* information to the verb."***** When students imitate the model, most will likely add an *–ly* word at the end, and you can seize the opportunity to discuss adverbs—how they often end with *–ly* but not always (for example, you could have written, *She laughed yesterday*, which answers the question When? And so on.

ASSESSING THIS:

- As always, we want students to demonstrate their grasp of these grammatical concepts in their own writing, first in sentences then in paragraphs. Provide several adjectives and adverbs that they must include in a paragraph about a text or topic they are studying, and tell them you will score the paragraph based on two things: 1) All sentences must be complete, and 2) These adjectives and adverbs must be used correctly.
- Cloze reading (text with blanks where, in this case, the proper adjectives and adverbs belong) is another useful way to check for understanding.

*See footnote[117] / **See footnote[118] / ***See footnote[119] / ****See footnote[120] / *****See footnote[121]

---

117 Diana Hacker and Nancy Sommers, *Rules for Writers* (Boston: Bedford/St. Martin's, 2016, 8th edition), 230 and 367-368.

118 Diana Hacker and Nancy Sommers, *Rules for Writers* (Boston: Bedford/St. Martin's, 2016, 8th edition), 230 and 368.

119 Diana Hacker and Nancy Sommers, *Rules for Writers* (Boston: Bedford/St. Martin's, 2016, 8th edition), 230.

120 Jeff Anderson, *Mechanically Inclined: Building Grammar, Usage, and Style into Writer's Workshop* (Portland, ME: Stenhouse Publishers, 2005), 65-67.

121 Jeff Anderson with Whitney La Rocca, *Patterns of Power: Inviting Young Writers into the Conventions of Language, Grades 1-5* (Portland, ME, Stenhouse Publishers, 2017), 285.

L 2.1.F: Produce, expand, and rearrange complete simple and compound sentences (e.g., The boy watched the movie; The little boy watched the movie; The action movie was watched by the little boy).

TEACHING THIS:

- This standard is obviously not a one-shot standard but one you will revisit repeatedly as students draft and revise writing. If you have been following my advice to assess most of these Language Standards by requiring students to write targeted sentences and paragraphs, then every time you collect their work, you have an opportunity to determine which aspects of their writing need revision. When you hand back the original drafts, you can praise and provide constructive feedback on student exemplars. Revision is the phase when we do the most work on expanding and rearranging, and your mini-lessons can convey this message most aptly.

- See Chapter 2, "Principle #4: Give Faster Feedback," for recommendations on how to provide effective feedback to the class, how to run efficient writing conferences, and how to maximize peer feedback.

ASSESSING THIS:

- Give students opportunities to revise their sentences and paragraphs. Establish targets for revision such as "Expand your paragraph with the 'Because-But-So' approach" or "Clarify and elaborate where your partner raised questions about your writing."

L 2.2.A: Capitalize holidays, product names, and geographic names.

TEACHING THIS:

- Capitalization is introduced in K (via *L K.1.A*, which is actually about printing capital letters, and *L K.2.A: Capitalize the first word in a sentence and the pronoun I*) and reinforced in grade 1 (via *L 1.1.B: Use common, proper, and possessive nouns* and *L 1.2.A: Capitalize dates and names of people*). So teaching this standard should entail a simple review.

- Show students examples in two columns:

Column 1	Column 2
1. Christmas/Thanksgiving	1. morning/evening
2. Nike/Pizza Hut	2. shoe/pizza
3. Florida/Texas	3. house/cottage

- Ask them to figure out what the relationship is between Column 1 and Column 2 and discuss this with a neighbor. Cold-calling should elicit that Column 1 lists proper nouns and Column 2 lists common nouns. If they don't also notice that the proper nouns are capitalized, ask them what else they notice, then steer them towards that realization.
- You should ask students to summarize the reasons why we use capital letters when writing: 1) to show we are starting a new sentence, 2) to show respect for a name of a person, place, or thing (AKA proper nouns), and 3) to show we are shouting ("IS ANYBODY HOME???").
- Students should practice writing sentences that use common and proper nouns.
- Remind students how to edit incorrect sentences: by double-underlining nouns that *should* be capitalized.

ASSESSING THIS:

- Give students sentences without nouns capitalized; they should double-underline the first letter of any word that should be capitalized. Also, either during the quiz or while going over it, they should also explain *why* that word should be capitalized, e.g., "Fido is the name of a particular dog, a proper noun, so it should be capitalized."
- As always, we want students to demonstrate their grasp of these grammatical concepts in their own writing, first in sentences then in paragraphs. Give them several nouns they must include in a paragraph about a text or topic they are studying, and tell them you will score the paragraph based on two things: 1) All sentences must be complete, and 2) Proper and common nouns should be written correctly.

L 2.2.B: Use commas in greetings and closings of letters.

TEACHING THIS:

- Find an authentic reason for students to write a letter to someone.
- Pitch: *There are many different ways in which people communicate with one another. We talk face-to-face, obviously; we talk on the phone. What else do we do to communicate?* Brainstorm a list of ways in which we communicate—in person, by phone, by text, by Email, by letter—*oh, by letter! That's what we're going to do today! We're going to write an old-fashioned letter! Now, before we do this, let's talk about WHY people write letters. What purposes are there for letter writing?* Brainstorm a list of reasons why we write letters. Point to today's purpose.

- Show students a model letter and explain the key features of the form (capitalize the salutation; use a comma if you know the person or a colon if you don't; and so on).
- Ask them to write the beginning of their letter, and circulate to ensure that they are following the model. Then allow them to proceed. PS: They will probably need to be reminded to indent for new paragraphs.

ASSESSING THIS:

- As always, we want students to demonstrate their grasp of these grammatical concepts in their own writing, first in sentences then in paragraphs. Give them several words they must include in a letter about a text or topic they are studying (e.g., they could write to a character in a story they've read, to a family member they feel grateful toward, or to a public figure to share their concerns about a topic of interest), and tell them you will score the letter based on two things: 1) All sentences must be complete, and 2) They must format their letter correctly, with proper punctuation and capitalization. (Note: You can always modify the suggested criteria; these are suggestions, not rules.)

L 2.2.C: Use an apostrophe to form contractions and frequently occurring possessives.

TEACHING THIS:

- This standard follows from *L 1.1.B: Use common, proper, and possessive nouns.* You should refer to the guidance for that standard: You will probably want to implement the described lesson, which helps students discover that possessive nouns are formed with apostrophe –s.
- Regarding contractions, I am not sure there is an optimal moment when you should introduce them. We use them all the time when speaking. I would try to find a teachable moment to toss in a quick demonstration of how contractions are formed—i.e., what letter(s) the apostrophe replaces.
- Students should practice writing sentences that include possessive nouns and contractions.

ASSESSING THIS:

- As always, we want students to demonstrate their grasp of these grammatical concepts in their own writing, first in sentences then in paragraphs. Provide several nouns and contractions that they must include in a paragraph about a text or topic they are studying, and tell them you will score the paragraph based on two things: 1) All sentences must be complete, and 2) The given nouns must be written as possessive nouns, and the contractions must be used correctly.
- Cloze reading (text with blanks where, in this case, the proper possessive nouns and contractions belong) is another useful way to check for understanding.

L 2.2.D: Generalize learned spelling patterns when writing words (e.g., cage → badge; boy → boil).

- This book does not explain phonics instruction but recommends its use for this standard.

L 2.2.E: Consult reference materials, including beginning dictionaries, as needed to check and correct spellings.

TEACHING THIS:

- I do not advocate telling students to "look it up" when you're reading a text with the whole class and someone asks, "What does that word mean?" Looking it up creates a distraction, and often when students look up word, they don't understand the definition anyway. Instead, you should ask them to look for context clues or word parts that they recognize, and if that doesn't work, give them a prepared sentence that provides ample instructive/directive context so they can figure it out. By wrestling with the context to infer the meaning of the word, students will then *own* the word. I'm not saying you should never just quickly tell them the meaning to keep things moving, but they are more likely to retain the word if they've had to figure it out.
- That said, sometimes students need to use reference materials such as dictionaries and thesauruses, and they need to learn how to use them.
- The pitch: *Sometimes when we're reading independently, we come upon or encounter a word that is unfamiliar. We can't figure it out from context clues, and we don't recognize any parts of the word. One thing we can do is use the dictionary to look it up. Let's try that…*

- Have students find a word, then discuss the features of the entry. If it includes an etymology, even better: This is a clue to the roots of the word.
- Since this may be a new skill for students, ask them what they find challenging about this process so you can address any concerns or confusion.
- Remind students that the dictionary can also help them find the spelling of a word, as long as they can begin to sound it out.

ASSESSING THIS:

- For a quick quiz, you can game-ify the process of looking up words and using dictionary skills while also reviewing content by simply giving them a few words to look up, with requirements about what information to capture.

L 2.3.A: Compare formal and informal uses of English.

TEACHING THIS:

- See Chapter 2—specifically "Principle #6: Provide Oral Support"—for suggestions on how to do this.

ASSESSING THIS:

- Ditto.

- How will you use the resources in this chapter?

- How did the ideas in this chapter challenge, change, or confirm what you previously believed about grammar and writing instruction (or instruction in general)?

- Which resources and ideas from this chapter will you share with colleagues? Why?

- What lingering concerns do you have about the K-2 standards, and how will you deal with them?

chapter
SIX

Grades 3-5 Writing and Language Instruction

GRADES 3-5 WRITING STANDARDS WITH INSTRUCTIONAL GUIDANCE

Next we'll look at the trajectory of Writing Standards for Grades 3-5 so that we can see how the Language Standards fit in with them. Note: If you want to see all of the ELA Common Core Standards in one place, check out the "K-12 ELA Common Core Standards Tracker" on the TLC Website.[122]

---

122 The "K-12 ELA Common Core Standards Tracker" is on the TLC "Using Grammar to Improve Writing" page found at https://www.literacycookbook.com/page.php?id=161. This and other

	Writing Anchor Standard #1: *Write arguments to support claims in an analysis of substantive topics or texts, using valid reasoning and relevant and sufficient evidence.*
W 3.1	Write opinion pieces on topics or texts, supporting a point of view with reasons. A) Introduce the topic or text they are writing about, state an opinion, and create an organizational structure that lists reasons. B) Provide reasons that support the opinion. C) Use linking words and phrases (e.g., because, therefore, since, for example) to connect opinion and reasons. D) Provide a concluding statement or section.
W 4.1	Write opinion pieces on topics or texts, supporting a point of view with reasons and information. A) Introduce a topic or text clearly, state an opinion, and create an organizational structure in which related ideas are grouped to support the writer's purpose. B) Provide reasons that are supported by facts and details. C) Link opinion and reasons using words and phrases (e.g., for instance, in order to, in addition). D) Provide a concluding statement or section related to the opinion presented.
W 5.1	Write opinion pieces on topics or texts, supporting a point of view with reasons and information. A) Introduce a topic or text clearly, state an opinion, and create an organizational structure in which ideas are logically grouped to support the writer's purpose. B) Provide logically ordered reasons that are supported by facts and details. C) Link opinion and reasons using words, phrases, and clauses (e.g., consequently, specifically). D) Provide a concluding statement or section related to the opinion presented.

standards-related resources can also be found on the TLC "Standards" page at https://www.literacy-cookbook.com/page.php?id=138.

Across grades 3 through 5, Writing Standard #1 (opinion writing) becomes increasingly demanding with regard to content and organization—and particularly in the use of logic to organize thoughts. In grade 3, students must "support a point of view with reasons," while in grades 4 and 5, that support must include reasons *and information*. And while the 3rd grade organizational structure merely "lists reasons," 4th-graders are expected to *group related ideas* and 5th-graders to *logically* group their ideas *to support the writer's purpose*. Of course, this does not mean that we should be satisfied with "listy" writing in 3rd grade.

Training students in Argument vs. Evidence Steps 1-3 (see Chapter 4) beginning in 3rd grade will help them support arguments with relevant evidence and explanation. By analyzing effective essays, they should be able to explain how logically composed paragraphs serve a writer's overall purpose. Again, it's crucial to show students effective models to imitate.

The standards provide little guidance on how to conclude, so you will need to show students examples of punchy concluding sentences to imitate.

	Writing Anchor Standard #2: *Write informative/explanatory texts to examine and convey complex ideas and information clearly and accurately through the effective selection, organization, and analysis of content.*
W 3.2	Write informative/explanatory texts to examine a topic and convey ideas and information clearly.
	A) Introduce a topic and group related information together; include illustrations when useful to aiding comprehension.
	B) Develop the topic with facts, definitions, and details.
	C) Use linking words and phrases (e.g., also, another, and, more, but) to connect ideas within categories of information.
	D) Provide a concluding statement or section.

W 4.2	Write informative/explanatory texts to examine a topic and convey ideas and information clearly.
	A) Introduce a topic clearly and group related information in paragraphs and sections; include formatting (e.g., headings), illustrations, and multimedia when useful to aiding comprehension.
	B) Develop the topic with facts, definitions, concrete details, quotations, or other information and examples related to the topic.
	C) Link ideas within categories of information using words and phrases (e.g., another, for example, also, because).
	D) Use precise language and domain-specific vocabulary to inform about or explain the topic.
	E) Provide a concluding statement or section related to the information or explanation presented.
W 5.2	Write informative/explanatory texts to examine a topic and convey ideas and information clearly.
	A) Introduce a topic clearly, provide a general observation and focus, and group related information logically; include formatting (e.g., headings), illustrations, and multimedia when useful to aiding comprehension.
	B) Develop the topic with facts, definitions, concrete details, quotations, or other information and examples related to the topic.
	C) Link ideas within and across categories of information using words, phrases, and clauses (e.g., in contrast, especially).
	D) Use precise language and domain-specific vocabulary to inform about or explain the topic.
	E) Provide a concluding statement or section related to the information or explanation presented.

With this standard's reliance on the word "topic," one might be misled into assigning *topic-driven* writing such as "The Dangers of Smoking" or "The Causes of the Civil War." No matter how compelling the topic, a topic-driven approach will almost inevitably lead students to plagiarize because the idea of topic-driven writing seems to be "Tell us as much about this topic as you can." So students dump information in and don't explain it. By contrast, **question-driven writing** such as "Why is it dangerous to smoke?" or "Why did Americans engage in the Civil War?" pushes students to explain their ideas and information. To make this approach work, review Reading Standard 2.1 (*Ask and answer such questions as who, what, where, when, why, and how to demonstrate understanding of key details in a text*), which is explained in Chapter 4 (see "The Most Important Writing Standard"). Also, show students high-quality mentor texts and invite *them* to explain what makes the texts so effective.

As with the progression in grades 3-5 for opinion writing, Writing Standard #2 (informative/explanatory writing) shows a noticeable uptick in expectations regarding content and organization. In grades 4 and 5, again, we see the shift to *grouping related ideas* then grouping related information *logically*. Again, teaching Argument vs. Evidence Steps 1-3 (see Chapter 4) will be helpful for grades 3 and up.

We also see in grades 4 and 5 new demands for using *precise language and domain-specific vocabulary* to inform about or explain the topic. This standard thus raises the question: "How will we teach vocabulary—not only in ELA but across the curriculum?" For guidance, see *The Literacy Cookbook*.[123]

Again, the standards are vague on how to conclude, so you will need to show students examples of punchy concluding sentences to imitate.

PS: This standard is relevant to the PARCC Research Simulation Task. If your state requires PARCC testing, see the TLC "PARCC Prep" page for more information.[124]

---

123 Sarah Tantillo, *The Literacy Cookbook: A Practical Guide to Effective Reading, Writing, Speaking, and Listening Instruction* (San Francisco: Jossey-Bass, 2012), 28-36. For online resources, see the TLC "Building Robust Vocabulary" page found at https://www.literacycookbook.com/page.php?id=4.

124 The TLC "PARCC Prep" page is found at https://www.literacycookbook.com/page.php?id=155.

	Writing Standard #3: *Write narratives to develop real or imagined experiences or events using effective technique, well-chosen details, and well-structured event sequences.*
W 3.3	Write narratives to develop real or imagined experiences or events using effective technique, descriptive details, and clear event sequences. A) Establish a situation and introduce a narrator and/or characters; organize an event sequence that unfolds naturally. B) Use dialogue and descriptions of actions, thoughts, and feelings to develop experiences and events or show the response of characters to situations. C) Use temporal words and phrases to signal event order. D) Provide a sense of closure.
W 4.3	Write narratives to develop real or imagined experiences or events using effective technique, descriptive details, and clear event sequences. A) Orient the reader by establishing a situation and introducing a narrator and/or characters; organize an event sequence that unfolds naturally. B) Use dialogue and description to develop experiences and events or show the responses of characters to situations. C) Use a variety of transitional words and phrases to manage the sequence of events. D) Use concrete words and phrases and sensory details to convey experiences and events precisely. E) Provide a conclusion that follows from the narrated experiences or events.

W 5.3	Write narratives to develop real or imagined experiences or events using effective technique, descriptive details, and clear event sequences.
	A) Orient the reader by establishing a situation and introducing a narrator and/or characters; organize an event sequence that unfolds naturally.
	B) Use narrative techniques, such as dialogue, description, and pacing, to develop experiences and events or show the responses of characters to situations.
	C) Use a variety of transitional words, phrases, and clauses to manage the sequence of events.
	D) Use concrete words and phrases and sensory details to convey experiences and events precisely.
	E) Provide a conclusion that follows from the narrated experiences or events.

For me, Writing Standard #3 (narrative writing) illustrates the notion that nobody is perfect, and with all due respect, standards writers are no exception. As someone who has written and studied short stories for decades, I find it stunning that there is no mention of a problem or conflict in the verbiage of this standard until grades 9-10. So let me begin with this tip: **Teach students—as early as you can—to base their narratives on a problem or conflict.** If they don't, they will end up writing a list of events; and while the events might be interesting, the ultimate product will be a *list*, not a story of growth, change, or insight. A list is not a story.

That said, in contrast with the grade 2 version of this standard which sounds more like a summary of an event or two (*"Write narratives in which they recount a well-elaborated event or short sequence of events, include details to describe actions, thoughts, and feelings, use temporal words to signal event order, and provide a sense of closure"*), grades 3-5 require students to write more what we think of as a regular story with a narrator and/or characters, dialogue, and all the fixin's.

The number one thing you can do to help students master this standard is to analyze great stories. For advice on how to teach close reading strategies, see *The Literacy Cookbook* and *Literacy and the Common Core.*[125] For additional resources to support reading and writing narratives, see the TLC "Analyzing Literature" and "Narrative Writing" pages.[126]

PS: If your state requires PARCC testing, you can find information on the PARCC Narrative Writing Task on the TLC "PARCC Prep" page.[127]

Brief Notes About Writing Standards #4-6:

Writing Anchor Standard #4: *Produce clear and coherent writing in which the development, organization, and style are appropriate to task, purpose, and audience.*

Writing Anchor Standard #5: *Develop and strengthen writing as needed by planning, revising, editing, rewriting, or trying a new approach.*

Writing Anchor Standard #6: *Use technology, including the Internet, to produce and publish writing and to interact and collaborate with others.*

In working on Writing Standards #4 and #5, teachers must establish the key steps of the writing process through modeling, practice, and feedback. This involves using mentor texts[128] and establishing classroom routines for working through the different steps of the writing process, whether with teacher or peer support, or independently. Revisit Chapter 2, particularly "Principle #3: Ask, 'What Do You *Like* About That Sentence?'" and "Principle #4: Give Faster Feedback," for detailed ideas about how to address these standards.

Writing Standard #6 speaks to the use of technology (especially keyboarding skills in grades 3-5) and Internet research.

---

125 Sarah Tantillo, *The Literacy Cookbook: A Practical Guide to Effective Reading, Writing, Speaking, and Listening Instruction* (San Francisco: Jossey-Bass, 2012); also *Literacy and the Common Core: Recipes for Action* (San Francisco: Jossey-Bass, 2014).

126 The TLC "Analyzing Literature" page is found at https://www.literacycookbook.com/page. php?id=2. The TLC "Narrative Writing" page is found at https://www.literacycookbook.com/page. php?id=150.

127 For more information on PARCC testing preparation, see the TLC "PARCC Prep" page found at https://www.literacycookbook.com/page.php?id=155.

128 Sarah Tantillo, *The Literacy Cookbook: A Practical Guide to Effective Reading, Writing, Speaking, and Listening Instruction* (San Francisco: Jossey-Bass, 2012), 95-104.

	Writing Anchor Standard #7: *Conduct short as well as more sustained research projects based on focused questions, demonstrating understanding of the subject under investigation.*
W 3.7	Conduct short research projects that build knowledge about a topic.
W 4.7	Conduct short research projects that build knowledge through investigation of different aspects of a topic.
W 5.7	Conduct short research projects that use several sources to build knowledge through investigation of different aspects of a topic.

	Writing Anchor Standard #8: *Gather relevant information from multiple print and digital sources, assess the credibility and accuracy of each source, and integrate the information while avoiding plagiarism.*
W 3.8	Recall information from experiences or gather information from print and digital sources; take brief notes on sources and sort evidence into provided categories.
W 4.8	Recall relevant information from experiences or gather relevant information from print and digital sources; take notes and categorize information, and provide a list of sources.
W 5.8	Recall relevant information from experiences or gather relevant information from print and digital sources; summarize or paraphrase information in notes and finished work, and provide a list of sources.

Writing Standards #7 and 8 (research writing) echo the work of Writing Standard #2 (informative/explanatory writing), so you should refer back to my comments on that standard, especially regarding the need for *question-driven* rather than *topic-driven* writing assignments. These standards also tie in with Writing Standard #6, which addresses the use of technology and Internet research.

For a full explanation of how to teach research paper writing, see *The Literacy Cookbook* and the TLC "Research Paper Guide" page.[129]

---

129 Sarah Tantillo, *The Literacy Cookbook: A Practical Guide to Effective Reading, Writing, Speaking, and Listening Instruction* (San Francisco: Jossey-Bass, 2012), 169-190. The TLC "Research Paper Guide" page is found at https://www.literacycookbook.com/page.php?id=24.

	Writing Anchor Standard #9: *Draw evidence from literary or informational texts to support analysis, reflection, and research.*
W 3.9	**Begins in grade 4.**
W 4.9	Draw evidence from literary or informational texts to support analysis, reflection, and research. A) Apply grade 4 Reading standards to literature (e.g., "Describe in depth a character, setting, or event in a story or drama, drawing on specific details in the text [e.g., a character's thoughts, words, or actions]."). B) Apply grade 4 Reading standards to informational texts (e.g., "Explain how an author uses reasons and evidence to support particular points in a text").
W 5.9	Draw evidence from literary or informational texts to support analysis, reflection, and research. A) Apply grade 5 Reading standards to literature (e.g., "Compare and contrast two or more characters, settings, or events in a story or a drama, drawing on specific details in the text [e.g., how characters interact]"). B) Apply grade 5 Reading standards to informational texts (e.g., "Explain how an author uses reasons and evidence to support particular points in a text, identifying which reasons and evidence support which point[s]").

Writing Standard #9 illustrates why some people say that the writing standards consist of 20 standards in one. The premise, beginning in grade 4 (although of course you could start sooner), is for students to use writing to demonstrate that they read well. Students must apply close reading and analysis skills (see *Literacy and the Common Core*[130] and the TLC "Analyzing Literature" page[131]) and Argument vs. Evidence Steps 1-3 (see Chapter 4).

Writing Anchor Standard #10: *Write routinely over extended time frames (time for research, reflection, and revision) and shorter time*

---

130 Sarah Tantillo, *Literacy and the Common Core: Recipes for Action* (San Francisco: Jossey-Bass, 2014), 107-127.

131 The TLC "Analyzing Literature" page is found at https://www.literacycookbook.com/page.php?id=2.

frames (a single sitting or a day or two) for a range of tasks, purposes, and audiences.

This standard does not need to be unpacked, but it should be duly noted. Teachers may want to use a checklist such as the following to ensure that students' writing assignments meet all of the stated criteria:

- Students write routinely.

- Students write over extended periods, with time for research, reflection, and revision.

- Students practice and are assessed on timed writing.

- Students write to complete a range of tasks.

- Students write for a range of audiences.

- Students write for various purposes.

GRADES 3-5 LANGUAGE STANDARDS

In this section, we'll look at the Grades 3-5 trajectory of key Language Standards first, then go through the standards grade by grade (so: all 3rd first, then all 4th, then all 5th) so that we can dive more deeply into effective instructional practices. Note: If you want to track student progress on the K-12 Language Standards, check out the "K-12 Selected Language CCS Tracker" in the Appendix and on the TLC Website.[132]

---

132 The "K-12 Selected Language CCS Tracker" can be downloaded from the TLC "Using Grammar to Improve Writing" page found at https://www.literacycookbook.com/page.php?id=161. Additional standards-related resources are available on the TLC "Standards" page found at https://www.literacy-cookbook.com/page.php?id=138.

	Language Anchor Standard #1: *Demonstrate command of the conventions of standard English grammar and usage when writing or speaking.*
L 3.1	A) Explain the function of nouns, pronouns, verbs, adjectives, and adverbs in general and their functions in particular sentences. B) Form and use regular and irregular plural nouns. C) Use abstract nouns (e.g., childhood). D) Form and use regular and irregular verbs. E) Form and use the simple (e.g., I walked; I walk; I will walk) verb tenses. F) Ensure subject-verb and pronoun-antecedent agreement. G) Form and use comparative and superlative adjectives and adverbs, and choose between them depending on what is to be modified. H) Use coordinating and subordinating conjunctions. I) Produce simple, compound, and complex sentences.
L 4.1	A) Use relative pronouns (who, whose, whom, which, that) and relative adverbs (where, when, why). B) Form and use the progressive (e.g., I was walking; I am walking; I will be walking) verb tenses. C) Use modal auxiliaries (e.g., can, may, must) to convey various conditions. D) Order adjectives within sentences according to conventional patterns (e.g., a small red bag rather than a red small bag). E) Form and use prepositional phrases. F) Produce complete sentences, recognizing and correcting inappropriate fragments and run-ons. G) Correctly use frequently confused words (e.g., to, too, two; there, their).
L 5.1	A) Explain the function of conjunctions, prepositions, and interjections in general and their function in particular sentences. B) Form and use the perfect (e.g., I had walked; I have walked; I will have walked) verb tenses. C) Use verb tense to convey various times, sequences, states, and conditions. D) Recognize and correct inappropriate shifts in verb tense. E) Use correlative conjunctions (e.g., either/or, neither/nor).

Next:

	Language Anchor Standard #2: *Demonstrate command of the conventions of standard English capitalization, punctuation, and spelling when writing.*
L 3.2	A) Capitalize appropriate words in titles. B) Use commas in addresses. C) Use commas and quotation marks in dialogue. D) Form and use possessives. E) Use conventional spelling for high frequency and other studied words and for adding suffixes to base words (e.g., sitting, smiled, cries, happiness). F) Use spelling patterns and generalizations (e.g., word families, position-based spellings, syllable patterns, ending rules, meaningful word parts) in writing words. G) Consult reference materials, including beginning dictionaries, as needed to check and correct spellings.
L 4.2	A) Use correct capitalization. B) Use commas and quotation marks to mark direct speech and quotations from a text. C) Use a comma before a coordinating conjunction in a compound sentence. D) Spell grade-appropriate words correctly, consulting references as needed.
L 5.2	A) Use punctuation to separate items in a series. B) Use a comma to separate an introductory element from the rest of the sentence. C) Use a comma to set off the words yes and no (e.g., Yes, thank you), to set off a tag question from the rest of the sentence (e.g., It's true, isn't it?), and to indicate direct address (e.g., Is that you, Steve?). D) Use underlining, quotation marks, or italics to indicate titles of works. E) Spell grade-appropriate words correctly, consulting references as needed.

Next:

	Language Anchor Standard #3: *Apply knowledge of language to understand how language functions in different contexts, to make effective choices for meaning or style, and to comprehend more fully when reading or listening.*
L 3.3	Use knowledge of language and its conventions when writing, speaking, reading, or listening. A) Choose words and phrases for effect. B) Recognize and observe differences between the conventions of spoken and written standard English.
L 4.3	Use knowledge of language and its conventions when writing, speaking, reading, or listening. A) Choose words and phrases to convey ideas precisely. B) Choose punctuation for effect. C) Differentiate between contexts that call for formal English (e.g., presenting ideas) and situations where informal discourse is appropriate (e.g., small-group discussion).
L 5.3	Use knowledge of language and its conventions when writing, speaking, reading, or listening. A) Expand, combine, and reduce sentences for meaning, reader/listener interest, and style. B) Compare and contrast the varieties of English (e.g., dialects, registers) used in stories, dramas, or poems.

(Note: Language Standards #4-6 deal primarily with vocabulary, so we will not analyze them here. For guidance on vocabulary instruction, see *The Literacy Cookbook*.[133])

---

133 Sarah Tantillo, *The Literacy Cookbook: A Practical Guide to Effective Reading, Writing, Speaking, and Listening Instruction* (San Francisco: Jossey-Bass, 2012), 28-36. For online resources, see the TLC "Building Robust Vocabulary" page found at https://www.literacycookbook.com/page.php?id=4.

GRADE 3 LANGUAGE STANDARDS: A DEEPER DIVE

In the next three sections, we'll dive more deeply into each grade's Language Standards and look at ways to teach and assess them more systematically, in conjunction with writing instruction. These are by no means the *only* ways to teach these standards, just a few to illustrate how to connect grammar with writing and reading. We begin with grade 3.

L 3.1.A: Explain the function of nouns, pronouns, verbs, adjectives, and adverbs in general and their functions in particular sentences.

TEACHING THIS:

Obviously, this is not a standard you can teach in one sitting. These parts of speech should have been introduced in earlier grades. Here are some standards to review, which include lessons you can recycle:

- NOUNS:
    - o L K.1.B: Use frequently occurring nouns and verbs.
    - o L 1.1.B: Use common, proper, and possessive nouns.
    - o L 2.1.A: Use collective nouns (e.g., group).
    - o L 3.1.C: Use abstract nouns (e.g., childhood).
- PRONOUNS:
    - o L 1.1.D: Use personal, possessive, and indefinite pronouns (e.g., I, me, my; they, them, their; anyone, everything).
    - o L 2.1.C: Use reflexive pronouns (e.g., myself, ourselves).
    - o L 3.1.F: Ensure subject-verb and pronoun-antecedent agreement.
- VERBS:
    - o L K.1.B: Use frequently occurring nouns and verbs.
    - o L 1.1.C: Use singular and plural nouns with matching verbs in basic sentences (e.g., He hops; We hop).
    - o L 1.1.E: Use verbs to convey a sense of past, present, and future (e.g., Yesterday I walked home; Today I walk home; Tomorrow I will walk home).
- ADJECTIVES:
    - o L 1.1.F: Use frequently occurring adjectives.
    - o L 2.1.E: Use adjectives and adverbs, and choose between them depending on what is to be modified.
    - o L 3.1.G: Form and use comparative and superlative adjectives and adverbs, and choose between them depending on what is to be modified.

- ADVERBS:
    - o L 2.1.E: Use adjectives and adverbs, and choose between them depending on what is to be modified.
    - o L 3.1.G: Form and use comparative and superlative adjectives and adverbs, and choose between them depending on what is to be modified.

- You will have daily opportunities to review these parts of speech as you encourage students to expand their sentences. It's important to consider words in context because many words can function as different parts of speech (e.g., "elaborate" can be a verb or an adjective).
- Asking students to identify parts of speech in random texts ("Circle all of the nouns in these sentences") is generally *not* helpful and definitely not sufficient. It's more productive for students to build sentences imitating various structures, using given parts of speech or specific words. Again, the point of learning grammar forms is not merely to be able to identify them, but to *use* them in writing.

ASSESSING THIS:

- As always, we want students to demonstrate their grasp of these grammatical concepts in their own writing, first in sentences then in paragraphs. Provide a list of words that they must include in a paragraph about a text or topic they are studying, and tell them you will score the paragraph based on two things: 1) All sentences must be complete, and 2) All given words must be used properly (and underlined).
- Cloze reading (text with blanks where, in this case, the various words from a word bank belong) is another useful way to check for understanding.

L 3.1.B: Form and use regular and irregular plural nouns.

TEACHING THIS: [*This follows from L K.1.C and L 2.1.B.*]

- This book does not explain phonics instruction but recommends its use for this standard. That said, this standard provides an opportunity to review how we form *regular* plural nouns (See *L K.1.C: Form regular plural nouns orally by adding /s/ or /es/ [e.g., dog, dogs; wish, wishes]*) and *irregular* plural nouns (See *L 2.1.B: Form and use frequently occurring irregular plural nouns [e.g., feet, children, teeth, mice, fish]*).
- And again, you can point out that English is a highly irregular language, so we often need to memorize irregular forms.
- PS: A quick Google search will produce a list of common irregular plural nouns.

ASSESSING THIS:

- As always, students need to practice writing with these forms, first in sentences then in paragraphs. Provide several singular nouns that they must include in a paragraph about a text or topic they are studying, and tell them you will score the paragraph based on two things: 1) All sentences must be complete, and 2) These nouns must be written properly in the plural form.

- You can design quick quizzes in which students choose the correct form when the correct and incorrect forms are provided in context like this:
  - o The dog/dogs sat on the floor and ate their biscuits.
  - o For my birthday, I made three wishes/wishs.
  - o All of the childs/children in first grade like cupcakes.

  PS: Make sure students underline any context clues.

L 3.1.C: Use abstract nouns (e.g., childhood).

TEACHING THIS:

- Remember that students should have been introduced to different types of nouns in 1st grade (*L 1.1.B: Use common, proper, and possessive nouns.*) and collective nouns in 2nd (*L 2.1.A: Use collective nouns [e.g., group]*).
- Show students two lists: concrete nouns (e.g., shoe, basketball, eggs) and abstract nouns (justice, honesty, caring). Ask them to discuss with a partner: "What do you think is different about the words in the two categories?" Cold-call to elicit that the List #1 nouns can be seen and touched, whereas the List #2 nouns cannot be touched; they are ideas. If your school is based on core values, this is an opportunity to point out that values are abstract nouns; people demonstrate them in different ways, and they cannot be measured with a ruler.
- Pitch: *Why do abstract nouns matter? Remember, nouns are "people, places, or things." An idea is a thing, and an abstract noun represents an idea. When you want to talk about ideas, you need abstract nouns. And interestingly, people often disagree on what they mean. For example, what is "justice"? What is "beauty"? People have different definitions for abstract nouns. Whereas, concrete nouns, like "concrete," which is what most sidewalks are made of, can easily be touched or pointed at.*
- Brainstorm a more complete list of abstract nouns, and make this an anchor chart. Students should practice writing sentences using abstract nouns.
- You can also review the difference between abstract and concrete nouns by providing examples of each and asking students to sort them, then explain their choices.

- Because abstract nouns are concepts, they are also useful when discussing themes in literature. You could invite students to create a thematic sentence about a current text using an abstract noun. For example, "selfishness" is an abstract noun. A theme of *How the Grinch Stole Christmas** might be: *People can overcome selfishness with love from the people around them.* See the "How to Infer Themes Organizer" that follows for a simple three-step strategy for inferring themes.

ASSESSING THIS:

- As always, we want students to demonstrate their grasp of these grammatical concepts in their own writing, first in sentences then in paragraphs. Ask them to write a paragraph about an abstract noun, using evidence from a text or topic they are studying, and tell them you will score the paragraph based on two things: 1) All sentences must be complete, and 2) The paragraph should make an argument about the abstract noun and should provide evidence from a text or topic they are studying.
- Ask students to explain the difference between abstract and concrete nouns and give several examples of each.
- Cloze reading (text with blanks where, in this case, abstract nouns belong) is another useful way to check for understanding.

*See footnote[134]

---

134 Dr. Seuss, *How the Grinch Stole Christmas* (New York: Random House, 1957).

How to Infer Themes Organizer[135]

NAME_____ DATE_____

TITLE OF TEXT:_____

AUTHOR:_____

1. What TOPICS/ISSUES does this text deal with? List as many as you can think of. *(Ex: How the Grinch Stole Christmas by Dr. Seuss* is about SELFISHNESS.)*

2. What QUESTIONS does the author raise about these topics/issues? Pick 1-2 topics to focus on. *(Ex.: Why are people selfish? What are the consequences of selfishness? How can people overcome selfishness?)*

3. What MESSAGE(S) does the author convey about your selected topic/issue? *(Ex.: People can overcome selfishness with love from the people around them.)*

*See footnote[136]

---

135 The "How to Infer Themes Organizer" is on the TLC "Using Grammar to Improve Writing" page found at https://www.literacycookbook.com/page.php?id=161. Along with other analytic tools, it can also be found on the TLC "Analyzing Literature" page at https://www.literacycookbook.com/page.php?id=2.

136 Dr. Seuss, *How the Grinch Stole Christmas* (New York: Random House, 1957).

L 3.1.D: Form and use regular and irregular verbs.

TEACHING THIS:

- This standard follows from *L 1.1.E: Use verbs to convey a sense of past, present, and future (e.g., Yesterday I walked home; Today I walk home; Tomorrow I will walk home)* and *L 2.1.D: Form and use the past tense of frequently occurring irregular verbs (e.g., sat, hid, told).* So, it should be review, but just in case, here is a reminder of how we addressed this in 2nd grade (when the focus was on *past* tense, whereas in 3rd grade, students should exhibit fluency with a wider range of tenses):

- Again, we have another opportunity to remark upon how irregular the English language is! Start with the regular forms of past tense verbs—e.g., *talk→ talked* and *ask→ asked*—and show students examples of present tense verbs they know, such as *sit, hide,* and *tell.* Then simply ask them: *How would you talk about having done these things yesterday? Would you say, "I sitted"?* Elicit the proper past tense forms for these examples, then show them a vocabulary list of others they will need to learn (easily found online).

- Pitch: *Why do we need to learn these tense forms? Because good writers know these forms and use them fluently. And once you know them, no one can take them away from you.*

- Students should practice incorporating these forms into sentences.

ASSESSING THIS:

- As always, we want students to demonstrate their grasp of these grammatical concepts in their own writing, first in sentences then in paragraphs. Give them several present-tense verbs they must include in a paragraph about a text or topic they are studying, and tell them you will score the paragraph based on two things: 1) All sentences must be complete, and 2) These verbs must be used properly in the past tense.

- Cloze reading (text with blanks where, in this case, the proper past tense forms of the regular and irregular verbs belong) is another useful way to check for understanding.

- Note: These examples focus on past tense. You can assess a wider range of tenses. See also *L 3.1.E: Form and use the simple (e.g., I walked; I walk; I will walk) verb tenses.)*

L 3.1.E: Form and use the simple (e.g., I walked; I walk; I will walk) verb tenses.

TEACHING THIS:

- This standard repeats *L 1.1.E: Use verbs to convey a sense of past, present, and future (e.g., Yesterday I walked home; Today I walk home; Tomorrow I will walk home)*, the guidance for which is repeated here. Also relevant are *L 2.1.D: Form and use the past tense of frequently occurring irregular verbs (e.g., sat, hid, told)* and *L 3.1.D: Form and use regular and irregular verbs.* You should review the lessons described for those standards in addition to the guidance here.

- **GENRE ALERT: Students will need to apply this standard when working on narrative writing (W 3.3).**

- Show students examples of different tenses. You can even use the exact words from this standard: *Yesterday I walked home; Today I walk home; Tomorrow I will walk home.* Invite them to explain how these sentences are different. Discuss the clues such as time-indicating words and different verb forms.

- Note that English is a challenging language with many exceptions to rules, so not all verbs are "regular." For example, even though we say, "I walked" and "I laughed," we don't say, "I runned" or "I haved." English contains numerous irregular verbs, and you simply have to learn them.

- Model writing a narrative paragraph in either past or future tense, inviting student input as you go. Be sure to point out transitions/signal words such as "then," "before," and "after." Remind students that transitions help readers steer through the text and follow what is going on; you can illustrate this by leaving out some transitions to show how confusing such writing can be.

- Let students imitate and practice sentences focused on different tenses, then move into paragraph writing.

ASSESSING THIS:

- As always, we want students to demonstrate their grasp of these grammatical concepts in their own writing, first in sentences then in paragraphs. For **past tense,** they could write a narrative paragraph about "what happened from when I entered school this morning till I arrived in this class" or some variation on that idea. For **future tense,** the topic could be "what I will do between leaving school and going to bed tonight." Tell them you will score the paragraph based on three things: 1) All sentences must be complete, 2) They should include transitions/signal words such as "then" and "after," and 3) All verbs must be written in the appropriate tense.

- Cloze reading (text with blanks where, in this case, the verbs or the transitions belong) is another useful way to check for understanding.

L 3.1.F: Ensure subject-verb and pronoun-antecedent agreement.

TEACHING THIS:

- The seeds for this standard are planted in grade 1 with *L 1.1.C: Use singular and plural nouns with matching verbs in basic sentences (e.g., He hops; We hop)* and *L 1.1.D: Use personal, possessive, and indefinite pronouns (e.g., I, me, my; they, them, their; anyone, everything).* You can recycle the guidance for those standards to teach/re-teach subject-verb agreement.

- To tackle **pronoun-antecedent agreement**, you could show students a sentence that illustrates the concept—e.g., "Mary and I went to the beach, then *we* went swimming." Then ask them, "Why couldn't I have used 'they' instead of 'we'?" Or: "How would the meaning be different if I wrote 'she' instead of 'we'?" Students should explain why to their partner. Cold-calling should elicit that in the first case, "we" makes sense, based on the antecedent "Mary and I." And in the second example, if "she" alone went swimming, it would mean that "I" did not. Incidentally, you can throw in some Latin and point out that "antecedent" literally means "the thing that goes before."

- Alternatively, or simply after that, you could give students a Cloze reading passage with blanks where the pronouns belong and walk through it with them, asking for their advice about which pronouns make the most sense and why. For an example, see "Cloze Reading Passage: Personal Pronouns" in Chapter 3.

ASSESSING THIS:

- As always, we want students to demonstrate their grasp of these grammatical concepts in their own writing, first in sentences then in paragraphs. List several pronouns they must include in a paragraph about a text or topic they are studying, and tell them you will score the paragraph based on two things: 1) All sentences must be complete, and 2) All pronouns must agree with their antecedents.

- Again, Cloze reading (text with blanks where, in this case, the pronouns belong) is another useful way to check for understanding.

L 3.1.G: Form and use comparative and superlative adjectives and adverbs, and choose between them depending on what is to be modified.

TEACHING THIS:

- Background: Adjectives and adverbs take three different forms: positive ("soft"), comparative ("softer"), and superlative ("softest").* Longer words and those ending with -ly should be modified by "more" or "most," respectively. Students will need to be reminded not to double the modification—that is, "most softest" is incorrect.

- Pitch: *As you know, good writers use adjectives and adverbs to make their writing more compelling. Sometimes they don't just want to DESCRIBE something, though. Sometimes they want to COMPARE it to something else. For example, maybe I want to establish that I used to run FASTER than my brother (I can't anymore, but that is besides the point). We can use "-er" or "more" to compare things or people. And sometimes we compare something to more than one thing, like when we say something is the "best" or the "most funny." Let's brainstorm a chart of adjectives and see if we can figure out what they look like in the "comparative" and "superlative" forms...*

- Brainstorm a three-column chart (e.g., "good-better-best"), then invite students to write sentences about a current text or topic using several of these forms.

ASSESSING THIS:

- As always, we want students to demonstrate their grasp of these grammatical concepts in their own writing, first in sentences then in paragraphs. Provide several adjectives or adverbs that they must include in a paragraph about a text or topic they are studying, and tell them you will score the paragraph based on two things: 1) All sentences must be complete, and 2) All adjectives or adverbs must be used in either the comparative or superlative form, and they must be used correctly.

- Again, Cloze reading (text with blanks where, in this case, the comparative and superlative forms belong) is another useful way to check for understanding.

- You can design quick quizzes in which students choose the correct form when the correct and incorrect forms are provided in context like this:

  o Which of the three dogs ate the biscuits *faster/fastest*?

  o I drew my illustration *more/most* carefully than he did.

  o The *goodest/best* cupcakes have icing on them.

  PS: Make sure students underline any context clues.

*See footnote[137]

---

137 Diana Hacker and Nancy Sommers, *Rules for Writers* (Boston: Bedford/St. Martin's, 2016, 8th edition), 234-235.

L 3.1.H: Use coordinating and subordinating conjunctions.

TEACHING THIS:

- This standard repeats *L 1.1.G: Use frequently occurring conjunctions (e.g., and, but, or, so, because)* and also moves into subordinating conjunctions beyond "because." You should review the guidance for L 1.1.G and recycle the lesson if needed.

- Pitch: *We know how to connect independent clauses with FANBOYS (For, And, Nor, But, Or, Yet, So), so we can write compound sentences like, "I went to the store,* but *I forgot to buy milk." Today we're going to move into more COMPLEX sentences. To write a complex sentence, you need an AAAWWUBBIS.*

- PS, here's some quick background: Jeff Anderson, author of *Mechanically Inclined*, helps his students remember the list of subordinating conjunctions by calling it a funny-sounding mnemonic: "AAAWWUBBIS" (As, Although, After, While, When, Unless, Because, Before, If, Since). He reminds them that if they start a sentence with an AAAWWUBBIS, "they are almost guaranteed to have a comma in the sentence." And the comma never immediately follows the AAAWWUBBIS.* In his more recent book, *Patterns of Power*, he provides a mnemonic chart showing the outlines of two hands, with "AAAWW" on the left and "UBBISS" on the right (and each word on a different finger), with this caption: "When you get your HANDS on a sentence, make it complex!" He also notes that if the AAAWWUBBIS isn't the first word of the sentence, it probably doesn't require a comma (e.g., "I will eat lunch *when I am hungry*.").**

- Resume pitch: *So let's write some sentences using AAAWWUBBIS!*

- Use a current topic or text to model how to write a sentence with subordinating conjunction (including the comma where it belongs), then invite students to create their own sentences using AAAWWUBBIS. Actively monitor their work, then use Show Call to share their exemplars (see Chapter 2, "Principle #4: Give Faster Feedback," to review Show Call).

- During Show Call, let students explain what makes the exemplary edits effective. Then send them back to their own writing with this advice: "Use what you now know about subordinating conjunctions in your own writing."

ASSESSING THIS:

- As always, we want students to demonstrate their grasp of these grammatical concepts in their own writing, first in sentences then in paragraphs. Direct them to use several conjunctions from FANBOYS and AAAWWUBBIS in a paragraph about a text or topic they are studying. Tell them you will score the paragraph based on two things: 1) All sentences must be complete, and 2) All conjunctions must be used correctly, with proper punctuation.

- Again, Cloze reading (text with blanks where, in this case, the proper coordinating or subordinating conjunctions belong) is another useful way to check for understanding.

L 3.1.I: Produce simple, compound, and complex sentences.

TEACHING THIS:

- This standard follows directly from *L 3.1.H: Use coordinating and subordinating conjunctions*, so if your students are working on 3rd-grade standards, you should feel confident that you are capturing this standard with the work you do for L 3.1.H.

- However, if your students are not operating on the 3rd-grade level yet, you should refer back to the following standards for more guidance and recycle the lessons there:

  o L 1.1.G: Use frequently occurring conjunctions (e.g., and, but, or, so, because).

  o L 1.1.J: Produce and expand complete simple and compound declarative, interrogative, imperative, and exclamatory sentences in response to prompts.

  o L 2.1.F: Produce, expand, and rearrange complete simple and compound sentences (e.g., The boy watched the movie; The little boy watched the movie; The action movie was watched by the little boy).

ASSESSING THIS:

- As always, we want students to demonstrate their grasp of these grammatical concepts in their own writing, first in sentences then in paragraphs. Direct them to use several conjunctions from FANBOYS (see L 1.1.G) and AAAWWUBBIS (see L 3.1.H) in a paragraph about a text or topic they are studying. Tell them you will score the paragraph based on two things: 1) All sentences must be complete, and 2) All conjunctions must be used correctly, with proper punctuation.

- Again, Cloze reading (text with blanks where, in this case, the proper coordinating or subordinating conjunctions belong) is another useful way to check for understanding.

*See footnote[138] / **See footnote[139]

---

138 Jeff Anderson, *Mechanically Inclined: Building Grammar, Usage, and Style into Writer's Workshop* (Portland, ME: Stenhouse Publishers, 2005), 38-39.

139 Jeff Anderson with Whitney La Rocca, *Patterns of Power: Inviting Young Writers into the Conventions of Language, Grades 1-5* (Portland, ME, Stenhouse Publishers, 2017), 398-399

L 3.2.A: Capitalize appropriate words in titles.

TEACHING THIS:

- **GENRE ALERT: Students will need to apply this standard when working on narrative writing (W 3.3).** And of course it can be discussed any time they *read* any text.
- The general rule for this standard is that you capitalize "the first, last, and all major words in titles and subtitles," which I take to mean "the first, last, and most words *but not prepositions, articles, or coordinating conjunctions.*"
- Show students a dozen examples of titles and ask them what they think the rule is for capitalizing titles. Create an anchor chart based on what they figure out.
- This is also a good time to discuss whether one should underline/italicize a title or put it in quotation marks. See *L 5.2.D: Use underlining, quotation marks, or italics to indicate titles of works.* You don't have to wait until students are in 5ᵗʰ grade to teach this!
- Remind students about the editing mark for capitalization: a double-underline under the lowercase letter.

ASSESSING THIS:

- Dictated quizzes, especially with erasable white boards, can quickly capture which students are "getting it" and which need more support.
- Give students titles in lowercase and have them either edit the titles with the double-underline mark or rewrite the titles altogether (or both) to apply this rule.
- Hold students accountable for proper capitalization of their own titled works.

*See footnote[140]

L 3.2.B: Use commas in addresses.

TEACHING THIS:

- The pitch: *Whenever we want to mail (snail-mail) a letter to someone or to pay a bill, we need to address the envelope, and we must do this properly; otherwise, the letter won't get there. Let's take a look at some examples of how to do this....*
- Letter writing should have been introduced in 2ⁿᵈ grade. See *L 2.2.B: Use commas in greetings and closings of letters.* Demonstrate how to address an envelope. Model with the school's address, then give students other addresses to practice with.

---

140 Diana Hacker and Nancy Sommers, *Rules for Writers* (Boston: Bedford/St. Martin's, 2016, 8th edition), 358.

L 3.2.C: Use commas and quotation marks in dialogue.

TEACHING THIS:

- **GENRE ALERT: Students will need to apply this standard when working on narrative writing (W 3.3).**
- **Reading prep work:** Teach students that writers reveal characters with "DDAT": direct description, dialogue, action, and thought. See the "DDAT Organizer" that follows for details.
- The pitch: *When writing stories or narratives, we want to include dialogue, or what the characters say to one another, because in real life people talk to each other and because in stories, dialogue also gives readers a clearer idea of what the characters are like. We saw this with our "DDAT Organizers." Today we're going to learn how to punctuate dialogue properly so that we won't accidentally confuse the reader. Let's take a look at some examples of dialogue....*
- Show students examples of dialogue from texts they have read (or not) and ask them to notice where the commas and quotation marks go. Derive rules for an anchor chart.
- Remind them that each new speaker's dialogue must be indented, or as I like to say (with a touch of attitude), "You wanna talk? Get your *own* paragraph!"
- Invite them to write a brief dialogue between two people, based on a current text or topic, then use Show Call to review the way students implemented the rules (see Chapter 2, "Principle #4: Give Faster Feedback," to review Show Call).
- During Show Call, let students explain what makes the exemplary edits effective. Then send them back to their own writing with this advice: "Use what you now know about punctuating and formatting dialogue effectively in your own writing."

ASSESSING THIS:

- As always, we want students to demonstrate their grasp of these grammatical concepts in their own writing. Ask them to write a brief dialogue between two people, based on a current text or topic, and tell them you will score the dialogue based on two things: 1) All sentences must be complete, and 2) The dialogue must be properly indented and punctuated.
- Quick editing quiz: Give students a dialogue that is missing commas and quotation marks, and instruct them to insert the proper punctuation.

DDAT Organizer[141]

DDAT is a simple mnemonic device to help readers remember how writers develop characters. It stands for description, dialogue, actions, and thoughts.

Direct Characterization:

- **Description:** Example: *He had a great sense of humor.* No inference is required.

Indirect Characterization:

- **Dialogue:** Example: *"I want to save the whales," she explained.* We can infer that she cares about animals and maybe that she is idealistic.
- **Actions:** Example: *The young man studied every night and earned straight A's in high school.* We can infer that he is hard-working and perseverant.
- **Thoughts:** Example: *The girl wondered if the boy would ask her to dance.* We can infer that she has a crush on him.

Let's try it…. **CHARACTER'S NAME:**_____

	QUOTE/EVIDENCE	INFERENCE
Description:		N/A because the evidence literally describes the character.
Dialogue:		
Actions:		
Thoughts:		

---

141 Sarah Tantillo, *Literacy and the Common Core: Recipes for Action* (San Francisco: Jossey-Bass, 2014), 113. The "DDAT Organizer" is on the TLC "Using Grammar to Improve Writing" page found at https://www.literacycookbook.com/page.php?id=161. Along with other analytic tools, it can also be found on the TLC "Analyzing Literature" page at https://www.literacycookbook.com/page.php?id=2.

L 3.2.D: Form and use possessives.

TEACHING THIS:

- This standard follows from *L 1.1.B: Use common, proper, and possessive nouns.* You should refer to the guidance for that standard: You will probably want to implement the described lesson, which helps students discover that possessive nouns are formed with apostrophe –s.

- For possessive pronouns, refer back to *L 1.1.D: Use personal, possessive, and indefinite pronouns (e.g., I, me, my; they, them, their; anyone, everything).*

- Students should practice writing sentences that include possessive nouns and pronouns.

ASSESSING THIS:

- As always, we want students to demonstrate their grasp of these grammatical concepts in their own writing, first in sentences then in paragraphs. Give them several singular and plural nouns they must include in a paragraph about a text or topic they are studying, and tell them you will score the paragraph based on two things: 1) All sentences must be complete, and 2) The given nouns must possess something and must be properly punctuated to show that possession.

- Alternatively, give them several possessive pronouns they must include in a paragraph about a text or topic they are studying, and tell them you will score the paragraph based on two things: 1) All sentences must be complete, and 2) All pronouns must be used properly.

- Cloze reading (text with blanks where, in this case, the possessive pronouns or possessive nouns belong) is another useful way to check for understanding.

- Quick editing quiz: Provide sentences with singular and plural possessive nouns that are missing apostrophes, and instruct students to insert the apostrophes where they belong.

L 3.2.E: Use conventional spelling for high frequency and other studied words and for adding suffixes to base words (e.g., sitting, smiled, cries, happiness).

- This book does not explain phonics instruction but recommends its use for this standard.

L 3.2.F: Use spelling patterns and generalizations (e.g., word families, position-based spellings, syllable patterns, ending rules, meaningful word parts) in writing words.

- This book does not explain phonics instruction but recommends its use for this standard.

L 3.2.G: Consult reference materials, including beginning dictionaries, as needed to check and correct spellings.

TEACHING THIS: *[This repeats L 2.2.E.]*

- I do not advocate telling students to "look it up" when you're reading a text with the class and someone asks, "What does that word mean?" Looking it up creates a distraction, and often when students look up word, they don't understand the definition anyway. Instead, you should ask them to look for context clues or word parts that they recognize, and if that doesn't work, give them a prepared sentence that provides ample instructive/directive context so they can figure it out. By wrestling with the context to infer the meaning of the word, students will then *own* the word. Although sometimes you need to quickly tell them the meaning to keep things moving, in general, they are more likely to retain the word if they've had to figure it out.

- That said, sometimes students need to use reference materials such as dictionaries and thesauruses, and they need to learn how to use them.

- The pitch: *Sometimes when we're reading independently, we come upon or encounter a word that is unfamiliar. We can't figure it out from context clues, and we don't recognize any parts of the word. One thing we can do is use the dictionary to look it up. Let's try that…*

- Have students find a word, then discuss the features of the entry. If it includes an etymology, even better: This is a clue to the roots of the word.

- Since this may be a new skill for students, ask them what they find challenging about this process so you can address any concerns or confusion.

- Remind students that the dictionary can also help them find the spelling of a word, as long as they can begin to sound it out.

ASSESSING THIS:

- For a quick quiz, you can game-ify the process of looking up words and using dictionary skills while also reviewing content by simply giving them a few words to look up, with requirements about what information to capture.

L 3.3: Use knowledge of language and its conventions when writing, speaking, reading, or listening. A) Choose words and phrases for effect. B) Recognize and observe differences between the conventions of spoken and written standard English.

TEACHING THIS:

- Regarding *L 3.3.A: Choose words and phrases for effect*, your vocabulary instruction should address the importance of paying attention to the nuances of words and using them for effect. For guidance on vocabulary instruction, see *The Literacy Cookbook.*

- Regarding *L 3.3.B: Recognize and observe differences between the conventions of spoken and written standard English*, see Chapter 2—specifically "Principle #6: Provide Oral Support"—for suggestions on how to compare and contrast varieties of English.

ASSESSING THIS:

- Ditto.

*See footnote[142]

GRADE 4 LANGUAGE STANDARDS: A DEEPER DIVE

Next, we'll dive more deeply into the Grade 4 Language Standards and look at how to teach and assess them more systematically, in conjunction with writing instruction. Again, these are by no means the *only* ways to teach these standards, just a few to illustrate how to connect grammar with writing and reading.

L 4.1.A: Use relative pronouns (who, whose, whom, which, that) and relative adverbs (where, when, why).

TEACHING THIS:

- Background: By the end of 3rd grade, students should have learned about subordinate clauses introduced by subordinating conjunctions. If they didn't or if you want to review that concept, you should revisit the guidance for *L 3.1.H: Use coordinating and subordinating conjunctions.* Then, you'll be able to point out that another way to form a subordinate clause is with a relative pronoun or a relative adverb.
- The pitch: *Good writers know how to write simple, compound, complex, and even compound-complex sentences. In order to write complex sentences, you need to know what "parts" you can add. We're going to remind ourselves about what we already know about complex sentences, then learn a new way to build them.*

---

142 Sarah Tantillo, *The Literacy Cookbook: A Practical Guide to Effective Reading, Writing, Speaking, and Listening Instruction* (San Francisco: Jossey-Bass, 2012), 28-36. For online resources, see the TLC "Building Robust Vocabulary" page found at https://www.literacycookbook.com/page.php?id=4.

- Pause to review examples of subordinating conjunctions. It could be as simple as showing them several sentences that begin with an AAAWWUBBIS word (show them the whole list on an anchor chart) and asking them to identify the subordinate clause (attached to the conjunction, of course), the comma, and the independent clause—e.g., "*Since* I like to read, I go to the library at least once a week."
- Continuing the pitch: *Now, here's where we learn the new stuff! Take a look at this complex sentence, and see if you can figure out which part is the subordinate clause and which part is the independent clause.*
- Show students a sentence like this (ideally on a handout they can mark up): "The quarterback who won the game lives in Haddonfield." They should identify the subject and verb first, to find the independent clause ("The quarterback lives in Haddonfield"). The remainder ("who won the game") is the subordinate clause. Remind students that **the subordinate clause can be removed and the sentence will still make sense.** Get students to imitate this structure by writing sentences about a current text or topic using "who," then "which" and "that."
- More explanation: *These are relative pronouns; just like other pronouns, they stand in for nouns. In our first example, "who" stands in for "the quarterback" because it would sound silly to say, "The quarterback the quarterback won the game lives in Haddonfield."*
- *There are also relative ADVERBS. Here's an example: "The woman visited the elementary school where she had first learned to read." See if you can pull out the independent clause first, then find the subordinate clause.* Again, get students to imitate this structure by writing sentences about a current text or topic using "where," then "when" and "why."

- For more advanced work (which will be revisited with *L 6.2.A: Use punctuation [commas, parentheses, dashes] to set off nonrestrictive/parenthetical elements*), dig into restrictive vs. nonrestrictive relative clauses (AKA adjective clauses). Restrictive clauses restrict the meaning of the word they modify, whereas nonrestrictive clauses are nonessential.
  - **Restrictive:** Her car has seats *that are made of leather.* (Obviously, her car has seats; the intended meaning is more limited. The sentence would sound silly without the qualifying clause.)
  - **Nonrestrictive:** Her car, *which is black,* has leather seats. (The fact that the car is black is not essential; the sentence would make sense without that clause.)
- Using a current text or topic, students should practice writing sentences using restrictive and nonrestrictive clauses.

ASSESSING THIS:

- Exit Ticket: 1) What two types of clauses make up a complex sentence? 2) What is our acronym for subordinating conjunctions? 3) Write three sentences [about a current text or topic] using relative pronouns. 4) Write three sentences [about a current text or topic] using relative adverbs.

- As always, we want students to demonstrate their grasp of these grammatical concepts in their own writing, first in sentences then in paragraphs. Direct them to write a paragraph about a current text or topic and include either a relative pronoun or a relative adverb in at least three sentences and tell them you will score the paragraph based on two things: 1) All sentences must be complete, and 2) The relative pronouns and relative adverbs must be used correctly.
- Cloze reading (text with blanks where, in this case, the subordinating conjunctions, relative pronouns, or relative adverbs belong) is another useful way to check for understanding.

L 4.1.B: Form and use the progressive (e.g., I was walking; I am walking; I will be walking) verb tenses.

TEACHING THIS:

- Give students a handout that includes this two-column chart:

	SIMPLE	PROGRESSIVE
PRESENT	1) I walk.	4) I am walking.
PAST	2) I walked.	5) I was walking.
FUTURE	3) I will walk.	6) I will be walking.

And these sentences to complete:

Add at least FIVE WORDS to each sentence, including TIME SIGNAL WORDS THAT MATCH THE TENSE:
1) Example: I walk <u>to school with my friends</u> *every day.*
2) I walked <u>home from school with my friends</u> *yesterday.*
3) I will walk
4) I am walking
5) I was walking
6) I will be walking

- Pitch: *The verb forms in the two columns might look pretty similar, but they are not exactly the same, and they are not interchangeable. We have to be careful and precise when using them, or else our readers will become confused. So here's my first challenge. In order to figure out how to use these forms properly, we're going to extend these sentences. You must add AT LEAST FIVE words, but you may add more than five, and you must include TIME SIGNAL WORDS THAT MATCH THE TENSE. Check out my models. Take 3 minutes to do this, and be prepared to discuss how these different verb forms work differently.*

- Actively monitor student work. When they are finished, ask them to discuss with a partner: "What did you figure out about how simple and progressive verb forms work differently?"

- Show students the following sentences and ask them to discuss what they notice, and what rules they can derive from these examples:

1) I walk to school with my friends *every day.*
2) I walked home from school with my friends *yesterday.*
3) I will walk home from school with my friends *later.*
4) I am walking to school with my friends *tomorrow.* [As in, *It is my intention to.*] I am walking home from school with my friends *now.*
5) I was walking home from school *when it began snowing.* [You might also want to share this: I *was going to* walk to school this morning, *but* it was raining torrentially.]
6) I will be walking home from school with my friends *later today.* [As in, *It is my intention to.*]

- Solicit student examples, as well.

- Give students more practice with these forms (with other verbs, possibly on a separate handout or with more charts on the same one).

- Exit Ticket: Write a paragraph about a current text or topic in which you include at least *three* examples of progressive verbs. Underline the verbs.

ASSESSING THIS:

- As always, we want students to demonstrate their grasp of these grammatical concepts in their own writing, first in sentences then in paragraphs. Give them several verbs they must include in a paragraph about a text or topic they are studying, and tell them you will score the paragraph based on two things: 1) All sentences must be complete, and 2) The given verbs must be used in the progressive form with proper context clues. They must circle the verbs and underline the context clues [i.e., time-related signal words].

- Cloze reading (text with blanks where, in this case, the verbs—whether simple or progressive—belong) is another useful way to check for understanding.

> • Quick editing quiz: Give students sentences and ask them to choose the proper form of the verb, based on context clues [e.g., *I talked/was talking to my mother when suddenly the power went out.*]

L 4.1.C: Use modal auxiliaries (e.g., can, may, must) to convey various conditions.

TEACHING THIS:

- On the board, show the following words: *can, could, may, might, must, shall, should, will, would.*
- Pitch: *These words are a special type of verb called a "modal verb." Let's write sentences using these words and try to figure out how they work!*
- Go through the list, either enlisting student examples or generating your own, and for each one, ask students to determine what the word is meant to convey. For example, in "I *can* type faster than my brother" the word "can" suggests "general ability." Whereas, "*Can* you help me find my lost cat?" is an informal request. "*Could* you pass the salt?" is slightly more polite, but still informal. "*May* I leave the table?" is more formal. And so on.*

ASSESSING THIS:

- Cloze reading (text with blanks where, in this case, the modal verbs belong) is another useful way to check for understanding. Note: Be sure that your sentences provide enough context clues to suggest proper use.
- As always, we want students to apply these grammatical forms in their own writing. One way to be playful about this particular standard would be to ask students to write sentences about situations in which they would use each modal verb, and why. For example: "I will finish writing this book even if it kills me. I am certain, so 'will' is the appropriate word choice."

*See footnote[143]

---

[143] For a more detailed explanation of the meanings of modal verbs, see Diana Hacker and Nancy Sommers, *Rules for Writers* (Boston: Bedford/St. Martin's, 2016, 8th edition), 261-263.

L 4.1.D: Order adjectives within sentences according to conventional patterns (e.g., a small red bag rather than a red small bag).

> **TEACHING THIS:**
>
> - This is a good standard to game-ify. Before class, photocopy the "Order of Cumulative Adjectives Handout" (following this box—PS, feel free to modify it!), then cut each example into separate strips. Put sets of these strips in envelopes to create one envelope for each pair of students in class. Don't forget to keep a copy of the original handout because it provides the proper sequence (although there are occasional exceptions).
>
> - First, you need to make the pitch: *Scholars, when we describe people, places, or things, we use adjectives, of course—like when we say, "I am wearing* brown shoes" *or "My shoes are* brown." *It's easy to do this when we are only using ONE adjective to describe the noun. But good writers sometimes want to use MULTIPLE adjectives, and this can be a little tricky. For example, you might want to say something like, "I'm wearing my* battered old brown *shoes." [Show this sentence on the board.] Notice how I didn't need any commas or "and" between these adjectives? That's because they are all different kinds of adjectives. Whereas, if I wrote "my smelly, dusty shoes" I would need a comma because when you use two or more adjectives of the same type, the general rule is that you need to separate them with a comma; those are called* **COORDINATE adjectives** *because you could combine them with "and," as in "my smelly and dusty shoes" (It may help to remember that "and" is a "coordinating conjunction").* * *Today we're going to figure out the rules for determining the order of* **CUMULATIVE adjectives**—*adjectives that add up, or accumulate—when you use one of each in a list to describe a noun.*
>
> - Distribute an envelope to each pair of students, and challenge students to create *one complete sentence* using at least one word from each slip (plus a verb, of course). They should write their sentences on looseleaf so that you can use Show Call later (see Chapter 2, "Principle #4: Give Faster Feedback," to review Show Call). How you incentivize the work is up to you. Maybe "The first three pairs to get the words in the proper sequence get an extra credit point" or something like that.
>
> - During Show Call, let students explain what makes the exemplary sentences effective. Then send them back to their own writing with this advice: "Use what you now know about cumulative adjectives in your own writing."
>
> - For variations, you can invite students to add appropriate words to the original lists so that everyone will have more words to choose from in subsequent rounds.
>
> - This makes a helpful anchor chart.

ASSESSING THIS:

- Invite students to write playful sentences with at least one adjective from each category on the "Order of Cumulative Adjectives Handout."

*See footnote[144]

Order of Cumulative Adjectives Handout[145]

ARTICLE OR OTHER NOUN MARKER: a, an, the, his, Jane's, some, three
EVALUATIVE WORD: beautiful, hard-working, tasty, smelly
SIZE: tiny, small, gigantic, large
LENGTH OR SHAPE: short, long, round, triangular
AGE: ancient, new, old, young
COLOR: red, orange, yellow, green
NATIONALITY: American, French, Mexican, Polish
RELIGION: Catholic, Jewish, Muslim, Protestant
MATERIAL: wood, wool, marble, copper
NOUN/ADJECTIVE: tree (as in *tree* house), kitchen, dog, window

---

144 For more information on the distinction between coordinate and cumulative adjectives, see Diana Hacker and Nancy Sommers, Rules for Writers (Boston: Bedford/St. Martin's, 2016, 8th edition), 297-298.

145 This sequence is from Diana Hacker and Nancy Sommers, *Rules for Writers* (Boston: Bedford/St. Martin's, 2016, 8th edition), 287; however, I have changed some of the word choices. The "Order of Cumulative Adjectives Handout" is on the TLC "Using Grammar to Improve Writing" page found at https://www.literacycookbook.com/page.php?id=161.

L 4.1.E: Form and use prepositional phrases.

TEACHING THIS: *[This repeats L K.1.E and L 1.1.I.]*

- Prepositions should be taught in kindergarten and 1ˢᵗ grade, but they can continue to be tricky, especially for ESL/ELL students who struggle with idioms (e.g., *"Is the ball IN the air, or ON the air?"*).* Prepositional phrases are simply prepositions followed by a noun (*on the chair*) or a noun equivalent (*by working hard*). In case you need to review this standard, here's that guidance:

- You will need a soft object such as a squoosh ball or a small pillow—something that won't hurt anyone. Place the object in various locations and emphasize the phrases that capture its location: "The ball is *ON the desk.* The ball is *IN the closet.* I brought this ball *TO school* today *FOR you.*" Invite students to generate their own sentences emphasizing the prepositional phrases.

- As always, reinforce oral language with visual support such as an anchor chart listing the prepositions you want them to use or a PowerPoint presentation that quizzes them.

ASSESSING THIS:

- First, read aloud sentences and invite students to identify the prepositional phrases (e.g., "to him"). You can engage the entire class in practice by doing this with a rapid-fire turn-and-talk approach. Don't forget to model this: "I'll say the sentence once, then Partner A will turn to Partner B and restate *only* the prepositional phrase to Partner B. For example, if I said, 'I gave the book to Joe,' Partner A would turn to Partner B and say, 'TO JOE.' Let's see a model pair try this...." Select a pair to demonstrate, then launch a whole-class attempt. Then cold-call and clarify if anyone was confused. Run a few rounds, then switch the partner roles.

- Students should move from identifying the phrases to imitating your sentences using prepositions, then writing their own.

- Cloze reading (text with blanks where, in this case, the prepositions belong) is another useful way to check for understanding.

*See footnote¹⁴⁶

---

146 For some helpful resources on teaching idioms, see the TLC "Idiom Power" page at https://www.literacycookbook.com/page.php?id=7.

L 4.1.F: Produce complete sentences, recognizing and correcting inappropriate fragments and run-ons.

TEACHING THIS:

- Students should have been saying and writing complete sentences since kindergarten, although if they are struggling to do so, you can find useful guidance with *L 3.1.I: Produce simple, compound, and complex sentences.*

- The challenge of this standard is more the second half: how to recognize and correct inappropriate fragments and run-ons. Incidentally, I appreciate how the authors of the standards included the word "inappropriate" as a way to acknowledge that sometimes we *choose* to use fragments or run-ons *for effect.*

- For students writing fragments unintentionally, you might want to revisit Jeff Anderson's notion of the two-word sentence described in "Principle #7: Model, Model, Model" in Chapter 2.* This means go back to the basics: subject + verb= sentence. If you notice trends such as students writing "unfinished" subordinate clauses such as "Because I like chocolate milkshakes" or "When I go to the store," you could review the "Demonstrated Grammar" skit in Chapter 2, found under "Principle #3: Ask, 'What Do You *Like* About That Sentence?'"

- Run-ons can be a bit more dicey because some students think that long sentences are automatically run-on sentences. A good place to start when clearing up this misconception is with the standards pertaining to conjunctions, especially *L 1.1.G: Use frequently occurring conjunctions (e.g., and, but, or, so, because)* and *L 3.1.H: Use coordinating and subordinating conjunctions.*

ASSESSING THIS:

- A quick quiz would give students examples of sentences, fragments, and run-ons and ask them to correct any that are not sentences.

- As always, we want students to demonstrate their grasp of these grammatical concepts in their own writing, first in sentences then in paragraphs. Give them either a "How" or "Why" question or an argument they must support about a topic or current text and require them to respond with a paragraph. Use the "Paragraph Response Scoring Checklist" in Chapter 3 or modify it to suit your needs. If you want to zero in on the punctuation, add that to the checklist.

*See footnote[147]

---

147 Jeff Anderson, *Mechanically Inclined: Building Grammar, Usage, and Style into Writer's Workshop* (Portland, ME: Stenhouse Publishers, 2005), 65-67.

L 4.1.G: Correctly use frequently confused words (e.g., to, too, two; there, their).

TEACHING THIS:

- Students frequently (and understandably) misspell homophones. A quick Google search will elicit a list. To help them remember how to spell and use these words, share mnemonic hints (e.g., "Too has too many o's in it!"), post them *in sentences with context clues*, and review them during editing mini-lessons. Always discuss them *in context* so that the spellings will stick to the meanings.

ASSESSING THIS:

- After teaching these commonly confused words, give students the list and direct them to write a paragraph (or a list of sentences) in which they use them correctly. Make sure they circle the words and underline the context clues to show that they can explain why they chose the spelling they did.
- Alternatively, give them a Cloze reading passage with blanks where these words belong. Again, it's a good idea for them to underline the context clues.

L 4.2.A: Use correct capitalization.

TEACHING THIS:

- Students should have been taught the rules of capitalization by 4th grade and should be applying them in their writing, but you may need to review some rules. Their writing will reveal their needs; however, if you would like to figure things out more quickly, you could administer a diagnostic assessment such as the one described below.
- Once you know which rules students need to review, check out the guidance for the following standards:
  - o L 1.1.A: Print all upper- and lowercase letters.
  - o L 1.1.B: Use common, proper, and possessive nouns.
  - o L 1.2.A: Capitalize dates and names of people.
  - o L 2.2.A: Capitalize holidays, product names, and geographic names.
  - o L 3.2.A: Capitalize appropriate words in titles.

- For quick diagnostic assessments, give students sentences that manifest capitalization errors and have them correct the errors.

- To fold this work into writing, direct students to write a paragraph about a current text or topic that includes the following: at least one proper noun, one date, one holiday, one product name, one city, and the title of a book; and they should underline these items. Tell them you will score the paragraph based on two things: 1) All sentences must be complete, and 2) All required items must be included. Note: You should *not* add "and they must be capitalized" because you want to see if students already know that.

L 4.2.B: Use commas and quotation marks to mark direct speech and quotations from a text.

TEACHING THIS:

- Although this standard echoes *L 3.2.C: Use commas and quotation marks in dialogue*, it also addresses how to quote evidence from a text, which, interestingly, is a 5th-grade reading standard (*RIT 5.1: Quote accurately from a text when explaining what the text says explicitly and when drawing inferences from the text*). You should review the guidance for L 3.2.C before addressing how to set up quoted text.

- Before you work on how to quote evidence, you should also review Argument vs. Evidence Steps 1-3. See Chapter 4 for a detailed explanation of how to teach these steps.

- Remember to make a pitch: *Why do we have to put quoted text in quotation marks? It's important for us to clarify which ideas are ours versus which ideas are the author's. Putting quotation marks around the author's exact words helps us do that.*

- Then you can start modeling with evidence from whatever text the class is reading.

ASSESSING THIS:

- As always, we want students to demonstrate their grasp of these grammatical concepts in their own writing, first in sentences then in paragraphs. Give them either a "How" or "Why" question or an argument they must support about a current text and require them to respond with a paragraph that includes quoted evidence and explanation. Use the "Paragraph Response Scoring Checklist" in Chapter 3 or modify it to suit your needs. If you want to zero in on the punctuation, add that to the checklist.

L 4.2.C: Use a comma before a coordinating conjunction in a compound sentence.

TEACHING THIS:

- In truth, this standard should be taught in 1ˢᵗ grade, with *L 1.1.G: Use frequently occurring conjunctions (e.g., and, but, or, so, because).* Here's a review of the guidance for that standard:

- Show students a pair of sentences that could be logically combined with a conjunction—e.g., "I like peanut butter. I don't like jelly." Ask them, "If you had to combine these sentences and turn them into one sentence, how could you do it? There is not one right answer here, but I will ask you to explain your thinking. Talk to your neighbor." Students might come up with "Insert a semi-colon!" (There's always one in the crowd), but at some point they will realize that inserting a comma then "but" makes the most sense. Note that "but" is called a "conjunction" [specifically, a coordinating conjunction], and move into the pitch: *Today we're going to start paying more attention to conjunctions because they help us build bigger, stronger sentences. And they help us vary our sentence structures so that we're not always writing short, choppy sentences. With a conjunction, we can combine two simple sentences to form a "compound sentence." Let's look at some more short sentences that we can combine with conjunctions— and let's see if we can figure out what the other conjunctions are, besides "but."*

- Provide pairs of sentences and ask students to combine them logically.

- Note the useful mnemonic FANBOYS for coordinating conjunctions: *for, and, nor, but, or, yet, so.*

- Model other uses of conjunctions—phrases such as "this or that" and "bread and butter"—to remind students that conjunctions provide the glue to combine not only sentences but also words and phrases.

- After working through the coordinating conjunctions, introduce "because," a subordinating conjunction, and have students practice Hochman and Wexler's "Because, But, So" approach (described in Chapter 5, in the "K-2 Writing Standards with Instructional Guidance" section).˙

ASSESSING THIS:

- Ultimately, of course, you want students to practice using FANBOYS in their own writing.

- Also, per Hochman and Wexler, students should expand sentences with *because, but,* and *so.*

- Cloze reading (text with blanks where, in this case, the conjunctions belong) is another useful way to check for understanding. Make sure students are also required to insert punctuation where needed.

*See footnote[148]

---

[148] Judith C. Hochman and Natalie Wexler, *The Writing Revolution: A Guide to Advancing Thinking Through Writing in All Subjects and Grades* (San Francisco: Jossey-Bass, 2017), 40-43.

L 4.2.D: Spell grade-appropriate words correctly, consulting references as needed.

TEACHING THIS:

- This book does not explain phonics instruction but recommends its use for students who struggle with spelling.
- For guidance on how to teach students to consult reference materials, see *L 3.2.G: Consult reference materials, including beginning dictionaries, as needed to check and correct spellings.*

ASSESSING THIS:

- See *L 3.2.G: Consult reference materials, including beginning dictionaries, as needed to check and correct spellings.*

L 4.3.A: Choose words and phrases to convey ideas precisely.

TEACHING THIS:

- Your vocabulary instruction should address the importance of paying attention to the nuances of words and using them for effect. For guidance on vocabulary instruction, see *The Literacy Cookbook.*

ASSESSING THIS:

- Ditto.

---

*See footnote[149]

---

149 Sarah Tantillo, *The Literacy Cookbook: A Practical Guide to Effective Reading, Writing, Speaking, and Listening Instruction* (San Francisco: Jossey-Bass, 2012), 28-36. For online resources, see the TLC "Building Robust Vocabulary" page found at https://www.literacycookbook.com/page.php?id=4.

L 4.3.B: Choose punctuation for effect.

TEACHING THIS:

- This standard reminds me of a 10th-grader named Don, who for several
  months in my English class ended *every sentence* with an exclamation point.
  I am not making this up. I always felt like he was shouting at me. His essays
  would begin, "Huckleberry Finn is an interesting character! He had a difficult
  upbringing! His dad was an alcoholic!" Because Don was such an energetic
  young man, it made a strange sort of sense that he wrote this way. However, I
  needed to point out to him (repeatedly) that not every sentence warrants such
  enthusiasm; he would need to dial it back a bit.

- The most obvious "effect" is how you end a sentence, which reveals your intent
  (whether to state, question, or exclaim), and you can review this, if needed,
  by recycling the guidance for *L 1.1.J: Produce and expand complete simple and
  compound declarative, interrogative, imperative, and exclamatory sentences in
  response to prompts.*

- Teaching other "effects" of punctuation will require close attention to sentences
  that do more than end. Moreover, some "effects" aren't mentioned until later
  grades. One of my favorites, which illustrates the power of punctuation, is part
  of *L 5.2.C: Use a comma to set off the words yes and no (e.g., Yes, thank you), to
  set off a tag question from the rest of the sentence (e.g., It's true, isn't it?), and to
  indicate direct address (e.g., Is that you, Steve?).* I love to point out the difference between "Let's eat, Grandma," and "Let's eat Grandma," asking students,
  "Do you *like* your grandmother? Or are you a *cannibal*?"

ASSESSING THIS:

- When conferring with students, you are most likely to find opportunities to
  reinforce the effect of punctuation decisions or oversights (as in, "Did you
  mean for this to be a question, or a statement?").

- As always, we want students to demonstrate their grasp of these grammatical
  concepts in their own writing. Provide prompts/scenarios for them to respond
  to with a sentence or two. For example: *Imagine someone accidentally spilled
  milk on your desk. What POLITE imperative sentence might you say? What
  POLITE exclamatory sentence might you say? What POLITE question might
  you ask?*

L 4.3.C: Differentiate between contexts that call for formal English (e.g., presenting ideas) and situations where informal discourse is appropriate (e.g., small-group discussion).

TEACHING THIS:

- See Chapter 2—specifically "Principle #6: Provide Oral Support"—for suggestions on how to compare and contrast varieties of English.

ASSESSING THIS:

- Ditto.

GRADE 5 LANGUAGE STANDARDS: A DEEPER DIVE

Next, we'll dive more deeply into the Grade 5 Language Standards and look at how to teach and assess them more systematically, in conjunction with writing instruction. Again, these are by no means the *only* ways to teach these standards, just a few to illustrate how to connect grammar with writing and reading.

L 5.1.A: Explain the function of conjunctions, prepositions, and interjections in general and their function in particular sentences.

TEACHING THIS:

- Pitch: *One way to build more sophisticated sentences (beyond two-word sentences) is to add more information. We can use a variety of strategies to do this. Today, we'll review* [fill in the blank with "conjunctions" or "prepositions"] *and practice developing more complex sentences.*
- You can then recycle the guidance for the following standards:
    - o L 3.1.H: Use coordinating and subordinating conjunctions.
    - o L 5.1.E: Use correlative conjunctions (e.g., either/or, neither/nor).
    - o L 4.1.E: Form and use prepositional phrases.

- Additional background: An interjection is a word used to express surprise or emotion (such as *Oh! Hey! Wow!*).* **GENRE ALERT: Interjections will most often be used in narrative writing (W 5.3).** Take advantage of teachable moments when reading stories or novels to point them out. Reinforce this work by giving students scenarios in which one might use an interjection (e.g., When you step in mud, you might say, "Ugh!") and asking them which interjection(s) would be appropriate. Conversely, you could ask them to generate scenarios appropriate for interjections that you provide. Be sure to move quickly into dialogue, though, so students see how interjections are used in context.

ASSESSING THIS:

- As always, we want students to demonstrate their grasp of these grammatical concepts in their own writing, first in sentences then in paragraphs. **For conjunctions:** Provide the anchor charts of coordinating, subordinating, and correlative conjunctions, and direct students to write a paragraph about a current text or topic using at least one example of each type of conjunction (which they should underline). **For prepositions:** Provide an anchor chart for prepositions, and direct students to write a paragraph about a current text or topic using three prepositional phrases (which they should underline). Tell them you will score the paragraph based on two things: 1) All sentences must be complete, and 2) All required items must be included and used properly.

- **For interjections:** Direct students to write a brief dialogue between two characters from a current story/novel in which they include at least two interjections (which they should underline). Tell them you will score the dialogue based on three things: 1) All sentences must be complete, 2) All required items must be included and used properly, and 3) All dialogue must be formatted correctly.

- For a quick quiz, give students a Cloze reading activity (text with blanks where, in this case, the conjunctions, prepositions, or interjections belong).

*See footnote[150]

---

150 Diana Hacker and Nancy Sommers, Rules for Writers (Boston: Bedford/St. Martin's, 2016, 8th edition), 371.

L 5.1.B: Form and use the perfect (e.g., I had walked; I have walked; I will have walked) verb tenses.

TEACHING THIS:

- **GENRE ALERT: Students will need to apply this standard when working on narrative writing (W 5.3).**
- For reasons that have to do with the use of informal language, some students misuse the perfect tense. They "over-past-ify" things, saying, "I *had* talked to him yesterday" when they really mean "I *talked* to him yesterday." The advice in Chapter 2 regarding "Principle #6: Provide Oral Support," which offers suggestions on how to compare and contrast varieties of English, is relevant here.
- You should also review the guidance for the following standards:
  - o L 1.1.E: Use verbs to convey a sense of past, present, and future (e.g., Yesterday I walked home; Today I walk home; Tomorrow I will walk home).
  - o L 2.1.D: Form and use the past tense of frequently occurring irregular verbs (e.g., sat, hid, told).
  - o L 3.1.E: Form and use the simple (e.g., I walked; I walk; I will walk) verb tenses.
- Pitch: *We're writing narratives/stories about events that happened in the past, and today I want to bring your attention to some important nuances. Not all past tenses are the same. So it's important to be sure you're using the one that captures exactly what you mean. You already know about the simple past tense: "I cheered, you cheered," and so on. Today we're going to examine the PERFECT tense.*
- Show students this chart:

	SIMPLE	PERFECT
PRESENT	1) I walk.	4) I have walked.
PAST	2) I walked.	5) I had walked.
FUTURE	3) I will walk.	6) I will have walked.

- Then show students the following sentences and ask them to discuss what they notice about each sentence: *How does it work?*

1) I have walked to school *every day since the beginning of September.*
2) I had walked home *before my mother remembered to pick me up.*
3) I will have walked home *before my mother remembers to pick me up.*

- As Sentence #1 suggests, the **present perfect tense** is useful when talking about something that is done continuously/repeatedly. Here's another example, "My mother *has asked* me five times to set the table." As Sentence #2 indicates, the **past perfect** is used when you are talking about two actions: one in the past, and one before it (also in the past). Another example: "My teammates *had scored* 40 points before I entered the game." Sentence #3 shows that the **future perfect tense** is a little trickier: You're talking about something that you can anticipate having done before something else happens. Example: "If I'm lucky, he *will have cooked* dinner by the time I get home."

ASSESSING THIS:

- As always, we want students to demonstrate their grasp of these grammatical concepts in their own writing, first in sentences then in paragraphs. After practicing with sentences, students should write a paragraph about a current text or topic in which they use at least one example of each perfect tense. Tell them you will score the paragraph based on two things: 1) All sentences must be complete, and 2) All required items must be included and used properly.

- For a quick quiz, you can give students a Cloze reading activity (text with blanks where, in this case, the various forms of perfect tense verbs belong).

L 5.1.C: Use verb tense to convey various times, sequences, states, and conditions.

TEACHING THIS:

- This is clearly not a standard you can teach in one day. It actually speaks to a review of standards that students should have already mastered. By analyzing their writing, you can determine which aspect(s) of this standard they need support with. You can then recycle guidance for the following standards:

  o L 1.1.E: Use verbs to convey a sense of past, present, and future (e.g., Yesterday I walked home; Today I walk home; Tomorrow I will walk home).

  o L 2.1.D: Form and use the past tense of frequently occurring irregular verbs (e.g., sat, hid, told).

  o L 3.1.E: Form and use the simple (e.g., I walked; I walk; I will walk) verb tenses.

  o L 4.1.B: Form and use the progressive (e.g., I was walking; I am walking; I will be walking) verb tenses.

  o L 5.1.B: Form and use the perfect (e.g., I had walked; I have walked; I will have walked) verb tenses.

- See "Principle #4: Give Faster Feedback" in Chapter 2 for suggestions about how to support students with revising and editing.

L 5.1.D: Recognize and correct inappropriate shifts in verb tense.

TEACHING THIS:

- This standard is, to some degree, a reiteration of *L 5.1.C: Use verb tense to convey various times, sequences, states, and conditions.* So you should review that guidance. However, it also suggests that students should *evaluate* sentences to apply what they know about verb tenses. Therefore, after reviewing L 5.1.C, you should zero in on inappropriate shifts in verb tense.

- Pitch: *We've been spending a fair amount of time talking about verbs, especially different verb tenses and how they are used. Because I will not be with you when you go to college, it's important for you to be able to evaluate your own writing to make sure you always use the appropriate verb tense. Sometimes we make mistakes; that's OK; we're human. But we need to be able to identify and fix those mistakes. So today we're going to see how much we've learned about verb tenses....*

- Show students an excerpt from a current text in which you have changed some of the verbs to the wrong tense. Give them a copy to write on while also projecting it on the board. Tell them that as detectives, it is their job to spot any verbs that need to be fixed. Then read through the passage sentence by sentence, and ask them to discuss with a partner whether anything needs to be corrected. Then cold-call. **It is not enough to get the right answer. Be sure to ask, "Why does that need to be changed?"** Welcome confusion and errors as opportunities to review rules.

- Repeat this work with another passage. This time, have students try to edit the whole thing before you ask them to compare their results with a partner. Then go through the passage sentence by sentence, cold-calling to elicit corrections and explanations. Again, remember to ask, "Why...?"

ASSESSING THIS:

- The Exit Ticket should be a third passage that needs to be corrected.

L 5.1.E: Use correlative conjunctions (e.g., either/or, neither/nor).

TEACHING THIS:

- Background: In order to use correlative conjunctions (listed below) properly, one must also employ parallel structure, which is a 9-10 standard (*L 9-10.1.A: Use parallel structure*).

- Pitch: *Today we're going to zero in on a third type of conjunctions. We already know about coordinating conjunctions, AKA FANBOYS, and subordinating conjunctions, AKA AAAWWUBBIS [see L 3.1.H: Use coordinating and subordinating conjunctions], and now we will turn to CORRELATIVE conjunctions. What root or roots do you see in that word, "correlative"? Tell your neighbor. [Pause, then cold call to elicit "relate" or "relative."] Yes. So that's a hint for us: These conjunctions are connected or related. In fact, we will only ever see them in pairs.*

- Show an anchor chart or Powerpoint slide that includes the following:
  o *either...or*
  o *neither...nor*
  o *not only...but also*
  o *whether...or*
  o *both...and*

- Show students several examples such as the ones below:
  1) She will *either* become a rock star *or* become a lawyer.
  2) She will become *either* a rock star *or* a lawyer.

- Note that both are correct, but #2 is more concise. Both are correct because they use PARALLEL STRUCTURE, which means the conjunctions are followed by the same type of word or phrase. If you wrote, "She will *either* become a rock star *or* a lawyer," you can see that the word after "either" is a verb, while what follows "or" is a noun. They are not the same, not parallel. So that would be incorrect.

- Show students more examples using correlative conjunctions correctly, and invite them to imitate those sentences, then do Show Call to share some good examples (see Chapter 2, "Principle #4: Give Faster Feedback," to review Show Call).

- During Show Call, let students explain what makes the exemplars effective. Then send them back to their own writing with this advice: "Use what you now know about correlative conjunctions in your own writing."

- Show them also some non-examples mixed in (later), and ask them to evaluate the sentences for parallel structure. In cases where parallel structure is missing, they should correct the sentence.

L 5.2.A: Use punctuation to separate items in a series.

TEACHING THIS:

- I am a big fan of the Oxford, or serial, comma because I believe it helps writers to ensure clarity. If you Google "serial comma funny examples," you will see why. For example, there's a magazine cover that shouts, "Rachel Ray [the Food Network star] finds inspiration in cooking her family and her dog."* Eww. For students, you could change that to, "I like cooking my family and my dog."

ASSESSING THIS:

- You might not have to spend much time reviewing this rule if students already know it. For a quick diagnostic, give them several sentences that are missing punctuation and ask them to correct the sentences. Then you can go from there.

*See footnote[151]

---

151 Sarah Henrich, "15 Reasons You Should Definitely Use the Oxford Comma," Buzzfeed, Feb. 22, 2015, found at https://www.buzzfeed.com/sarahhenrich/15-reasons-why-you-should-use-the-oxford-comma-yr75?utm_term=.cjeva9a2n#.xyxqB1BwM

L 5.2.B: Use a comma to separate an introductory element from the rest of the sentence.

TEACHING THIS:

- This standard is best taught when you are supporting students in editing. Show a sentence that lacks the needed comma (e.g., "When he was trying to get some rest [missing comma] a mosquito kept buzzing around his ear.") and tell students that while you read it aloud, their job is to pay attention to when you pause. Note: *When you pause, you need a comma. When you stop, you probably need a period.* Try it again with a few more sentences to have students figure out where the commas belong.

- Pitch: *Why does this comma matter? Because it shows us how the sentence works. You can take out the dependent clause (or the prepositional phrase, such as "In the beginning,"), and the sentence will still make sense. Why? Because what's left is the INDEPENDENT clause, which, as we know, is a complete sentence.*

- You should review the guidance for *L 3.1.H: Use coordinating and subordinating conjunctions*, which addresses the acronym AAAWWUBBIS. Clauses that begin with an AAAWWUBBIS are dependent/subordinate clauses and should end with a comma.

- For practice, give students a paragraph to edit. Include some sentences that are already properly punctuated along with a few that are not.

ASSESSING THIS:

- Give students a paragraph to edit. Include some sentences that are already properly punctuated (vis-→-vis the introductory comma) along with a few that are not.

- As always, we want students to demonstrate their grasp of these grammatical concepts in their own writing, first in sentences then in paragraphs. Give them the AAAWWUBBIS list and tell them that they must include several subordinating conjunctions in a paragraph about a current text or topic. Use the "Paragraph Response Scoring Checklist" in Chapter 3 or modify it to suit your needs. If you want to zero in on the punctuation, add that to the checklist.

L 5.2.C: Use a comma to set off the words yes and no (e.g., Yes, thank you), to set off a tag question from the rest of the sentence (e.g., It's true, isn't it?), and to indicate direct address (e.g., Is that you, Steve?).

TEACHING THIS:

- **GENRE ALERT: Students will need to apply this standard when working on narrative writing (W 5.3).**

- As you may have noticed from the comma-related examples embedded in this standard, they fit nicely in dialogue because we use them when one person is addressing another. Dialogue format is a 3rd-grade standard (*L 3.2.C: Use commas and quotation marks in dialogue*), but let's face it: it's a constant battle. When you review it, you should make a point of showing students these examples.
- Pro tip #1: Omitting the comma can sound rude when you say, "No thank you." As in, "I refuse to thank you."
- Pro tip #2: "It's true" and "Isn't it?" are both independent clauses, so omitting the comma would create a run-on.
- Pro tip #3: As noted in the guidance for *L 4.3.B: Choose punctuation for effect*, I love to point out the difference between "Let's eat, Grandma," and "Let's eat Grandma," asking students, "Do you *like* your grandmother? Or are you a *cannibal?*"

ASSESSING THIS:

- As always, we want students to demonstrate their grasp of these grammatical concepts in their own writing, first in sentences then in paragraphs. Ask them to write a brief dialogue between two people, based on a current text or topic, which must include a Yes/No question, an answer, and both characters' names in the dialogue. Tell them you will score the dialogue based on two additional things: 1) All sentences must be complete, and 2) The dialogue must be properly indented and punctuated.
- Quick editing quiz: Give students a dialogue that is missing commas and quotation marks, and instruct them to insert the proper punctuation.

L 5.2.D: Use underlining, quotation marks, or italics to indicate titles of works.

TEACHING THIS:

- **GENRE ALERT: Students will apply this standard when writing literary analysis essays (W 5.9.A), research papers (W 5.1, W 5.2, W 5.7, W 5.8, and W 5.9.B), or book/movie reviews (W 5.9.A).**
- Ideally, the 3rd grade teacher will have addressed this standard when discussing how to capitalize titles (*L 3.2.A: Capitalize appropriate words in titles*), but if that didn't happen, you should probably revisit the guidance for L 3.2.A, too.
- Background: We underline or italicize the titles of *whole* works (e.g., books, movies), while we put the *parts* of works (stories, songs, poems) in quotation marks.
- The best way to teach this standard is when students are writing something that requires them to refer to the title of a book or movie—in other words, when they need to know it.

- Show students titles of books and movies that are italicized/underlined vs. titles of poems, songs, or short stories that are in quotation marks. Ask them to discuss with a neighbor what they think the rule is about how to format different kinds of titles, "For example, what should we do with book titles?" Cold-calling should elicit the rules.
- Pitch: *One way I remember to underline or italicize the title of a WHOLE work is that I think of publishing a book or producing a movie as a BIG DEAL, so you have to do something to make it stand out: Make it **lean forward** to show it's powerful (like it could mow less powerful things down) or give it a "red carpet" by underlining it. And if it's a PART of the work, it still needs to be acknowledged—like, it's not as big a deal, but it still needs to be set off in some way—so that's why we use quotation marks.*

ASSESSING THIS:

- As always, we want students to demonstrate their grasp of these grammatical concepts in their own writing, first in sentences then in paragraphs. Ask them to write a paragraph about a current text (and they must include the title). See the discussion of paragraph responses and the "Paragraph Response Scoring Checklist" in Chapter 3. You can modify the Checklist to focus on the punctuation.
- For a quick diagnostic quiz, give students sentences that include various titles, and direct them to punctuate them properly.

L 5.2.E: Spell grade-appropriate words correctly, consulting references as needed.

TEACHING THIS:

- This book does not explain phonics instruction but recommends its use for students who struggle with spelling.
- For guidance on how to teach students to consult reference materials, see *L 3.2.G: Consult reference materials, including beginning dictionaries, as needed to check and correct spellings.*

ASSESSING THIS:

- See *L 3.2.G: Consult reference materials, including beginning dictionaries, as needed to check and correct spellings.*

L 5.3.A: Expand, combine, and reduce sentences for meaning, reader/listener interest, and style.

TEACHING THIS:

- This standard is best taught when you are supporting students in revising. Model with anonymous student examples how to expand, combine, and reduce sentences—but not all at once because they are three different skills. Indeed, you could spend weeks on each one.

- For **expanding**, refer to the guidance for the following standards:
    - o L 1.1.F: Use frequently occurring adjectives.
    - o L 1.1.I: Use frequently occurring prepositions (e.g., during, beyond, toward).
    - o L 2.1.E: Use adjectives and adverbs, and choose between them depending on what is to be modified.
    - o L 3.1.H: Use coordinating and subordinating conjunctions.
    - o L 4.1.A: Use relative pronouns (who, whose, whom, which, that) and relative adverbs (where, when, why).
    - o L 4.1.D: Order adjectives within sentences according to conventional patterns (e.g., a small red bag rather than a red small bag).
    - o L 5.1.E: Use correlative conjunctions (e.g., either/or, neither/nor).
    - o Also, introduce **appositives**: nouns or noun phrases that rename a nearby noun. For example, "My sister, an artist, has created stained glass windows for almost all of my windows."

- For **combining**, refer to the guidance for the following standards:
    - o L 1.1.G: Use frequently occurring conjunctions (e.g., and, but, or, so, because).
    - o L 3.1.H: Use coordinating and subordinating conjunctions.
    - o L 4.2.C: Use a comma before a coordinating conjunction in a compound sentence.

- For **reducing**, challenge students to rewrite a given sentence with fewer words. For example: "Ben Franklin once said, 'Those who would give up essential liberty to purchase a little temporary safety deserve neither liberty nor safety.' Rewrite this quotation in 10 words or fewer." (Incidentally, this makes a great Do Now, and then you can ask, "Why would Mr. Franklin say that?" Students will have to use their background knowledge to draw an inference.)

ASSESSING THIS:

- Give students a sample paragraph to revise. They must *expand* at least one sentence, *combine* two, and *reduce* one. Note: When creating this model, do not include any grammatical errors. The focus should be on sentence building or tightening.

- Give students opportunities to revise their sentences and paragraphs. Establish targets for revision such as "Expand your paragraph with the 'Because-But-So' approach," or "Expand your paragraph by introducing appositives," or "Clarify and elaborate where your partner raised questions about your writing."

- As always, we want students to demonstrate their grasp of these grammatical concepts in their own writing, first in sentences then in paragraphs. Ask them to write a paragraph about a current text or topic. Tell them you will score the paragraph based on how effectively the sentences are crafted, with clarity being the top priority.

L 5.3.B: Compare and contrast the varieties of English (e.g., dialects, registers) used in stories, dramas, or poems.

TEACHING THIS:

- Background: Dialects tend to be based on demographic tendencies (i.e., where/how one is raised), whereas registers are based on the situation in which one is speaking (e.g., using a more formal register when applying for a job than when hanging out with friends).

- See Chapter 2—specifically "Principle #6: Provide Oral Support"—for suggestions on how to compare and contrast varieties of English. You can apply the T-chart idea in that chapter to compare different uses of dialects or registers within or among different texts.

ASSESSING THIS:

- Ditto.

- How will you use the resources in this chapter?

- How did the ideas in this chapter challenge, change, or confirm what you previously believed about grammar and writing instruction (or instruction in general)?

- Which resources and ideas from this chapter will you share with colleagues? Why?

- What lingering concerns do you have about the standards for grades 3-5, and how will you deal with them?

chapter
SEVEN

Grades 6-8 Writing and Language Instruction

GRADES 6-8 WRITING STANDARDS WITH INSTRUCTIONAL GUIDANCE

Next we'll look at the trajectory of Writing Standards for Grades 6-8 so that we can see how the Language Standards fit in with them. Note: If you want to see all of the ELA Common Core Standards in one place, check out the "K-12 ELA Common Core Standards Tracker" on the TLC Website.[152]

---

152 The "K-12 ELA Common Core Standards Tracker" is on the TLC "Using Grammar to Improve Writing" page found at https://www.literacycookbook.com/page.php?id=161. This and other standards-related resources can also be found on the TLC "Standards" page at https://www.literacycookbook.com/page.php?id=138.

	Writing Anchor Standard #1: *Write arguments to support claims in an analysis of substantive topics or texts, using valid reasoning and relevant and sufficient evidence.*
W 6.1	Write arguments to support claims with clear reasons and relevant evidence. A) Introduce claim(s) and organize the reasons and evidence clearly. B) Support claim(s) with clear reasons and relevant evidence, using credible sources and demonstrating an understanding of the topic or text. C) Use words, phrases, and clauses to clarify the relationships among claim(s) and reasons. D) Establish and maintain a formal style. E) Provide a concluding statement or section that follows from the argument presented.
W 7.1	Write arguments to support claims with clear reasons and relevant evidence. A) Introduce claim(s), acknowledge alternate or opposing claims, and organize the reasons and evidence logically. B) Support claim(s) with logical reasoning and relevant evidence, using accurate, credible sources and demonstrating an understanding of the topic or text. C) Use words, phrases, and clauses to create cohesion and clarify the relationships among claim(s), reasons, and evidence. D) Establish and maintain a formal style. E) Provide a concluding statement or section that follows from and supports the argument presented.
W 8.1	Write arguments to support claims with clear reasons and relevant evidence. A) Introduce claim(s), acknowledge and distinguish the claim(s) from alternate or opposing claims, and organize the reasons and evidence logically. B) Support claim(s) with logical reasoning and relevant evidence, using accurate, credible sources and demonstrating an understanding of the topic or text. C) Use words, phrases, and clauses to create cohesion and clarify the relationships among claim(s), counterclaims, reasons, and evidence. D) Establish and maintain a formal style. E) Provide a concluding statement or section that follows from and supports the argument presented.

Across grades 6 through 8, Writing Standard #1 (opinion writing) becomes increasingly demanding with regard to the use of sources, counterclaims, and logic. Beginning in grade 6, students are expected to cite "credible sources" to support claims (which fits in with *RIT 6.1: Cite textual evidence to support analysis of what the text says explicitly as well as inferences drawn from the text*), and beginning in grade 7, students must "acknowledge alternate or opposing claims" and "organize the reasons and evidence *logically*" (as opposed to "clearly," in grade 6).

Reviewing Argument vs. Evidence Steps 1-3 (see Chapter 4) will help students support arguments with relevant evidence and explanation. By analyzing effective essays, they should be able to explain how logically composed paragraphs serve a writer's overall purpose. And beginning in grade 7 (if not sooner), you should show them essays that acknowledge counterclaims. You will also need to teach students how to evaluate sources for credibility and how to use MLA format. See the TLC "Research Paper Guide" page for support on teaching those skills.[153]

The standards provide little guidance on how to conclude, so you will need to show students examples of punchy concluding sentences to imitate.

---

153 The TLC "Research Paper Guide" page is found at https://www.literacycookbook.com/page.php?id=24.

	Writing Anchor Standard #2: *Write informative/explanatory texts to examine and convey complex ideas and information clearly and accurately through the effective selection, organization, and analysis of content.*
W 6.2	Write informative/explanatory texts to examine a topic and convey ideas, concepts, and information through the selection, organization, and analysis of relevant content.
	A) Introduce a topic; organize ideas, concepts, and information, using strategies such as definition, classification, comparison/contrast, and cause/effect; include formatting (e.g., headings), graphics (e.g., charts, tables), and multimedia when useful to aiding comprehension.
	B) Develop the topic with relevant facts, definitions, concrete details, quotations, or other information and examples.
	C) Use appropriate transitions to clarify the relationships among ideas and concepts.
	D) Use precise language and domain-specific vocabulary to inform about or explain the topic.
	E) Establish and maintain a formal style.
	F) Provide a concluding statement or section that follows from the information or explanation presented.
W 7.2	Write informative/explanatory texts to examine a topic and convey ideas, concepts, and information through the selection, organization, and analysis of relevant content.
	A) Introduce a topic clearly, previewing what is to follow; organize ideas, concepts, and information, using strategies such as definition, classification, comparison/contrast, and cause/effect; include formatting (e.g., headings), graphics (e.g., charts, tables), and multimedia when useful to aiding comprehension.
	B) Develop the topic with relevant facts, definitions, concrete details, quotations, or other information and examples.
	C) Use appropriate transitions to create cohesion and clarify the relationships among ideas and concepts.
	D) Use precise language and domain-specific vocabulary to inform about or explain the topic.
	E) Establish and maintain a formal style.
	F) Provide a concluding statement or section that follows from and supports the information or explanation presented.

W 8.2	Write informative/explanatory texts to examine a topic and convey ideas, concepts, and information through the selection, organization, and analysis of relevant content.
	A) Introduce a topic clearly, previewing what is to follow; organize ideas, concepts, and information into broader categories; include formatting (e.g., headings), graphics (e.g., charts, tables), and multimedia when useful to aiding comprehension.
	B) Develop the topic with relevant, well-chosen facts, definitions, concrete details, quotations, or other information and examples.
	C) Use appropriate and varied transitions to create cohesion and clarify the relationships among ideas and concepts.
	D) Use precise language and domain-specific vocabulary to inform about or explain the topic.
	E) Establish and maintain a formal style.
	F) Provide a concluding statement or section that follows from and supports the information or explanation presented.

With this standard's reliance on the word "topic," one might be misled into assigning *topic-driven* writing such as "The Dangers of Smoking" or "The Causes of the Civil War." No matter how compelling the topic, a topic-driven approach will almost inevitably lead students to plagiarize because the idea of topic-driven writing seems to be "Tell us as much about this topic as you can." So students dump information in and don't explain it. By contrast, **question-driven writing** such as "Why is it dangerous to smoke?" and "Why did Americans engage in the Civil War?" pushes students to explain their ideas and information. To make this approach work, review Reading Standard 2.1 (*Ask and answer such questions as who, what, where, when, why, and how to demonstrate understanding of key details in a text*), which is explained in Chapter 4 (see "The Most Important Writing Standard"). Also, show students high-quality mentor texts and invite *them* to explain what makes the texts so effective.

As with the progression in grades 6-8 for opinion writing, Writing Standard #2 shows a noticeable uptick in expectations regarding analysis. Beginning in grade 6, students are expected to "write informative/explanatory texts to examine a topic and convey ideas, concepts, and information *through the selection, organization, and analysis of relevant content*" (italics mine). Again, reviewing Argument vs. Evidence Steps 1-3 (see Chapter 4) will be helpful. Pay particular attention to Step 2.5, which deals with selecting the most relevant evidence.

In grades 6 and 7, students should practice writing strategies such as definition, classification, comparison/contrast, and cause/effect.

In all three grades, students must not only use transitions but also use them to greater effect. By grade 8, they must "use appropriate and varied transitions to create cohesion and clarify the relationships among ideas and concepts."

The standards are once again vague on how to conclude, so you will need to show students examples of punchy concluding sentences to imitate.

	Writing Standard #3: *Write narratives to develop real or imagined experiences or events using effective technique, well-chosen details, and well-structured event sequences.*
W 6.3	Write narratives to develop real or imagined experiences or events using effective technique, relevant descriptive details, and well-structured event sequences. A) Engage and orient the reader by establishing a context and introducing a narrator and/or characters; organize an event sequence that unfolds naturally and logically. B) Use narrative techniques, such as dialogue, pacing, and description, to develop experiences, events, and/or characters. C) Use a variety of transition words, phrases, and clauses to convey sequence and signal shifts from one time frame or setting to another. D) Use precise words and phrases, relevant descriptive details, and sensory language to convey experiences and events. E) Provide a conclusion that follows from the narrated experiences or events.

W 7.3	Write narratives to develop real or imagined experiences or events using effective technique, relevant descriptive details, and well-structured event sequences.
	A) Engage and orient the reader by establishing a context and point of view and introducing a narrator and/or characters; organize an event sequence that unfolds naturally and logically.
	B) Use narrative techniques, such as dialogue, pacing, and description, to develop experiences, events, and/or characters.
	C) Use a variety of transition words, phrases, and clauses to convey sequence and signal shifts from one time frame or setting to another.
	D) Use precise words and phrases, relevant descriptive details, and sensory language to capture the action and convey experiences and events.
	E) Provide a conclusion that follows from and reflects on the narrated experiences or events.
W 8.3	Write narratives to develop real or imagined experiences or events using effective technique, relevant descriptive details, and well-structured event sequences.
	A) Engage and orient the reader by establishing a context and point of view and introducing a narrator and/or characters; organize an event sequence that unfolds naturally and logically.
	B) Use narrative techniques, such as dialogue, pacing, description, and reflection, to develop experiences, events, and/or characters.
	C) Use a variety of transition words, phrases, and clauses to convey sequence, signal shifts from one time frame or setting to another, and show the relationships among experiences and events.
	D) Use precise words and phrases, relevant descriptive details, and sensory language to capture the action and convey experiences and events.
	E) Provide a conclusion that follows from and reflects on the narrated experiences or events.

As I noted in the commentary for grades 3-5, Writing Standard #3 (narrative writing) illustrates the notion that nobody is perfect, and with all due respect, standards writers are no exception. As someone who has written and studied narratives for decades, I find it stunning that there is no mention of a problem or conflict in the verbiage of this standard until grades 9-10. So let me begin with this tip: **Teach students—as early as you can—to base their narratives on a problem or conflict.** If they don't, they will end up writing a list of events; and while the events might be interesting, the ultimate product will be a *list*, not a story of growth, change, or insight. A list is not a story.

That said, grades 6-8 require students to write what we think of as a regular story with a narrator and/or characters, dialogue, and all the fixin's.

The number one thing you can do to help students master this standard is to analyze great stories. For advice on how to teach close reading strategies, see *The Literacy Cookbook* and *Literacy and the Common Core*.[154] For additional resources to support reading and writing narratives, see the TLC "Analyzing Literature" and "Narrative Writing" pages.[155]

PS: If your state requires PARCC testing, you can find information on the PARCC Narrative Writing Task on the TLC "PARCC Prep" page.[156]

Brief Notes About Writing Standards #4-6:

Writing Anchor Standard #4: *Produce clear and coherent writing in which the development, organization, and style are appropriate to task, purpose, and audience.*

Writing Anchor Standard #5: *Develop and strengthen writing as needed by planning, revising, editing, rewriting, or trying a new approach.*

Writing Anchor Standard #6: *Use technology, including the Internet, to produce and publish writing and to interact and collaborate with others.*

In working on Writing Standards #4 and #5, teachers must establish the key steps of the writing process through modeling, practice, and feedback. This involves using mentor texts[157] and establishing classroom routines for working through the different steps of the writing process,

---

154 Sarah Tantillo, *The Literacy Cookbook: A Practical Guide to Effective Reading, Writing, Speaking, and Listening Instruction* (San Francisco: Jossey-Bass, 2012); also *Literacy and the Common Core: Recipes for Action* (San Francisco: Jossey-Bass, 2014).

155 The TLC "Analyzing Literature" page is found at https://www.literacycookbook.com/page.php?id=2. The TLC "Narrative Writing" page is found at https://www.literacycookbook.com/page.php?id=150.

156 For more information on PARCC testing preparation, see the TLC "PARCC Prep" page found at https://www.literacycookbook.com/page.php?id=155.

157 Sarah Tantillo, *The Literacy Cookbook: A Practical Guide to Effective Reading, Writing, Speaking, and Listening Instruction* (San Francisco: Jossey-Bass, 2012), 95-104.

whether with teacher or peer support, or independently. Revisit Chapter 2, particularly "Principle #3: Ask, 'What Do You *Like* About That Sentence?'" and "Principle #4: Give Faster Feedback," for detailed ideas about how to address these standards.

Writing Standard #6 speaks to the use of technology (especially keyboarding skills in grade 6) and Internet research.

	Writing Anchor Standard #7: *Conduct short as well as more sustained research projects based on focused questions, demonstrating understanding of the subject under investigation.*
W 6.7	Conduct short research projects to answer a question, drawing on several sources and refocusing the inquiry when appropriate.
W 7.7	Conduct short research projects to answer a question, drawing on several sources and generating additional related, focused questions for further research and investigation.
W 8.7	Conduct short research projects to answer a question (including a self-generated question), drawing on several sources and generating additional related, focused questions that allow for multiple avenues of exploration.

	Writing Anchor Standard #8: *Gather relevant information from multiple print and digital sources, assess the credibility and accuracy of each source, and integrate the information while avoiding plagiarism.*
W 6.8	Gather relevant information from multiple print and digital sources; assess the credibility of each source; and quote or paraphrase the data and conclusions of others while avoiding plagiarism and providing basic bibliographic information for sources.
W 7.8	Gather relevant information from multiple print and digital sources, using search terms effectively; assess the credibility and accuracy of each source; and quote or paraphrase the data and conclusions of others while avoiding plagiarism and following a standard format for citation.
W 8.8	SAME AS W 7.8

Writing Standards #7 and 8 (research writing) echo the work of Writing Standard #2 (informative/explanatory writing), so you should refer back to my comments on that standard, especially regarding the need for *question-driven* rather than *topic-driven* writing assignments. These standards also tie in with Writing Standard #6, which addresses the use of technology and Internet research.

For a full explanation of how to teach research paper writing, see *The Literacy Cookbook* and the TLC "Research Paper Guide" page.[158]

	Writing Anchor Standard #9: *Draw evidence from literary or informational texts to support analysis, reflection, and research.*
W 6.9	Draw evidence from literary or informational texts to support analysis, reflection, and research.
	A) Apply grade 6 Reading standards to literature (e.g., "Compare and contrast texts in different forms or genres [e.g., stories and poems; historical novels and fantasy stories] in terms of their approaches to similar themes and topics").
	B) Apply grade 6 Reading standards to literary nonfiction (e.g., "Trace and evaluate the argument and specific claims in a text, distinguishing claims that are supported by reasons and evidence from claims that are not").
W 7.9	Draw evidence from literary or informational texts to support analysis, reflection, and research.
	A) Apply grade 7 Reading standards to literature (e.g., "Compare and contrast a fictional portrayal of a time, place, or character and a historical account of the same period as a means of understanding how authors of fiction use or alter history").
	B) Apply grade 7 Reading standards to literary nonfiction (e.g. "Trace and evaluate the argument and specific claims in a text, assessing whether the reasoning is sound and the evidence is relevant and sufficient to support the claims").

158 Sarah Tantillo, *The Literacy Cookbook: A Practical Guide to Effective Reading, Writing, Speaking, and Listening Instruction* (San Francisco: Jossey-Bass, 2012), 169-190. The TLC "Research Paper Guide" page is found at https://www.literacycookbook.com/page.php?id=24.

W 8.9	Draw evidence from literary or informational texts to support analysis, reflection, and research.
	A) Apply grade 8 Reading standards to literature (e.g., "Analyze how a modern work of fiction draws on themes, patterns of events, or character types from myths, traditional stories, or religious works such as the Bible, including describing how the material is rendered new").
	B) Apply grade 8 Reading standards to literary nonfiction (e.g., "Delineate and evaluate the argument and specific claims in a text, assessing whether the reasoning is sound and the evidence is relevant and sufficient; recognize when irrelevant evidence is introduced").

Writing Standard #9 is why some people say that the writing standards are 20 (or even 30) standards in one. The premise is for students to use writing to demonstrate that they read well. Students must apply close reading and analysis skills (see *Literacy and the Common Core*[159] and the TLC "Analyzing Literature" page[160]) and Argument vs. Evidence Steps 1-3 (see Chapter 4).

For W 6.9.A , W 7.9.A, and W 8.9.A—AKA literary response writing—see the TLC "Literary Response Paper Guide" page.[161]

For W 6.9.B, W 7.9.B, and W 8.9.B—AKA research paper writing— see the TLC "Research Paper Guide" page.[162]

Writing Anchor Standard #10: *Write routinely over extended time frames (time for research, reflection, and revision) and shorter time frames (a single sitting or a day or two) for a range of tasks, purposes, and audiences.*

---

159 Sarah Tantillo, *Literacy and the Common Core: Recipes for Action* (San Francisco: Jossey-Bass, 2014), 107-127.

160 The TLC "Analyzing Literature" page is found at https://www.literacycookbook.com/page.php?id=2.

161 The TLC "Literary Response Paper Guide" page is found at https://www.literacycookbook.com/page.php?id=19.

162 The TLC "Research Paper Guide" page is found at https://www.literacycookbook.com/page.php?id=24.

This standard does not need to be unpacked, but it should be duly noted. Teachers may want to use a checklist such as the following to ensure that students' writing assignments meet all of the stated criteria:

- Students write routinely.
- Students write over extended periods, with time for research, reflection, and revision.
- Students practice and are assessed on timed writing.
- Students write to complete a range of tasks.
- Students write for a range of audiences.
- Students write for various purposes.

GRADES 6-8 LANGUAGE STANDARDS

In this section, we'll look at the Grades 6-8 trajectory of key Language Standards first, then go through the standards grade by grade (so: all 6th first, then all 7th, then all 8th) so that we can dive more deeply into effective instructional practices. Note: If you want to track student progress on the K-12 Language Standards, check out the "K-12 Selected Language CCS Tracker" in the Appendix and on the TLC Website.[163]

	Language Anchor Standard #1: *Demonstrate command of the conventions of standard English grammar and usage when writing or speaking.*

---

163 The "K-12 Selected Language CCS Tracker" can be downloaded from the TLC "Using Grammar to Improve Writing" page found at https://www.literacycookbook.com/page.php?id=161. Additional standards-related resources are available on the TLC "Standards" page found at https://www.literacy-cookbook.com/page.php?id=138.

L 6.1	A) Ensure that pronouns are in the proper case (subjective, objective, possessive). B) Use intensive pronouns (e.g., myself, ourselves). C) Recognize and correct inappropriate shifts in pronoun number and person. D) Recognize and correct vague pronouns (i.e., ones with unclear or ambiguous antecedents). E) Recognize variations from standard English in their own and others' writing and speaking, and identify and use strategies to improve expression in conventional language.
L 7.1	A) Explain the function of phrases and clauses in general and their function in specific sentences. B) Choose among simple, compound, complex, and compound-complex sentences to signal differing relationships among ideas. C) Place phrases and clauses within a sentence, recognizing and correcting misplaced and dangling modifiers.
L 8.1	A) Explain the function of verbals (gerunds, participles, infinitives) in general and their function in particular sentences. B) Form and use verbs in the active and passive voice. C) Form and use verbs in the indicative, imperative, interrogative, conditional, and subjunctive mood. D) Recognize and correct inappropriate shifts in verb voice and mood.

Next:

	Language Anchor Standard #2: *Demonstrate command of the conventions of standard English capitalization, punctuation, and spelling when writing.*
L 6.2	A) Use punctuation (commas, parentheses, dashes) to set off nonrestrictive/parenthetical elements. B) Spell correctly.
L 7.2	A) Use a comma to separate coordinate adjectives (e.g., It was a fascinating, enjoyable movie but not He wore an old[,] green shirt). B) Spell correctly.

L 8.2	A) Use punctuation (comma, ellipsis, dash) to indicate a pause or break. B) Use an ellipsis to indicate an omission. C) Spell correctly.

Next:

	Language Anchor Standard #3: *Apply knowledge of language to understand how language functions in different contexts, to make effective choices for meaning or style, and to comprehend more fully when reading or listening.*
L 6.3	Use knowledge of language and its conventions when writing, speaking, reading, or listening. A) Vary sentence patterns for meaning, reader/ listener interest, and style. B) Maintain consistency in style and tone.
L 7.3	Use knowledge of language and its conventions when writing, speaking, reading, or listening. A) Choose language that expresses ideas precisely and concisely, recognizing and eliminating wordiness and redundancy.
L 8.3	Use knowledge of language and its conventions when writing, speaking, reading, or listening. A) Use verbs in the active and passive voice and in the conditional and subjunctive mood to achieve particular effects (e.g., emphasizing the actor or the action; expressing uncertainty or describing a state contrary to fact).

(Note: Language Standards #4-6 deal primarily with vocabulary, so we will not analyze them here. For guidance on vocabulary instruction, see *The Literacy Cookbook*.[164])

GRADE 6 LANGUAGE STANDARDS: A DEEPER DIVE

In the next three sections, we'll dive more deeply into each grade's Language Standards and look at ways to teach and assess them more systematically,

---

164 Sarah Tantillo, *The Literacy Cookbook: A Practical Guide to Effective Reading, Writing, Speaking, and Listening Instruction* (San Francisco: Jossey-Bass, 2012), 28-36. For online resources, see the TLC "Building Robust Vocabulary" page found at https://www.literacycookbook.com/page.php?id=4.

in conjunction with writing instruction. These are by no means the *only* ways to teach these standards, just a few to illustrate how to connect grammar with writing and reading. We begin with grade 6.

L 6.1.A: Ensure that pronouns are in the proper case (subjective, objective, possessive).

TEACHING THIS:

- Grade 6 grammar could be titled "All About Pronouns." As you will see, there is significant overlap among standards L 6.1.A, L 6.1.B, L 6.1.C, and L 6.1.D.

- Pronouns are introduced in 1ˢᵗ grade: *L 1.1.D: Use personal, possessive, and indefinite pronouns (e.g., I, me, my; they, them, their; anyone, everything).* This section reviews that guidance, with additional notes about proper case.

- See Chapter 2, "Principle #1: Treat Students Like Detectives," for a description of how to introduce **personal pronouns.** See also Chapter 3 for "Cloze Reading Passage: Personal Pronouns."

- Following from that introduction, which includes the sentence "I met Christine and Rochelle for dinner," here's the pitch: *Good writers use pronouns to avoid repeating themselves. Imagine how silly it would sound if I wrote an entire paragraph about dinner with Christine and Rochelle and never used "they" or "them"! "Christine and Rochelle ordered lasagna. Christine and Rochelle liked the garlic bread. Christine and Rochelle talked about their jobs...."* Based on this pitch, students should infer that pronouns should agree with their antecedents (i.e., "they" agrees with "Christine and Rochelle"), but you may need to emphasize this point if students seem confused.

- Use a current text as the base from which to translate nouns into pronouns (e.g., replace "Olivia" with "she"). Invite students to help with this.

- Modeling and having students imitate sentences is the key. PS: Students don't need to know about your golf game. Use sentences from their current text(s) to reinforce content while simultaneously illustrating the grammar points you want to teach.

- A few technical points:

  o When you're ready to turn to **possessive pronouns** (*my, mine, your, yours, her, hers, his, its, our, ours, your, yours, their, theirs*), remember that some function as *adjectives* (e.g., *my* laptop).

  o Regarding **indefinite pronouns** (*anything, anyone, some*, etc.), most are always singular (*everyone, each*); some are always plural (*both, many*); and a few may be either. Most indefinite pronouns substitute for nouns, but some also function as adjectives (*All* campers must check in....).˙

- **Regarding pronoun case,** students need to analyze sentences that include pronouns functioning as subjects and objects. For example, in "*He* bought breakfast for *them*," the subject is *he* and the object (of the preposition *for*) is *them*. You wouldn't say, "*Them* bought breakfast for *he*." On a related point, *who* is the subject pronoun and *whom* is the object. So you would write, "*Who* knows the address?" or "To *whom* should I address this letter?"

- As always, we want students to demonstrate their grasp of these grammatical concepts in their own writing, first in sentences then in paragraphs. Give them several pronouns they must include in a paragraph about a text or topic they are studying, and tell them you will score the paragraph based on two things: 1) All sentences must be complete, and 2) All pronouns must be used properly.
- Cloze reading (text with blanks where, in this case, the pronouns belong) is another useful way to check for understanding. See Chapter 3 for "Cloze Reading Passage: Personal Pronouns."

*See footnote[165]

L 6.1.B: Use intensive pronouns (e.g., myself, ourselves).

TEACHING THIS:

- As noted above, grade 6 grammar could be titled "All About Pronouns." There is significant overlap among standards L 6.1.A, L 6.1.B, L 6.1.C, and L 6.1.D.
- Intensive pronouns are identical to reflexive pronouns, but they are used in a different way. **To review reflexive pronouns, which are used when one does something to oneself,** see the guidance for *L 2.1.C: Use reflexive pronouns (e.g., myself, ourselves).* Here's a quick example: "I dressed *myself.*"
- **By contrast, intensive pronouns are used for emphasis,** as in "Bruce Springsteen *himself* sang at her brother's wedding.'"
- Caveat: Be careful not to replace personal pronouns with reflexive pronouns. "Sandy and myself went swimming" is incorrect. It should be "Sandy and I went swimming."
- Students should practice writing sentences about a current text or topic using reflexive and intensive pronouns.

ASSESSING THIS:

- Cloze reading (text with blanks where, in this case, the proper reflexive or intensive pronouns belong) is another useful way to check for understanding.

*See footnote[166]

---

165 Diana Hacker and Nancy Sommers, Rules for Writers (Boston: Bedford/St. Martin's, 2016, 8th edition), 364. See this page for a list of indefinite pronouns.

166 Diana Hacker and Nancy Sommers, Rules for Writers (Boston: Bedford/St. Martin's, 2016, 8th edition), 363-364.

L 6.1.C: Recognize and correct inappropriate shifts in pronoun number and person.

> **TEACHING THIS:**
>
> - As noted above, grade 6 grammar could be titled "All About Pronouns." There is significant overlap among standards L 6.1.A, L 6.1.B, L 6.1.C, and L 6.1.D.
> - This standard can be challenging for English Language Learners. While it refers to the problem when a writer mentions, say, a girl, and then refers to her as "he" or "him," it also overlaps with *L 3.1.F: Ensure subject-verb and pronoun-antecedent agreement.* This section reviews that guidance.
> - To tackle **pronoun-antecedent agreement**, you could show students a sentence that illustrates the concept—e.g., "Mary and I went to the beach, then *we* went swimming." Then ask them, "Why couldn't I have used 'they' instead of 'we'?" Or: "How would the meaning be different if I wrote 'she' instead of 'we'?" Students should explain why to their partner. Cold-calling should elicit that in the first case, "we" makes sense, based on the antecedent "Mary and I." And in the second example, if "she" alone went swimming, it would mean that "I" did not. Incidentally, you can throw in some Latin and point out that "antecedent" literally means "the thing that goes before."
> - Alternatively, or simply after that, you could give students a Cloze reading passage with blanks where the pronouns belong and walk through it with them, asking for their advice about which pronouns make the most sense and why.

> **ASSESSING THIS:**
>
> - As always, we want students to demonstrate their grasp of these grammatical concepts in their own writing, first in sentences then in paragraphs. Give them several pronouns they must include in a paragraph about a text or topic they are studying, and tell them you will score the paragraph based on two things: 1) All sentences must be complete, and 2) All pronouns must agree with their antecedents.
> - Again, Cloze reading (text with blanks where, in this case, the pronouns belong) is another useful way to check for understanding. See Chapter 3 for "Cloze Reading Passage: Personal Pronouns."

L 6.1.D: Recognize and correct vague pronouns (i.e., ones with unclear or ambiguous antecedents).

TEACHING THIS:

- As noted above, grade 6 grammar could be titled "All About Pronouns." There is significant overlap among standards L 6.1.A, L 6.1.B, L 6.1.C, and L 6.1.D.
- This standard calls in particular for a review of its predecessor, *L 6.1.C: Recognize and correct inappropriate shifts in pronoun number and person.*
- **Ambiguous pronoun reference** occurs when a pronoun could refer to two possible antecedents. For example, "When Gloria set the pitcher on the glass-topped table, it broke."* We can't tell which thing broke.
- In addition, one must be vigilant when using "this" and "that" and "some" as pronouns. If a reader asks, "This what?" then the writer should realize there's a problem. In the interest of clarity, it's advisable to avoid using "this" as a pronoun altogether. Tell us what the "this" is. To explain this standard to students, you might compare "This might be confusing for some" to "This standard might be confusing for some people."
- For practice, give students sentences in which "this," "that," and "some" are used as pronouns and ask them to turn the pronouns into adjectives by inserting logical nouns.

ASSESSING THIS:

- For a quick quiz, provide some sentences that exhibit ambiguous pronoun usage and some that do not. Ask students to revise the sentences for clarity as needed.
- As always, we want students to demonstrate their grasp of these grammatical concepts in their own writing, first in sentences then in paragraphs. Provide several pronouns that they must include in a paragraph about a text or topic they are studying, and tell them you will score the paragraph based on two things: 1) All sentences must be complete, and 2) All pronouns must agree with their antecedents.
- Again, Cloze reading (text with blanks where, in this case, the pronouns belong) is another useful way to check for understanding.

*See footnote[167]

167 Diana Hacker and Nancy Sommers, *Rules for Writers* (Boston: Bedford/St. Martin's, 2016, 8th edition), 218.

9L 6.1.E: Recognize variations from standard English in their own and others' writing and speaking, and identify and use strategies to improve expression in conventional language.

TEACHING THIS:

- See Chapter 2—specifically "Principle #6: Provide Oral Support"—for suggestions on how to compare and contrast varieties of English.

ASSESSING THIS:

- Ditto.

L 6.2.A: Use punctuation (commas, parentheses, dashes) to set off non-restrictive/parenthetical elements.

TEACHING THIS:

- Go back to *L 4.1.A: Use relative pronouns (who, whose, whom, which, that) and relative adverbs (where, when, why)* and recycle that guidance, which discusses restrictive and nonrestrictive adjective clauses.
- Also revisit *L 5.3.A: Expand, combine, and reduce sentences for meaning, reader/listener interest, and style,* which includes **appositives.**
- For the remaining elements, show students examples and ask them to infer how parentheses and dashes are used. See examples and rules below. Co-create some additional example sentences, then let students practice more on their own.
- **Parentheses** are used to enclose supplemental material, minor digressions, and afterthoughts.˙ For example: "Our coach brought healthy snacks (carrots, celery, and oranges) to share on the long bus ride."
- Use a **dash** (two hyphens together) to set off parenthetical material that warrants emphasis or appositives that contain commas.˙˙
  - o **For emphasis:** "The photocopier—the heart of the school—died before teachers finished copying their exams."
  - o **With an appositive that contains comma**s: "The junk drawer in the kitchen contained numerous items—pencils, pens, rubber bands, shoe laces, batteries, matches, a flashlight, a roll of masking tape, and a pair of scissors—but, oddly, not a single paper clip."

- As always, we want students to demonstrate their grasp of these grammatical concepts in their own writing, first in sentences then in paragraphs. Direct them to write a paragraph about a text or topic they are studying, and tell them you will score the paragraph based on two things: 1) All sentences must be complete, and 2) The paragraph must include parentheses, dashes, and an appositive, all used properly.

- For a quick quiz, you can give students sentences that are missing punctuation such as parentheses, dashes, and commas and require them to insert the proper punctuation marks.

*See footnote[168] / **See footnote[169]

L 6.2.B: Spell correctly.

TEACHING THIS:

- This book does not explain phonics instruction but recommends its use for students who struggle with spelling.

- For guidance on how to teach students to consult reference materials, see *L 3.2.G: Consult reference materials, including beginning dictionaries, as needed to check and correct spellings.*

ASSESSING THIS:

- See *L 3.2.G: Consult reference materials, including beginning dictionaries, as needed to check and correct spellings.*

---

168 Diana Hacker and Nancy Sommers, *Rules for Writers* (Boston: Bedford/St. Martin's, 2016, 8th edition), 333.

169 Diana Hacker and Nancy Sommers, *Rules for Writers* (Boston: Bedford/St. Martin's, 2016, 8th edition), 332.

L 6.3.A: Vary sentence patterns for meaning, reader/listener interest, and style.

> **TEACHING THIS:**
>
> - To teach this standard, you must keep your eyes peeled for captivating texts that vary sentence patterns for meaning, reader/listener interest, and style. While previewing texts to create lesson plans, keep this notion (discussed in "How to Carry Soup" in Chapter 2) in mind: **Good writers write one good sentence after another.** Note examples of such sentences when you find them, and don't forget to note the context in which they appear. Because writers also think about the cumulative effects of the sentences they write. You must then deliver this notion via these exemplars to your students when discussing ideas for revision.
> - Here's another thought: **Every so often, include an "Attention to Sentences" Do Now** in which students must explain what they like about these sentences (see Chapter 2, "Principle #3: Ask 'What Do You *Like* About That Sentence?'").
> - You should also revisit the guidance for *L 5.3.A: Expand, combine, and reduce sentences for meaning, reader/listener interest, and style.*
>
> **ASSESSING THIS:**
>
> - For the explicit purpose of zeroing in on good sentences, you could modify the partner feedback protocol described in Chapter 2, "Principle #4: Give Faster Feedback." Simply drop the "clarifying" and "elaborating" questions and limit the feedback to "sentences I like."

L 6.3.B: Maintain consistency in style and tone.

> **TEACHING THIS:**
>
> - There are many ways to support this standard, but my favorite is to show students exemplars that exhibit a clear, consistent tone. My current favorite text for this purpose is "Cat vs. Dog: War of the Diaries" (available online).·
> - Ask students what differences they notice in the dog's and cat's perspectives. The dog begins, "8:00am: Dog food! My favorite thing! 9:30am- A car ride! My favorite thing!" and continues to repeat itself in a way that suggests a dopey, sweet, overly enthusiastic dog. The contrast with the cat's point of view is evident even by the title of its diary, "Day 983 of My Captivity." Students will also recognize that the cat seems more intelligent, as evidenced by its sophisticated vocabulary: "My captors continue to taunt me with bizarre little dangling objects. They dine lavishly on fresh meat, while the other inmates and I are fed hash or some sort of dry nuggets."

- Pitch: *Whenever you're trying to convey a particular message, it's important to use tone effectively, and it's crucial that you maintain a consistent tone. How do these diaries convey tone? What can you infer about each narrator?*
- Connect the discussion to whatever writing students are working on. *Take a look at your writing and ask yourself, "How can I ensure that my tone is consistent?" Think about the strategies we identified in our analysis of the two diaries. The tone of your writing doesn't have to be anything like either of those, but it does have to serve whatever purpose you're aiming for.*
- As students write, either circulate or make yourself available for writing conferences to provide feedback and support.

ASSESSING THIS:

- Obviously you have to look at student writing to assess this standard. One way you might kick things up at notch is to ask students to reflect on strategies they used in a particular piece to achieve the tone they were aiming for.

*See footnote[170]

GRADE 7 LANGUAGE STANDARDS: A DEEPER DIVE

Next, we'll dive more deeply into the Grade 7 Language Standards and look at how to teach and assess them more systematically, in conjunction with writing instruction. Again, these are by no means the *only* ways to teach these standards, just a few to illustrate how to connect grammar with writing and reading.

L 7.1.A: Explain the function of phrases and clauses in general and their function in specific sentences.

TEACHING THIS:

- This standard should be handled in conjunction (no pun intended) with *L 7.1.C: Place phrases and clauses within a sentence, recognizing and correcting misplaced and dangling modifiers.*

---

170 JOKE: Cat vs. Dog: War of the Diaries," Huffington Post, Dec. 6, 2017, found at https://www.huffingtonpost.com/2012/05/21/joke-cat-vs-dog----war-of_n_1534447.html

- By 7th grade, students should have been exposed to various phrase and clause types, so to me, this is more a "review" than a "teach-something-new" standard. To ensure students can explain the function of phrases and clauses in general and their function in specific sentences, you should revisit the guidance for the following standards:
  - o L 4.1.A: Use relative pronouns (who, whose, whom, which, that) and relative adverbs (where, when, why).
  - o L 5.1.A: Explain the function of conjunctions, prepositions, and interjections in general and their function in particular sentences.
  - o L 5.3.A: Expand, combine, and reduce sentences for meaning, reader/listener interest, and style.
- You may also need to recycle the guidance for the following standards:
  - o L 3.1.H: Use coordinating and subordinating conjunctions.
  - o L 5.1.E: Use correlative conjunctions (e.g., either/or, neither/nor).
  - o L 4.1.E: Form and use prepositional phrases.

ASSESSING THIS:

- See the assessment guidance for the standards you choose to revisit.

L 7.1.B: Choose among simple, compound, complex, and compound-complex sentences to signal differing relationships among ideas.

TEACHING THIS:

- This standard recycles the following standards:
  - o L 1.1.J: Produce and expand complete simple and compound declarative, interrogative, imperative, and exclamatory sentences in response to prompts.
  - o L 2.1.F: Produce, expand, and rearrange complete simple and compound sentences (e.g., The boy watched the movie; The little boy watched the movie; The action movie was watched by the little boy).
  - o L 3.1.I: Produce simple, compound, and complex sentences.
  - o L 5.1.A: Explain the function of conjunctions, prepositions, and interjections in general and their function in particular sentences.
  - o L 5.3.A: Expand, combine, and reduce sentences for meaning, reader/listener interest, and style.
  - o L 6.3.A: Vary sentence patterns for meaning, reader/listener interest, and style.

ASSESSING THIS:

- See the assessment guidance for the standards you choose to revisit.

L 7.1.C: Place phrases and clauses within a sentence, recognizing and correcting misplaced and dangling modifiers.

TEACHING THIS:

- This standard should be handled in conjunction (no pun intended) with *L 7.1.A: Explain the function of phrases and clauses in general and their function in specific sentences.*
- By 7th grade, students should have been exposed to various phrase and clause types. However, you might need to revisit the guidance for the following standards:
  - o L 3.1.H: Use coordinating and subordinating conjunctions.
  - o L 4.1.A: Use relative pronouns (who, whose, whom, which, that) and relative adverbs (where, when, why).
  - o L 4.1.E: Form and use prepositional phrases.
  - o L 5.1.A: Explain the function of conjunctions, prepositions, and interjections in general and their function in particular sentences.
  - o L 5.1.E: Use correlative conjunctions (e.g., either/or, neither/nor).
  - o L 5.3.A: Expand, combine, and reduce sentences for meaning, reader/listener interest, and style.
- After reviewing those standards, show two sentences—one that uses a modifier correctly and one incorrectly. Ask students to explain what is different about the two sentences, identify which one is incorrect, and explain how they would fix it. PS: My favorite example of a misplaced modifier is in Strunk & White's *Elements of Style*: "Wondering irresolutely what to do next, the clock struck midnight."
- For practice, give students a few more examples to evaluate and correct. Make sure they can explain why misplaced/dangling modifiers are a problem!

ASSESSING THIS:

- Give students a paragraph that includes several modifiers—some correct, some misplaced—and ask them to correct any that are misplaced.
- As always, we want students to demonstrate their grasp of these grammatical concepts in their own writing, first in sentences then in paragraphs. Ask them to write a descriptive/informative/narrative paragraph about a text or topic they are studying, and tell them you will score the paragraph based on two things: 1) All sentences must be complete, and 2) The paragraph must include at least *three* modifiers used correctly.

*See footnote[171]

---

171 William Strunk Jr. and E.B. White, The Elements of Style (New York: Allyn & Bacon, 2000, 4th ed.), 25.

L 7.2.A: Use a comma to separate coordinate adjectives (e.g., It was a fascinating, enjoyable movie but not He wore an old[,] green shirt).

TEACHING THIS:

- To teach this standard, you should recycle *L 4.1.D: Order adjectives within sentences according to conventional patterns (e.g., a small red bag rather than a red small bag)*, which focuses on cumulative adjectives but also points out how coordinate adjectives work. In short, **coordinate adjectives** can be combined with "and" (a *coordinating* conjunction: a useful mnemonic) or a comma. So "a fascinating, enjoyable movie" is equivalent to "a fascinating and enjoyable movie."
- Note: If students need more background on adjectives, go back to the guidance for *L 1.1.F: Use frequently occurring adjectives*.

ASSESSING THIS:

- An early quiz might give students bare-bones sentences and ask them to insert pairs of adjectives to make them more compelling.
- As always, we want students to demonstrate their grasp of these grammatical concepts in their own writing, first in sentences then in paragraphs. Ask them to write a descriptive paragraph about a text or topic they are studying, and tell them you will score the paragraph based on two things: 1) All sentences must be complete, and 2) The paragraph must include at least *three* pairs of adjectives.
- A later quiz might give students a paragraph that includes both cumulative and coordinate adjectives; their job would be to insert commas if needed.

L 7.2.B: Spell correctly.

TEACHING THIS:

- This book does not explain phonics instruction but recommends its use for students who struggle with spelling.
- For guidance on how to teach students to consult reference materials, see *L 3.2.G: Consult reference materials, including beginning dictionaries, as needed to check and correct spellings*.

ASSESSING THIS:

- See *L 3.2.G: Consult reference materials, including beginning dictionaries, as needed to check and correct spellings*.

L 7.3.A: Choose language that expresses ideas precisely and concisely, recognizing and eliminating wordiness and redundancy.

TEACHING THIS:

- Part of this standard deals with vocabulary, for which your instruction should address the importance of paying attention to the nuances of words and using them for effect. For guidance on vocabulary instruction, see *The Literacy Cookbook.**

- The other part deals with my favorite sentence in Strunk and White's *Elements of Style*: "Omit needless words."** Show students a paragraph that you have modified to inject wordiness and redundancy (post it on the board and give them a copy to mark up).

- Pitch: *The sign of a good writer is someone who uses words well, but more than that—someone who doesn't use unnecessary words. Good writers ruthlessly remove words they don't need, words that don't serve their purpose or repeat ideas for no reason. Today we're going to see how ruthless you can be. Your job, should you choose to accept it, is to tighten/condense this paragraph as much as you can. You can cross out words or add them, whichever does the trick. Sometimes one word can say the same thing as three. Every sentence must make sense, and you cannot remove key ideas or information. If anything is repeated for no reason, however, feel free to remove it. Be ruthless. Let's see what you can do.*

- Give students a few minutes to edit while you actively monitor the room and identify a few exemplars for Show Call (see Chapter 2, "Principle #4: Give Faster Feedback," to review Show Call).

- During Show Call, let students explain what makes the exemplary edits effective. Then send them back to their own writing with this advice: "Use what you now know about omitting needless words to tighten up your own writing."

ASSESSING THIS:

- Give students another wordy paragraph to edit.
- Collect their writing and focus your grading on how clear it is.

*See footnote[172] / **See footnote[173]

---

172 Sarah Tantillo, *The Literacy Cookbook: A Practical Guide to Effective Reading, Writing, Speaking, and Listening Instruction* (San Francisco: Jossey-Bass, 2012), 28-36. For online resources, see the TLC "Building Robust Vocabulary" page found at https://www.literacycookbook.com/page.php?id=4.

173 William Strunk Jr. and E.B. White, *The Elements of Style* (New York: Allyn & Bacon, 2000, 4th ed.), 32.

GRADE 8 LANGUAGE STANDARDS: A DEEPER DIVE

Next, we'll dive more deeply into the Grade 8 Language Standards and look at how to teach and assess them more systematically, in conjunction with writing instruction. Again: these are by no means the *only* ways to teach these standards, just a few to illustrate how to connect grammar with writing and reading.

L 8.1.A: Explain the function of verbals (gerunds, participles, infinitives) in general and their function in particular sentences.

TEACHING THIS:

- Let's face it: Although most of us probably use gerunds, participles, and infinitives every day, we're a little hazy (OK, maybe a lot hazy) on what they are. That's not a crime. But we need to be able to explain them to our students—not just because this is an 8th grade standard but also because this knowledge can enliven their writing.

- Pitch: [Note: I would not introduce all three forms—gerunds, participles, and infinitives—in one day. You can re-use this pitch or some variation of it each time you dive into a new form.] *Today we're going to learn about a high-level grammatical form that—I'm not going to lie to you—many educated adults use but probably cannot explain. It's a form we use all the time without realizing it. But the more you know about this form, the more you can use it to make your writing catchier and more lively.*

- **Generic mini-lesson:** Show students sentences in which the form is underlined, and ask them how the phrase works in each sentence. (FYI, these three forms are known as "verbals." **Ironically, a verbal is a verb form that *does not function as the verb* of a clause.** Instead, it functions as a noun, an adjective, or an adverb.*) See the examples below.

- **GERUND** (*–ing* form of verb *always used as a NOUN):*
    o The baby's incessant crying annoyed the passengers on the plane. [subject]
    o The secret to a great essay is ending with a punchy conclusion. [subject complement]
    o Most athletes enjoy running. [direct object]
    o My sister is a genius at throwing super-fun parties. [object of preposition]
    o As you can see, a gerund, *like a noun,* can function as the subject, subject complement, direct object, or object of the preposition.

- **PARTICIPLE** (AKA "participial phrase": present= -*ing* form of verb; past= -*ed* or –*en* form of verb; *always used as an ADJECTIVE*):
  - o *That book*, <u>written 50 years ago</u>, is still relevant today.
  - o <u>Being extremely obese</u>, *my cat Lulu* doesn't walk downstairs very often.
  - o The *car* <u>driven by the man who was texting</u> hit the pedestrian.
  - o Note: I italicized the *nouns* <u>being modified</u> (See what I just did there?). Participles/Participial phrases can be moved. And if you remove them, you should still have a complete sentence (e.g., "I italicized the nouns.").
- **INFINITIVE** ("to" plus the base form of the verb; e.g., "to talk"; *can function as NOUNS, ADJECTIVES, or ADVERBS*):
  - o NOUN: <u>To send thank-you notes</u> is polite. [subject]
  - o ADJECTIVE: She expressed a strong desire <u>to win</u>. [Which desire?]
  - o ADVERB: I poured cat food into the bowl <u>to lure Lulu out from under the bed</u>. [Why?]

ASSESSING THIS:

- As always, we want students to demonstrate their grasp of these grammatical concepts in their own writing, first in sentences then in paragraphs. They will need lots of practice in imitating sentences that use the forms. Have them include several of the forms (underlined to show they know they're using them) in a paragraph about a text or topic they are studying. Tell them you will score the paragraph based on two things: 1) All sentences must be complete, and 2) They must use the forms correctly.

*See footnote[174]

L 8.1.B: Form and use verbs in the active and passive voice.

TEACHING THIS:

- This is a fun one! As most experts will tell you, it's preferable to use the active voice in order to show who/what is doing the action. For example, "The teenagers <u>spoke up about</u> the need for gun control" sounds more coherent and less clumsy than, "The need for gun control <u>was spoken up about</u> by the teenagers." That said, sometimes it is more appropriate to use the passive, such as when you want to emphasize the receiver of the action or to minimize the importance of the actor, as follows:
  - o "The students and teachers <u>were forced</u> to seek shelter when the gunman opened fire" emphasizes the victims.

---

174 Diana Hacker and Nancy Sommers, *Rules for Writers* (Boston: Bedford/St. Martin's, 2016, 8th edition), 385-387. My examples are derived from the explanations on these pages.

- o "Lemons and oranges <u>are grown</u> in warm climates" minimizes the importance of the actor (We don't need to know the names of the farmers).

- Also, some academic/scientific writing requires the use of the passive voice (because we don't need to know who collected the data, or we already know, and a lab report is not a memoir).

- Show students two sentences: one in the active voice, the other rewritten awkwardly in the passive (as in the first example above). Ask them which is preferable, and why.

- Pitch: *Even though both sentences say the same thing, that second example sounds very clumsy. That's because it's in the passive voice, as opposed to the active voice we see in the first sentence. Today we're going to explore when and how to use the active or passive voice so that you can be sure your writing emphasizes what you want to emphasize and is as clear as possible.*

- Show them some more pairs of contrasting sentences to evaluate. Then give them some sentences written in the passive to convert to active, and vice versa.

- Pitch continues: *OK, so now we have the hang of the difference between active and passive voice, and we can see how awkward the passive can be. Now let's look at some examples of APPROPRIATE use of the passive. Because sometimes the passive is preferable. Let's see if we can figure out some rules for when it's better to use the passive.*

- Show students the second set of examples from above (or your own imitations) with a few more that mimic them, and let them try to figure out 1) what is being emphasized or minimized and 2) why the passive is preferable in such a situation. Students should write their own sentences mimicking the appropriate usage of the passive voice.

ASSESSING THIS:

- As always, we want students to demonstrate their grasp of these grammatical concepts in their own writing, first in sentences then in paragraphs. Give them lots of practice in imitating sentences that use the forms. Then have them include several of the passive and active verb forms (underlined and labeled to show they know they're using them) in a paragraph about a text or topic they are studying. Tell them you will score the paragraph based on two things: 1) All sentences must be complete, and 2) They must use the passive and active forms correctly and *appropriately*.

- For a quick diagnostic, give students two paragraphs: one in which all of the sentences are written in the passive voice, the other in the active. They should rewrite the paragraphs in the opposite voice. For a follow-up question, they should identify any sentences that would be more appropriately left in the passive and explain why.

*See footnote[175]

---

175 Diana Hacker and Nancy Sommers, *Rules for Writers* (Boston: Bedford/St. Martin's, 2016, 8th edition), 126-127. My examples are derived from the explanations on these pages.

L 8.1.C: Form and use verbs in the indicative, imperative, interrogative, conditional, and subjunctive mood.

> **TEACHING THIS:**
>
> - Students should learn how to form verbs in the **indicative**, **interrogative**, and **imperative** moods well before grade 8. For guidance, see these:
>   - o L K.1.B: Use frequently occurring nouns and verbs.
>   - o L K.1.D: Understand and use question words (interrogatives) (e.g., who, what, where, when, why, how).
>   - o L 1.1.E: Use verbs to convey a sense of past, present, and future (e.g., Yesterday I walked home; Today I walk home; Tomorrow I will walk home).
>   - o L 1.1.J: Produce and expand simple and compound declarative, interrogative, imperative, and exclamatory sentences in response to prompts.
> - **The conditional mood** (or what I like to think of as the "*if, when,* or *unless* mood") will take some time because it pops up in a variety of—well, conditions. Before you dive into it, you should review the following guidance:
>   - o L 3.1.H: Use coordinating and subordinating conjunctions.
>   - o L 3.1.I: Produce simple, compound, and complex sentences.
>   - o L 4.1.C: Use modal auxiliaries (e.g., can, may, must) to convey various conditions.
> - **Conditional sentences** contain two clauses: **a subordinate clause** (usually beginning with *if, when,* or *unless*) and **an independent clause.** The subordinate clause states the condition or cause; the independent clause states the result or effect.˙ For example: "*When* that book became available in the library [subordinate clause], I checked it out [independent clause]."
> - To teach conditional sentences, here's one approach: Give students several factual conditional sentences, and point out that the purpose of these sentences is **factual** (i.e., to state a fact). "Conditional sentences have several other purposes. Let's look at a few more sentences and see if we can figure out those other purposes." Then show them **predictive** sentences, such as:
>   - o *Unless* you buy a train ticket, you will not be able to take that train home.
>   - o *If* the weather is cold enough, it should snow tomorrow.
> - Conditional sentences can also be **speculative.** This type expresses conditions that are unlikely, contrary-to-fact, or impossible/did not happen. For example:
>   - o *If* my father won the lottery, he would retire. [Winning the lottery is unlikely.]
>   - o *If* I *were* the governor, I would focus on improving schools. [This is contrary to fact. The notes on the subjunctive mood below explain why we must say "If I *were*" instead of "If I *was*."]
>   - o *If* my grandfather had lived longer, he would have seen me graduate from college. [Since he died too soon, it was impossible/did not happen.]

- **The subjunctive mood** can be a little tricky. It is used to express wishes, requests, and conditions contrary to fact, as follows:**
  - o **Wish:** She wished she *were* [not *was*] in Paris instead of New Jersey.
  - o **Request:** The accountant requested that Mr. Jones *file* [not *files*] his taxes prior to March 15. [Note: The subjunctive is used in *that* clauses following verbs such as *ask, insist, recommend, request*, and *suggest*.]
  - o **Condition contrary to fact:** If I *were* [not *was*] a millionaire, I would... (fill in the blank).
- **To teach the subjunctive**, show models and invite students to figure out which type of condition (wish, request, or condition contrary to fact) is being manifested. Then let them write sentences to imitate these conditions.

- **ASSESSING THIS:**
- For a quick diagnostic, use a Cloze reading passage full of conditional sentences with blanks where the proper verbs belong. Make sure there are enough context clues to suggest which condition is being addressed, if any.
- As always, we want students to demonstrate their grasp of these grammatical concepts in their own writing, first in sentences then in paragraphs. They will need lots of practice in imitating sentences that use the various verb forms. Then have them include several conditional and subjunctive verb forms (underlined and labeled to show they know they're using them) in a paragraph about a text or topic they are studying. Tell them you will score the paragraph based on two things: 1) All sentences must be complete, and 2) They must use the conditional and subjunctive verb forms correctly and *appropriately*.

*See footnote[176] / **See footnote[177]

L 8.1.D: Recognize and correct inappropriate shifts in verb voice and mood.

TEACHING THIS:

- This requires students to apply *L 8.1.B: Form and use verbs in the active and passive voice* and *L 8.1.C: Form and use verbs in the indicative, imperative, interrogative, conditional, and subjunctive mood*. See the guidance for those standards.

ASSESSING THIS:

- See the assessment guidance for the standards noted above.

---

176 Diana Hacker and Nancy Sommers, *Rules for Writers* (Boston: Bedford/St. Martin's, 2016, 8th edition), 265-266. My examples are derived from the explanations on these pages.

177 Diana Hacker and Nancy Sommers, *Rules for Writers* (Boston: Bedford/St. Martin's, 2016, 8th edition), 252-253. My examples are derived from the explanations on these pages.

L 8.2.A: Use punctuation (comma, ellipsis, dash) to indicate a pause or break.

TEACHING THIS:

- **For relevant guidance on commas,** revisit the follow standards:
    - o L 3.1.H: Use coordinating and subordinating conjunctions.
    - o L 4.2.C: Use a comma before a coordinating conjunction in a compound sentence.
    - o L 5.2.C: Use a comma to set off the words yes and no (e.g., Yes, thank you), to set off a tag question from the rest of the sentence (e.g., It's true, isn't it?), and to indicate direct address (e.g., Is that you, Steve?).
    - o L 6.2.A: Use punctuation (commas, parentheses, dashes) to set off non-restrictive/parenthetical elements.
- **For guidance on the ellipsis,** refer to *L 8.2.B: Use an ellipsis to indicate an omission.*
- **For guidance on dashes,** refer to *L 6.2.A: Use punctuation (commas, parentheses, dashes) to set off nonrestrictive/parenthetical elements.*

ASSESSING THIS:

- See the assessment guidance for standards noted above.

L 8.2.B: Use an ellipsis to indicate an omission.

TEACHING THIS:

- **GENRE ALERT: This standard is particularly useful when writing research papers (W 8.1, W 8.2, W 8.7, W 8.8, and W 8.9.B) or literary analysis essays (W 8.9.A).**
- The ellipsis mark (…) is used to indicate that words have been removed from a verbatim quote. Unfortunately, many students use ellipses more like a machete than a scalpel: They cut out so much of the quote that it becomes difficult to understand how the quote supports their argument.
- Pitch: *When we're providing evidence to support our arguments, we don't always have to include the entire paragraph in which the evidence appears. In fact, depending on the situation, we can use sentences or even excerpts—short clips— from sentences to be most efficient, so our explanations can flow most smoothly. Today we're going to review how to do that properly.*
- In anticipation of the problem of inappropriate ellipsis usage, you could give students an argument (e.g., if you were reading *To Kill a Mockingbird:* "Atticus teaches Scout several important life lessons.") and show students a few quotes that could support that argument (or invite them to find that evidence first). Then discuss how ellipses could be useful to trim sentences that are not needed. Then show what happens when you trim too much: The evidence comes across as incomplete and/or garbled.

*See footnote[178]

L 8.2.C: Spell correctly.

TEACHING THIS:

- This book does not explain phonics instruction but recommends its use for students who struggle with spelling.
- For guidance on how to teach students to consult reference materials, see *L 3.2.G: Consult reference materials, including beginning dictionaries, as needed to check and correct spellings.*

ASSESSING THIS:

- See *L 3.2.G: Consult reference materials, including beginning dictionaries, as needed to check and correct spellings.*

L 8.3A: Use verbs in the active and passive voice and in the conditional and subjunctive mood to achieve particular effects (e.g., emphasizing the actor or the action; expressing uncertainty or describing a state contrary to fact).

TEACHING THIS:

- This standard requires students to apply L 8.1.B and L 8.1.C. See the guidance for those standards.

ASSESSING THIS:

- See the assessment guidance for L 8.1.B and L 8.1.C.

---

178 Harper Lee, *To Kill a Mockingbird* (New York: Random House, 1960).

- How will you use the resources in this chapter?

- How did the ideas in this chapter challenge, change, or confirm what you previously believed about grammar and writing instruction (or instruction in general)?

- Which resources and ideas from this chapter will you share with colleagues? Why?

- What lingering concerns do you have about the standards for grades 6-8, and how will you deal with them?

chapter
EIGHT

Grades 9-12 Writing and Language Instruction

GRADES 9-12 WRITING STANDARDS WITH INSTRUCTIONAL GUIDANCE

Next we'll look at the trajectory of Writing Standards for Grades 9-12 so that we can see how the Language Standards fit in with them. Note: If you want to see all of the ELA Common Core Standards in one place, check out the "K-12 ELA Common Core Standards Tracker" on the TLC Website.[179]

Writing Anchor Standard #1: *Write arguments to support claims in an analysis of substantive topics or texts, using valid reasoning and relevant and sufficient evidence.*

---

179 The "K-12 ELA Common Core Standards Tracker" is on the TLC "Using Grammar to Improve Writing" page found at https://www.literacycookbook.com/page.php?id=161. This and other standards-related resources can also be found on the TLC "Standards" page at https://www.literacycookbook.com/page.php?id=138.

W 9-10.1	Write arguments to support claims in an analysis of substantive topics or texts, using valid reasoning and relevant and sufficient evidence.
	A) Introduce precise claim(s), distinguish the claim(s) from alternate or opposing claims, and create an organization that establishes clear relationships among claim(s), counterclaims, reasons, and evidence.
	B) Develop claim(s) and counterclaims fairly, supplying evidence for each while pointing out the strengths and limitations of both in a manner that anticipates the audience's knowledge level and concerns.
	C) Use words, phrases, and clauses to link the major sections of the text, create cohesion, and clarify the relationships between claim(s) and reasons, between reasons and evidence, and between claim(s) and counterclaims.
	D) Establish and maintain a formal style and objective tone while attending to the norms and conventions of the discipline in which they are writing.
	E) Provide a concluding statement or section that follows from and supports the argument presented.
W 11-12.1	Write arguments to support claims in an analysis of substantive topics or texts, using valid reasoning and relevant and sufficient evidence.
	A) Introduce precise, knowledgeable claim(s), establish the significance of the claim(s), distinguish the claim(s) from alternate or opposing claims, and create an organization that logically sequences claim(s), counterclaims, reasons, and evidence.
	B) Develop claim(s) and counterclaims fairly and thoroughly, supplying the most relevant evidence for each while pointing out the strengths and limitations of both in a manner that anticipates the audience's knowledge level, concerns, values, and possible biases.
	C) Use words, phrases, and clauses as well as varied syntax to link the major sections of the text, create cohesion, and clarify the relationships between claim(s) and reasons, between reasons and evidence, and between claim(s) and counterclaims.
	D) Establish and maintain a formal style and objective tone while attending to the norms and conventions of the discipline in which they are writing.
	E) Provide a concluding statement or section that follows from and supports the argument presented.

In grades 9-10, we see an increase in the requirements for sophistication of reasoning in argumentative writing, particularly with respect to the use of counterclaims. In grade 8, students must "introduce claim(s), acknowledge and distinguish the claim(s) from alternate or opposing claims, and organize the reasons and evidence logically," whereas in grades 9-10, they are expected to "introduce *precise* claim(s), distinguish the claim(s) from alternate or opposing claims, and *create an organization that establishes clear relationships among claim(s), counterclaims, reasons, and evidence*" (italics mine).

The progression from 9-10 to 11-12 focuses on **being thorough.** In grades 9-10, students must "develop claim(s) and counterclaims fairly, supplying evidence for each while pointing out the strengths and limitations of both in a manner that anticipates the audience's knowledge level and concerns," while in 11-12, they must "develop claim(s) and counterclaims fairly *and thoroughly*, supplying *the most relevant* evidence for each while pointing out the strengths and limitations of both in a manner that anticipates the audience's knowledge level, concerns, *values, and possible biases*" (italics mine).

To achieve such levels of sophistication in their writing, students will need to analyze complex text and highly effective, sophisticated models.

	Writing Anchor Standard #2: *Write informative/explanatory texts to examine and convey complex ideas and information clearly and accurately through the effective selection, organization, and analysis of content.*
W 9-10.2	Write informative/explanatory texts to examine and convey complex ideas, concepts, and information clearly and accurately through the effective selection, organization, and analysis of content.
	A) Introduce a topic; organize complex ideas, concepts, and information to make important connections and distinctions; include formatting (e.g., headings), graphics (e.g., figures, tables), and multimedia when useful to aiding comprehension.
	B) Develop the topic with well-chosen, relevant, and sufficient facts, extended definitions, concrete details, quotations, or other information and examples appropriate to the audience's knowledge of the topic.
	C) Use appropriate and varied transitions to link the major sections of the text, create cohesion, and clarify the relationships among complex ideas and concepts.
	D) Use precise language and domain-specific vocabulary to manage the complexity of the topic.

	E) Establish and maintain a formal style and objective tone while attending to the norms and conventions of the discipline in which they are writing.
	F) Provide a concluding statement or section that follows from and supports the information or explanation presented (e.g., articulating implications or the significance of the topic).
W 11-12.2	Write informative/explanatory texts to examine and convey complex ideas, concepts, and information clearly and accurately through the effective selection, organization, and analysis of content.
	A) Introduce a topic; organize complex ideas, concepts, and information so that each new element builds on that which precedes it to create a unified whole; include formatting (e.g., headings), graphics (e.g., figures, tables), and multimedia when useful to aiding comprehension.
	B) Develop the topic thoroughly by selecting the most significant and relevant facts, extended definitions, concrete details, quotations, or other information and examples appropriate to the audience's knowledge of the topic.
	C) Use appropriate and varied transitions and syntax to link the major sections of the text, create cohesion, and clarify the relationships among complex ideas and concepts.
	D) Use precise language, domain-specific vocabulary, and techniques such as metaphor, simile, and analogy to manage the complexity of the topic.
	E) Establish and maintain a formal style and objective tone while attending to the norms and conventions of the discipline in which they are writing.
	F) Provide a concluding statement or section that follows from and supports the information or explanation presented (e.g., articulating implications or the significance of the topic).

As I noted in previous grades for Writing Standard #2, this standard's reliance on the word "topic" might mislead teachers into assigning *topic-driven* writing such as "The Dangers of Smoking" or "The Causes of the Civil War." No matter how compelling the topic, a topic-driven approach will almost inevitably lead students to plagiarize because the idea of topic-driven writing seems to be "Tell us as much about this topic as you can." So students dump information in and don't explain it. By contrast, **question-driven writing** such as "Why is it dangerous to smoke?" and "Why did Americans engage in the Civil War?" pushes students to explain their ideas and information. To make this approach work, review Reading Standard 2.1 (*Ask and answer such questions as who, what, where, when,* *why, and how to demonstrate understanding of key details in a text*), which is explained in Chapter 4 (see "The Most Important Writing Standard"). Also, show students high-quality mentor texts and invite *them* to explain what makes the texts so effective.

As with grades 6-8, Writing Standard #2 for grades 9-12 requires analysis. In grades 9-12, students are expected to "write informative/ explanatory texts to examine and convey complex ideas, concepts, and information clearly and accurately through the effective selection, organization, and analysis of content."

Reviewing Argument vs. Evidence Steps 1-3 (see Chapter 4) will be helpful, and you should pay particular attention to Step 2.5, which deals with selecting the most relevant evidence.

One noticeable elevation from grades 9-10 to 11-12 can be seen in the use of language. Whereas in 9-10 students must use "precise language and domain-specific vocabulary to manage the complexity of the topic," grades 11-12 require "precise language, domain-specific vocabulary, *and techniques such as metaphor, simile, and analogy* to manage the complexity of the topic" (italics mine).

Finally, unlike in earlier grades, in 9-12 we see a parenthetical piece of guidance on how to conclude: "Provide a concluding statement or section that follows from and supports the information or explanation presented (*e.g., articulating implications or the significance of the topic*)" (italics mine).

	Writing Standard #3: *Write narratives to develop real or imagined experiences or events using effective technique, well-chosen details, and well-structured event sequences.*
W 9-10.3	Write narratives to develop real or imagined experiences or events using effective technique, well-chosen details, and well-structured event sequences. A) Engage and orient the reader by setting out a problem, situation, or observation, establishing one or multiple point(s) of view, and introducing a narrator and/or characters; create a smooth progression of experiences or events. B) Use narrative techniques, such as dialogue, pacing, description, reflection, and multiple plot lines, to develop experiences, events, and/ or characters.

	C) Use a variety of techniques to sequence events so that they build on one another to create a coherent whole.
	D) Use precise words and phrases, telling details, and sensory language to convey a vivid picture of the experiences, events, setting, and/or characters.
	E) Provide a conclusion that follows from and reflects on what is experienced, observed, or resolved over the course of the narrative.
W 11-12.3	Write narratives to develop real or imagined experiences or events using effective technique, well-chosen details, and well-structured event sequences. A) Engage and orient the reader by setting out a problem, situation, or observation and its significance, establishing one or multiple point(s) of view, and introducing a narrator and/or characters; create a smooth progression of experiences or events. B) Use narrative techniques, such as dialogue, pacing, description, reflection, and multiple plot lines, to develop experiences, events, and/or characters. C) Use a variety of techniques to sequence events so that they build on one another to create a coherent whole and build toward a particular tone and outcome (e.g., a sense of mystery, suspense, growth, or resolution). D) Use precise words and phrases, telling details, and sensory language to convey a vivid picture of the experiences, events, setting, and/or characters. E) Provide a conclusion that follows from and reflects on what is experienced, observed, or resolved over the course of the narrative.

The requirements for an effective narrative in grades 9-10 are more rigorous than those in grade 8. Whereas in grade 8 students must "engage and orient the reader by establishing a context and point of view and introducing a narrator and/or characters; organize an event sequence that unfolds naturally and logically," in grades 9-10 they must "engage and orient the reader *by setting out a problem, situation, or observation, establishing one or multiple point(s) of view,* and introducing a narrator and/or characters; *create a smooth progression of experiences or events*" (italics mine). While it still stuns me that the narrative standards do not explicitly mention "conflict," the word "problem" is at least a step in the right direction.

From grades 9-10 to 11-12, the standards require an increase in sophistication—even elegance. In grades 9-10, students must "use a variety of techniques to sequence events so that they build on one another to create a coherent whole," while in grades 11-12, they must "use a variety of techniques to sequence events so that they build on one another to create a coherent whole *and build toward a particular tone and outcome (e.g., a sense of mystery, suspense, growth, or resolution)*" (italics mine).

Brief Notes About Writing Standards #4-6:

Writing Anchor Standard #4: *Produce clear and coherent writing in which the development, organization, and style are appropriate to task, purpose, and audience.*

Writing Anchor Standard #5: *Develop and strengthen writing as needed by planning, revising, editing, rewriting, or trying a new approach.*

Writing Anchor Standard #6: *Use technology, including the Internet, to produce and publish writing and to interact and collaborate with others.*

In working on Writing Standards #4 and #5, teachers must establish the key steps of the writing process through modeling, practice, and feedback. This involves using mentor texts[180] and establishing classroom routines for working through the different steps of the writing process, whether with teacher or peer support, or independently. Revisit Chapter 2, particularly "Principle #3: Ask, 'What Do You *Like* About That Sentence?'" and "Principle #4: Give Faster Feedback," for detailed ideas about how to address these standards.

Writing Standard #6 speaks to the use of technology and Internet research.

Writing Anchor Standard #7: *Conduct short as well as more sustained research projects based on focused questions, demonstrating understanding of the subject under investigation.*

---

180 Sarah Tantillo, *The Literacy Cookbook: A Practical Guide to Effective Reading, Writing, Speaking, and Listening Instruction* (San Francisco: Jossey-Bass, 2012), 95-104.

W 9-10.7	Conduct short as well as more sustained research projects to answer a question (including a self-generated question) or solve a problem; narrow or broaden the inquiry when appropriate; synthesize multiple sources on the subject, demonstrating understanding of the subject under investigation.
W 11-12.7	Conduct short as well as more sustained research projects to answer a question (including a self-generated question) or solve a problem; narrow or broaden the inquiry when appropriate; synthesize multiple sources on the subject, demonstrating understanding of the subject under investigation.
	Writing Anchor Standard #8: *Gather relevant information from multiple print and digital sources, assess the credibility and accuracy of each source, and integrate the information while avoiding plagiarism.*
W 9-10.8	Gather relevant information from multiple authoritative print and digital sources, using advanced searches effectively; assess the usefulness of each source in answering the research question; integrate information into the text selectively to maintain the flow of ideas, avoiding plagiarism and following a standard format for citation.
W 11-12.8	Gather relevant information from multiple authoritative print and digital sources, using advanced searches effectively; assess the strengths and limitations of each source in terms of the task, purpose, and audience; integrate information into the text selectively to maintain the flow of ideas, avoiding plagiarism and over-reliance on any one source and following a standard format for citation.

Writing Standards #7 and 8 (research writing) echo the work of Writing Standard #2 (informative/explanatory writing), so you should refer back to my comments on that standard, especially regarding the need for *question-driven* rather than *topic-driven* writing assignments. These standards also tie in with Writing Standard #6, which addresses the use of technology and Internet research.

For a full explanation of how to teach research paper writing, see *The Literacy Cookbook* and the TLC "Research Paper Guide" page.[181]

---

181 Sarah Tantillo, *The Literacy Cookbook: A Practical Guide to Effective Reading, Writing, Speaking, and Listening Instruction* (San Francisco: Jossey-Bass, 2012), 169-190. The TLC "Research Paper Guide" page is found at https://www.literacycookbook.com/page.php?id=24.

	Writing Anchor Standard #9: *Draw evidence from literary or informational texts to support analysis, reflection, and research.*
W 9-10.9	Draw evidence from literary or informational texts to support analysis, reflection, and research. A) Apply grades 9–10 Reading standards to literature (e.g., "Analyze how an author draws on and transforms source material in a specific work [e.g., how Shakespeare treats a theme or topic from Ovid or the Bible or how a later author draws on a play by Shakespeare]"). B) Apply grades 9–10 Reading standards to literary nonfiction (e.g., "Delineate and evaluate the argument and specific claims in a text, assessing whether the reasoning is valid and the evidence is relevant and sufficient; identify false statements and fallacious reasoning").
W 11-12.9	Draw evidence from literary or informational texts to support analysis, reflection, and research. A) Apply grades 11–12 Reading standards to literature (e.g., "Demonstrate knowledge of eighteenth-, nineteenth- and early-twentieth-century foundational works of American literature, including how two or more texts from the same period treat similar themes or topics"). B) Apply grades 11–12 Reading standards to literary nonfiction (e.g., "Delineate and evaluate the reasoning in seminal U.S. texts, including the application of constitutional principles and use of legal reasoning [e.g., in U.S. Supreme Court Case majority opinions and dissents] and the premises, purposes, and arguments in works of public advocacy [e.g., The Federalist, presidential addresses]").

Writing Standard #9 is why some people say that the writing standards are 20—or or even 30—standards in one. The premise is for students to use writing to demonstrate that they read well. Students must apply close reading and analysis skills (see *Literacy and the Common Core*[182] and the TLC "Analyzing Literature" page[183]) and Argument vs. Evidence Steps 1-3 (see Chapter 4).

For W 9-10.9.A and W 11-12.9.A—AKA literary response writing—see the TLC "Literary Response Paper Guide" page.[184]

---

182 Sarah Tantillo, *Literacy and the Common Core: Recipes for Action* (San Francisco: Jossey-Bass, 2014), 107-127.

183 The TLC "Analyzing Literature" page is found at https://www.literacycookbook.com/page.php?id=2.

184 The TLC "Literary Response Paper Guide" page is found at https://www.literacycookbook.com/page.php?id=19.

For W 9-10.9.B and W 11-12.9.B—AKA research paper writing—see the TLC "Research Paper Guide" page.[185]

Writing Anchor Standard #10: *Write routinely over extended time frames (time for research, reflection, and revision) and shorter time frames (a single sitting or a day or two) for a range of tasks, purposes, and audiences.*

This standard does not need to be unpacked, but it should be duly noted. Teachers may want to use a checklist such as the following to ensure that students' writing assignments meet all of the stated criteria:

- Students write routinely.
- Students write over extended periods, with time for research, reflection, and revision.
- Students practice and are assessed on timed writing.
- Students write to complete a range of tasks.
- Students write for a range of audiences.
- Students write for various purposes.

GRADES 9-12 LANGUAGE STANDARDS

In this section, we'll look at the Grades 9-12 trajectory of key Language Standards first, then go through the standards grade by grade (so: all 9-10 first, then all 11-12) so that we can dive more deeply into effective instructional practices. Note: If you want to track student progress on the K-12 Language Standards, check out the "K-12 Selected Language CCS Tracker" in the Appendix and on the TLC Website.[186]

---

185 The TLC "Research Paper Guide" page is found at https://www.literacycookbook.com/page.php?id=24.

186 The "K-12 Selected Language CCS Tracker" can be downloaded from the TLC "Using Grammar to Improve Writing" page found at https://www.literacycookbook.com/page.php?id=161. Additional standards-related resources are available on the TLC "Standards" page found at https://www.literacycookbook.com/page.php?id=138.

	Language Anchor Standard #1: *Demonstrate command of the conventions of standard English grammar and usage when writing or speaking.*
L 9-10.1	A) Use parallel structure. B) Use various types of phrases (noun, verb, adjectival, adverbial, participial, prepositional, absolute) and clauses (independent, dependent; noun, relative, adverbial) to convey specific meanings and add variety and interest to writing or presentations.
L 11-12.1	A) Apply the understanding that usage is a matter of convention, can change over time, and is sometimes contested. B) Resolve issues of complex or contested usage, consulting references (e.g., Merriam-Webster's *Dictionary of English Usage*, Garner's *Modern American Usage*) as needed.

Next:

	Language Anchor Standard #2: *Demonstrate command of the conventions of standard English capitalization, punctuation, and spelling when writing.*
L 9-10.2	A) Use a semicolon (and perhaps a conjunctive adverb) to link two or more closely related independent clauses. B) Use a colon to introduce a list or quotation. C) Spell correctly.
L 11-12.2	A) Observe hyphenation conventions. B) Spell correctly.

Next:

	Language Anchor Standard #3: *Apply knowledge of language to understand how language functions in different contexts, to make effective choices for meaning or style, and to comprehend more fully when reading or listening.*
L 9-10.3	Apply knowledge of language to understand how language functions in different contexts, to make effective choices for meaning or style, and to comprehend more fully when reading or listening. A) Write and edit work so that it conforms to the guidelines in a style manual (e.g., *MLA Handbook*, Turabian's *Manual for Writers*) appropriate for the discipline and writing type.
L 11-12.3	Apply knowledge of language to understand how language functions in different contexts, to make effective choices for meaning or style, and to comprehend more fully when reading or listening. A) Vary syntax for effect, consulting references (e.g., Tufte's *Artful Sentences*) for guidance as needed; apply an understanding of syntax to the study of complex texts when reading.

(Note: Language Standards #4-6 deal primarily with vocabulary, so we will not analyze them here. For guidance on vocabulary instruction, see *The Literacy Cookbook.*[187])

GRADES 9-10 LANGUAGE STANDARDS: A DEEPER DIVE

In the next two sections, we'll dive more deeply into each paired grade's Language Standards and look at ways to teach and assess them more systematically, in conjunction with writing instruction. These are by no means the *only* ways to teach these standards, just a few to illustrate how to connect grammar with writing and reading. We begin with grades 9-10.

L 9-10.1.A: Use parallel structure.

> **TEACHING THIS:**
>
> - Pitch: *When you're trying to make a point and want the reader to be strongly convinced, you have various rhetorical tools at your disposal. You can use literary devices such as similes, metaphors, hyperbole, analogies, and so on, of course. And you can also use the way you structure your sentences to make an impact. Repetition—repeating words, phrases, or ideas—is one way to do that. Another way—somewhat related—is to suggest similarities amongst different ideas by using parallel structure. Grammatically, that means you express the ideas in the same grammatical format. For example, I might write [show this on the board], "She loved reading, writing, and Boogie boarding." Notice how all three verbs end with –ing. That creates a smooth, clear effect. Notice how awkward it would sound if I wrote this: "She loved reading, writing, and to ride her Boogie board." Sounds clumsy, right? Using parallel structure strengthens the impact your writing will have on the reader. Today we're going to dig into this concept further.*
>
> - We tend to pay the most attention to parallel structure when discussing correlative conjunctions (see *L 5.1.E: Use correlative conjunctions (e.g., either/ or, neither/nor)*, but let's not forget that independent clauses joined by coordinating conjunctions are also a form of parallel structure (see *L 1.1.G: Use frequently occurring conjunctions [e.g., and, but, or, so, because]*). Also, when paired ideas using coordinating conjunctions are expressed in parallel form, it shows that they are of equal importance: e.g., "Unfortunately, publishers began *to reduce* their promotional efforts and *to abandon* authors whose books didn't sell a million copies."

---

187 Sarah Tantillo, *The Literacy Cookbook: A Practical Guide to Effective Reading, Writing, Speaking, and Listening Instruction* (San Francisco: Jossey-Bass, 2012), 28-36. For online resources, see the TLC "Building Robust Vocabulary" page found at https://www.literacycookbook.com/page.php?id=4.

- Show students various sentences—some using parallel structure, some not—and invite them to evaluate the sentences to determine if the structure is parallel or not. Be sure to discuss the effect of "how it sounds"—either smooth or awkward. In cases where parallel structure is missing, they should correct the sentence.
- Show students more examples using parallel structure, and invite them to imitate those sentences, then do Show Call to share some good examples (see Chapter 2, "Principle #4: Give Faster Feedback," to review Show Call).
- During Show Call, let students explain what makes the exemplars effective. Then send them back to their own writing with this advice: "Use what you now know about parallel structure in your own writing."

ASSESSING THIS:

- For a quick diagnostic, give students some sentences that use correlative conjunctions or coordinating conjunctions with parallel structure and some that do not. Have them identify which are correct and fix any that are incorrect.
- As always, we want students to demonstrate their grasp of these grammatical concepts in their own writing, first in sentences then in paragraphs. Provide anchor charts of correlative conjunctions and coordinating conjunctions. Direct students to write a paragraph about a current text or topic using at least three examples of parallel structure (which they should underline). Tell them you will score the paragraph based on two things: 1) All sentences must be complete, and 2) All required items must be included and used properly.

L 9-10.1.B: Use various types of phrases (noun, verb, adjectival, adverbial, participial, prepositional, absolute) and clauses (independent, dependent; noun, relative, adverbial) to convey specific meanings and add variety and interest to writing or presentations.

TEACHING THIS:

- This standard obviously cannot be taught in one lesson. To ensure students master all aspects of this standard, review the notes here and revisit the guidance from earlier standards as noted.

- **NOUN PHRASES:**

  o **Noun phrases are also known as appositives,** as in "Mrs. Jones, *our math teacher*, asked us to memorize the times tables for homework." See *L 5.3.A: Expand, combine, and reduce sentences for meaning, reader/ listener interest, and style.*

- **VERB PHRASES:**

  o **Verb phrases are combinations of words that act as a verb,** as in "I *will mow* the lawn tomorrow." The verbs in a verb phrase are not always contiguous: "*Does* he *like* to read?" (Note: In that sentence, "to read" is not a verb but a *verbal*—in this case, an infinitive functioning as a direct object.) See the following standards for additional guidance:

    - L 1.1.E: Use verbs to convey a sense of past, present, and future (e.g., Yesterday I walked home; Today I walk home; Tomorrow I will walk home).

    - L 4.1.B: Form and use the progressive (e.g., I was walking; I am walking; I will be walking) verb tenses.

    - L 4.1.C: Use modal auxiliaries (e.g., can, may, must) to convey various conditions.

    - L 5.1.B: Form and use the perfect (e.g., I had walked; I have walked; I will have walked) verb tenses.

  o **Reminder: Verb phrases and verbals are NOT THE SAME THING.** For an explanation of verbals, see *L 8.1.A: Explain the function of verbals (gerunds, participles, infinitives) in general and their function in particular sentences.*

- **ADJECTIVAL PHRASES:**

  o **Adjectival (or adjective) phrases are prepositional phrases or verbal phrases that function as adjectives.** They may be restrictive (with no commas), as in "Her bedroom closet was filled with shoes *dating from the 1970s*" [verbal]. Or they may be nonrestrictive (with commas), as in "Her house, *with its thousands and thousands of books*, is like a library that you can sleep in" [prepositional].

---

o **For more on adjectives, see these standards:**

§ L 1.1.F: Use frequently occurring adjectives.

§ L 2.1.E: Use adjectives and adverbs, and choose between them depending on what is to be modified.

- **ADVERBIAL PHRASES:**

  o Like adverbs—which answer the questions *When? Where? Why? How? Under what condition?*—**adverbial (or adverb) phrases may take the form of prepositional phrases:** "The pulled pork *in that restaurant* made me want to move to Atlanta." [Where?] See *L 4.1.E: Form and use prepositional phrases.*

  o **They may also take the form of infinitive phrases:** "I poured cat food into the bowl *to lure Lulu out from under the bed.*" [Why?] See *L 8.1.A: Explain the function of verbals (gerunds, participles, infinitives) in general and their function in particular sentences.*

- **PARTICIPIAL PHRASES:**

  o **Participial phrases always function as adjectives.** They are either present participles (e.g., *laughing*) or past participles (e.g., *written*).*

  o See *L 8.1.A: Explain the function of verbals (gerunds, participles, infinitives) in general and their function in particular sentences.*

  o **To work on avoiding or correcting dangling participles or modifiers,** see *L 7.1.C: Place phrases and clauses within a sentence, recognizing and correcting misplaced and dangling modifiers.*

- **PREPOSITIONAL PHRASES:**

  o Students should be introduced to prepositions in kindergarten. See *L K.1.E: Use the most frequently occurring prepositions (e.g., to, from, in, out, on, off, for, of, by, with).*

  o See also *L 4.1.E: Form and use prepositional phrases.*

- **ABSOLUTE PHRASES:**

  o **An absolute phrase modifies a whole clause or sentence.**** It consists of a noun or noun equivalent followed by a participial phrase, as in "*His leg muscles cramping up*, the runner stopped by the side of the road." Mnemonic tip: One way to remember absolutes is that they "absolutely leave out the verb *to be* and only include the participial phrase." (In the example above, "were" was left out.)

  o As with other grammatical forms, students should practice using absolutes in sentences and paragraphs dealing with whatever text or topic they are studying.

- **INDEPENDENT OR DEPENDENT CLAUSES:**

  o Review the "Demonstrated Grammar" skit in Chapter 2 (found under "Principle #3: Ask, 'What Do You *Like* About That Sentence?'") for a physical way to demonstrate the difference between dependent (or subordinate) and independent clauses.

o Students learn how to write independent clauses—i.e., complete sentences—beginning in kindergarten (see *L K.1.F: Produce and expand complete sentences in shared language activities*). Here are additional standards that deal with independent and dependent clauses:

- L 1.1.G: Use frequently occurring conjunctions (e.g., and, but, or, so, because).
- L 1.1.J: Produce and expand complete simple and compound declarative, interrogative, imperative, and exclamatory sentences in response to prompts.
- L 2.1.F: Produce, expand, and rearrange complete simple and compound sentences (e.g., The boy watched the movie; The little boy watched the movie; The action movie was watched by the little boy).
- L 3.1.H: Use coordinating and subordinating conjunctions.
- L 3.1.I: Produce simple, compound, and complex sentences.
- L 4.1.F: Produce complete sentences, recognizing and correcting inappropriate fragments and run-ons.
- L 4.2.C: Use a comma before a coordinating conjunction in a compound sentence.
- L 5.3.A: Expand, combine, and reduce sentences for meaning, reader/listener interest, and style.
- L 6.3.A: Vary sentence patterns for meaning, reader/ listener interest, and style.

- **NOUN CLAUSES:**
  o **A noun clause functions exactly like a single-word noun.** It usually begins with *how, if, that, what, whatever, when, where, whether, which, who, whoever, whom, whomever, whose,* or *why.*``` For example: "I will be happy to eat *whatever she cooks*." [In this case, the noun clause functions as a direct object.]

  o **For a review of nouns and how they are used, see the following standards:**
  - L K.1.B: Use frequently occurring nouns and verbs.
  - L 1.1.B: Use common, proper, and possessive nouns.
  - L 2.1.A: Use collective nouns (e.g., group).
  - L 3.1.C: Use abstract nouns (e.g., childhood).

- **RELATIVE CLAUSES:**
  o Relative clauses—AKA adjective clauses—are patterned like sentences, but they function within sentences to modify nouns or pronouns.```` They can be restrictive (without commas), as in "The mouse *that escaped from the basement* was found later in the kitchen," or nonrestrictive (with commas), as in "His books, *which have sold more than a million copies,* have revolutionized teacher training."

  o See *L 4.1.A: Use relative pronouns (who, whose, whom, which, that) and relative adverbs (where, when, why).*

- **ADVERBIAL CLAUSES:**
  - o **Adverbial (or adverb) clauses begin with a subordinate conjunction.** Like adverbs, they tend to answer one of these questions: *When? Where? Why? How? Under what conditions?* For example: *"After we finished running up and down the boardwalk*, we stopped for water."***** [When?]
  - o See *L 3.1.H: Use coordinating and subordinating conjunctions.*

ASSESSING THIS:

- See the assessment guidance for the recommended standards.

*See footnote[188] / **See footnote[189] / ***See footnote[190] / ****See footnote[191] /
*****See footnote[192]

L 9-10.2.A: Use a semicolon (and perhaps a conjunctive adverb) to link two or more closely related independent clauses.

TEACHING THIS:

- Pitch: *Most people use conjunctive adverbs (which sound like a contagious disease!) often and don't even realize it. We're talking about words like "finally," "indeed," and "however." Incidentally (you see what I did there?), these words tend to link closely related independent clauses, which are best joined with a semi-colon. For example: "She liked to write; however, it hurt her back to sit for too long." What are the two independent clauses here? How could we write a different sentence that says the same thing?* ["She liked to write, but it hurt her back to sit for too long."]

- Invite students to help you create another example (i.e., We Do), then give them a list of conjunctive adverbs so that they can create their own. Kolln et al. note that conjunctive adverbs can indicate result, concession, apposition, addition, time, contrast, summary, or reinforcement, as follows:*

---

188 Diana Hacker and Nancy Sommers, *Rules for Writers* (Boston: Bedford/St. Martin's, 2016, 8th edition), 386.

189 Diana Hacker and Nancy Sommers, *Rules for Writers* (Boston: Bedford/St. Martin's, 2016, 8th edition), 388.

190 Diana Hacker and Nancy Sommers, *Rules for Writers* (Boston: Bedford/St. Martin's, 2016, 8th edition), 391.

191 Diana Hacker and Nancy Sommers, *Rules for Writers* (Boston: Bedford/St. Martin's, 2016, 8th edition), 301.

192 Diana Hacker and Nancy Sommers, *Rules for Writers* (Boston: Bedford/St. Martin's, 2016, 8th edition), 390-391.

- o **Result**: *therefore, consequently, of course*
- o **Concession**: *nevertheless, yet, still, after all, of course*
- o **Apposition**: *for example, for instance, that is, namely, in other words*
- o **Addition**: *moreover, furthermore, also, in addition, likewise, further*
- o **Time**: *meanwhile, in the meantime*
- o **Contrast**: *however, instead, on the contrary, on the other hand, in contrast, rather*
- o **Summary**: *thus, in conclusion, then*
- o **Reinforcement**: *further, in particular, indeed, above all, in fact*

- Using a current topic or text, students should practice writing sentences and then paragraphs with these conjunctive adverbs. Use Show Call to review their work and reinforce the importance of providing ample context clues in the sentences to show how the adverbs are used logically (see Chapter 2, "Principle #4: Give Faster Feedback," to review Show Call).

ASSESSING THIS:

- Give students a word bank of conjunctive adverbs and require them to insert the words where they belong in the blanks in a Cloze reading passage.
- As always, we want students to demonstrate their grasp of these grammatical concepts in their own writing, first in sentences then in paragraphs. Provide several conjunctive adverbs that they must include in a paragraph about a text or topic they are studying, and tell them you will score the paragraph based on two things: 1) All sentences must be complete, and 2) All of the conjunctive adverbs should be used logically, with appropriate context clues underlined. (You can always modify these requirements. My point is to ensure that your assessment is targeted to the concept you're teaching.)

*See footnote[193]

193 Martha J. Kolln, Loretta S. Gray, and Joseph Salvatore Understanding English Grammar (10th edition, New York: Pearson Publishing, 2015), 237.

L 9-10.2.B: Use a colon to introduce a list or quotation.

TEACHING THIS:

- Pitch: *I like to think of a colon as a set of stereo speakers, announcing something. Here's an example: "I'm going on a picnic, and I'm bringing four things: water, sandwiches, iced tea, and chips." Let's analyze this sentence.* [Show it on the board, and students should have it on a handout, as well.] *Please underline ANY independent clauses you see.* [Give students a moment, then ask them to compare with their neighbor.] *Let's see what you found.* [Solicit independent clauses: *I'm going on a picnic,* and *I'm bringing four things.*] *OK, I'm glad you found the independent clauses, which in this case are separated by a comma and a coordinating conjunction* [see *L 1.1.G: Use frequently occurring conjunctions (e.g., and, but, or, so, because)* and *L 3.1.H: Use coordinating and subordinating conjunctions.*]. **Notice that the list follows an independent clause. So does a quotation,** *like this:*
  - o The coach had just two words to say: "We won."
- *We also need an independent clause before a colon in two other instances: with an appositive and with a summary or explanation.* Let's look at these examples:
  - o The library was populated primarily by two types of people: children and senior citizens. ["Children and senior citizens" constitute the appositive. For more information on appositives, see "How to Carry Soup" in Chapter 2.]
  - o Aqua fitness classes are more challenging than they might seem: From the surface, you can't see how difficult it is to run underwater. [When a complete sentence follows a colon, it must be capitalized.]
- Give students time to systematically practice imitating these sentences using a current text or topic. Use Show Call to highlight their examples (see Chapter 2, "Principle #4: Give Faster Feedback," to review Show Call).
- **Note that the colon is commonly misused because too many people don't realize that they must put a *complete sentence* (independent clause) before the colon.** Here's an example of a common error:
  - o We went to the movies and bought: soda, candy, and popcorn. [There should not be a colon between "bought" and "soda" because "We went to the movies and bought" is not a complete sentence.]

ASSESSING THIS:

- For a quick diagnostic, you can give students sentences in which they should insert the colon where it belongs (*if* it belongs).

- As always, we want students to demonstrate their grasp of these grammatical concepts in their own writing, first in sentences then in paragraphs. Require them to include *four* colons in a paragraph about a text or topic they are studying, and tell them you will score the paragraph based on two things: 1) All sentences must be complete, and 2) The colons must set up a list, a quotation, an appositive, and a summary/explanation. (Of course, you can always modify these requirements. My point is to ensure that your assessment is targeted to the concept you're teaching.)

*See footnote[194]

L 9-10.2.C: Spell correctly.

TEACHING THIS:

- This book does not explain phonics instruction but recommends its use for students who struggle with spelling.
- For guidance on how to teach students to consult reference materials, see *L 3.2.G: Consult reference materials, including beginning dictionaries, as needed to check and correct spellings.*

ASSESSING THIS:

- See *L 3.2.G: Consult reference materials, including beginning dictionaries, as needed to check and correct spellings.*

L 9-10.3
Apply knowledge of language to understand how language functions in different contexts, to make effective choices for meaning or style, and to comprehend more fully when reading or listening.

Write and edit work so that it conforms to the guidelines in a style manual (e.g., *MLA Handbook*, Turabian's *Manual for Writers*) appropriate for the discipline and writing type.

TEACHING THIS:

- **GENRE ALERT: This standard is particularly useful when launching research papers (W 9-10.1, W 9-10.2, W 9-10.7, W 9-10.8, and W 9-10.9.B) or literary analysis essays (W 9-10.9.A).**

---

194 Diana Hacker and Nancy Sommers, *Rules for Writers* (Boston: Bedford/St. Martin's, 2016, 8th edition), 317-318. My examples are derived from the explanations on these pages.

- Pitch: *When you go to college, you will need to write your papers according to certain requirements. Depending on the discipline (in other words, depending on which academic department you're writing for), you might have to use the MLA Guide, APA Guide, or the Chicago Manual of Style to format your paper and, in particular, your citations. Different disciplines have different requirements. English departments typically use MLA (Modern Language Association); psychology and sociology departments tend to use APA (American Psychological Association); and business, history, and fine arts often use Chicago/Turabian. We're going to use MLA in this class.*
- Show students examples of papers written in MLA format.
- For resources to support teaching literary analysis papers, see the TLC "Literary Response Paper Guide" page.*
- For resources to support teaching research papers, see the TLC "Research Paper Guide" page.**

ASSESSING THIS:

- The ultimate product will be a paper written in proper format; however, you should scaffold the writing process to check student work as they move through the project to ensure they are on track.

*See footnote[195] / *See footnote[196]

GRADES 11-12 LANGUAGE STANDARDS: A DEEPER DIVE

Next, we'll dive more deeply into the Grades 11-12 Language Standards and look at how to teach and assess them more systematically, in conjunction with writing instruction. Again, these are by no means the *only* ways to teach these standards, just a few to illustrate how to connect grammar with writing and reading.

---

195 The TLC "Literary Response Paper Guide" page is found at https://www.literacycookbook.com/page.php?id=19.

196 The TLC "Research Paper Guide" page is found at https://www.literacycookbook.com/page.php?id=24.

L 11-12.1.A: Apply the understanding that usage is a matter of convention, can change over time, and is sometimes contested.

> **TEACHING THIS:**
>
> - My sense is that when they wrote this standard, the authors of the Common Core State Standards were probably thinking of conventions such as "Never end a sentence with a preposition" or "Don't split an infinitive" or "Don't use 'their' to refer to an individual." I don't think there is one way to teach this standard; I think if you spend enough time looking at mentor texts and student work with your students, such questions about usage will arise naturally, and you can discuss them then.
>
> **ASSESSING THIS:**
>
> - Let me know if you think of something for this one!

L 11-12.1.B: Resolve issues of complex or contested usage, consulting references (e.g., Merriam-Webster's *Dictionary of English Usage*, Garner's *Modern American Usage*) as needed.

> **TEACHING THIS:**
>
> - This standard follows from the preceding standard. Again, I think issues of "complex or contested usage" will arise when you and your students are analyzing mentor texts or student work, and at that point, you can discuss sources that could help resolve the issues.
>
> **ASSESSING THIS:**
>
> - N/A

L 11-12.2.A: Observe hyphenation conventions.

> **TEACHING THIS:**
>
> - *This is a true story: The copy editor of one of my previous books apparently was not a fan of hyphens. She deleted virtually every hyphen in the manuscript and sent it back to me. As a result, I had to spend eight hours combing through her edits, re-hyphenating the entire text. Oy. So to anyone who thinks hyphens don't matter that much, I disagree. Not knowing hyphenation rules can take hours off of your life—or someone else's.* (That would be my pitch. You'll have to create your own. Perhaps tell this story about an author you know.)
> - Whenever you decide to discuss hyphens with your students, be sure to cover the following points:

- o **Hyphenate two (or more) words used together as an adjective before a noun.** For example: "The chef's *fast-moving* hands produced a meal almost before we could blink." Also: "He is a *one-of-a-kind* culinary expert."
- o **DO NOT hyphenate those words used as an adjective if they appear AFTER the noun.** So you could say, "That chef was *world famous.*" Or you could refer to the "*world-famous* chef."
- o **DO NOT hyphenate *–ly* adverbs to the words they modify.** So: "His *quickly moving* hands mesmerized us."
- o Use a hyphen with the following prefixes: *all-*, *ex-*, and *self-*.
- o Use a hyphen with the suffix *–elect.*
- o Hyphenate words that would look weird if you didn't, such as *cross-stitch* and *anti-intellectual.*

ASSESSING THIS:

- Give students sentences that need or do not need hyphens and direct them to insert hyphens if needed.

L 11-12.2.B: Spell correctly.

TEACHING THIS:

- This book does not explain phonics instruction but recommends its use for students who struggle with spelling.
- For guidance on how to teach students to consult reference materials, see *L 3.2.G: Consult reference materials, including beginning dictionaries, as needed to check and correct spellings.*

ASSESSING THIS:

- See *L 3.2.G: Consult reference materials, including beginning dictionaries, as needed to check and correct spellings.*

*See footnote[197]

---

197 Diana Hacker and Nancy Sommers, *Rules for Writers* (Boston: Bedford/St. Martin's, 2016, 8th edition), 354-355. My examples are derived from the explanations on these pages.

L 11-12.3

Apply knowledge of language to understand how language functions in different contexts, to make effective choices for meaning or style, and to comprehend more fully when reading or listening.

A) **Vary syntax for effect, consulting references (e.g., Tufte's *Artful Sentences*) for guidance as needed; apply an understanding of syntax to the study of complex texts when reading.**

TEACHING THIS:

- This standard has two parts: 1) "Vary syntax for effect"—meaning, show control over your own writing; and 2) "Apply an understanding of syntax to the study of complex texts"—meaning, closely analyze someone else's writing. I've demonstrated both of these approaches to some degree in Chapter 2, in the section called "Principle #3: Ask, "What Do You *Like* About That Sentence?"" My dream is that students who are taught *all* of the Language Standards discussed in this book will be able to meet this standard by the time they arrive in 11th grade.

- Check out *Literacy and the Common Core* for ideas about how to teach close reading strategies.*

- Of course, you will want to use effective mentor texts to demonstrate the artful use of syntax. And now I must confess that in spite of having had an excellent education, until I read this standard, I had never heard of Tufte's *Artful Sentences.*** It turns out that Virginia Tufte, who presents and comments on more than a thousand excellent sentences (chosen from the works of authors in the twentieth and twenty-first centuries) is truly a kindred spirit. She focuses on sentences that succeed. And as you have surely realized by now, that is the goal of this book, too.

ASSESSING THIS:

- Effective syntax will need to be woven into paragraphs, essays, and narratives. Although this is not a simple, concrete item to assess, you could offer suggestions or a checklist to support students as they write, then incorporate those items in the rubric.

---

*See footnote[198] / **See footnote[199]

---

198 Sarah Tantillo, *Literacy and the Common Core: Recipes for Action* (San Francisco: Jossey-Bass, 2014).

199 Virginia Tufte, *Artful Sentences: Syntax as Style* (Cheshire, CT: Graphics Press LLC, 2017, 4th printing).

- How will you use the resources in this chapter?

- How did the ideas in this chapter challenge, change, or confirm what you previously believed about grammar and writing instruction (or instruction in general)?

- Which resources and ideas from this chapter will you share with colleagues? Why?

- What lingering concerns do you have about the standards for grades 9-12, and how will you deal with them?

Part Three:
Additional Resources

These Desserts provide sweet resources, including recommended reading and the K-12 Selected Language CCS Tracker, which will enable you to identify where your students actually are so that you can target their needs and push them forward. This part also includes sample overviews of weekly ELA routines and a sample week of lesson plans to illustrate "how to fit everything in" with a mini-unit on poetry analysis and paragraph writing. Last but definitely not least, you'll find out how to access free bonus content and a free 30-day trial to The Literacy Cookbook (TLC) Website, www.literacycookbook.com, which includes all of the files referenced in this book plus hundreds and hundreds more.

chapter
NINE

Recommended Reading

FOUNDATIONAL TEXTS

This book leans heavily on three resources in particular, so even though I have cited them throughout, I want to acknowledge my gratitude again here. No matter what you teach, you will want these books on your desk:

- Diana Hacker and Nancy Sommers, *Rules for Writers* (Boston: Bedford/St. Martin's, 2016, 8th edition).

- Doug Lemov, *Teach Like a Champion 2.0: 62 Techniques That Put Students on the Path to College* (San Francisco: Jossey-Bass, 2015).

- Anders Ericsson and Robert Pool, *Peak: Secrets from the New Science of Expertise* (Boston: Houghton Mifflin Harcourt, 2016).

Three others also inspired me, largely because of their focus on how to build good sentences:

- Jeff Anderson, *Mechanically Inclined: Building Grammar, Usage, and Style into Writer's Workshop* (Portland, ME: Stenhouse Publishers, 2005).

- Gerald Graff and Cathy Birkenstein, *They Say/I Say: The Moves That Matter in Academic Writing* (New York: W.W. Norton, 2010, 2nd edition).

- Judith C. Hochman and Natalie Wexler, *The Writing Revolution: A Guide to Advancing Thinking Through Writing in All Subjects and Grades* (San Francisco: Jossey-Bass, 2017).

OTHER GRAMMAR BOOKS OF INTEREST

If you are a grammar/sentence-writing junkie, consider these, too:

- Lynne Dorfman and Diane Dougherty, *Grammar Matters: Lessons, Tips, and Conversation Using Mentor Texts, K-6* (Portsmouth, ME: Stenhouse Publishers, 2014).

- Stanley Fish, *How to Write a Sentence and How to Read One* (New York: HarperCollins, 2011).

- Harry Noden, *Image Grammar: Using Grammatical Structures to Teach Writing* (Portsmouth, NH: Heinemann, 1999).

- Bruce Saddler, *The Teacher's Guide to Effective Sentence Writing* (New York: The Guilford Press, 2012).

- Virginia Tufte, *Artful Sentences: Syntax as Style* (Cheshire, CT: Graphics Press LLC, 2017, 4th printing).

- Constance Weaver, *Teaching Grammar in Context* (Portsmouth, NH: Boynton/Cook, 1996), 134-135.

- Constance Weaver and Jonathan Bush, *Grammar to Enrich and Enhance Writing* (Portsmouth, NH: Heinemann, 2008).

WHERE TO FIND MENTOR TEXTS FOR STUDENTS

There are probably a million places to find excellent mentor texts. Here are just a few:

- Lynne Dorfman and Diane Dougherty, *Grammar Matters: Lessons, Tips, and Conversation Using Mentor Texts, K-6* (Portsmouth, ME: Stenhouse Publishers, 2014). See pp. 261-264 for "A Treasure Chest of Children's Books for Teaching Grammar and Conventions" with an annotated list of resources.

- Virginia Tufte, *Artful Sentences: Syntax as Style* (Cheshire, CT: Graphics Press LLC, 2017, 4th printing). This book contains more than a thousand excellent sentences chosen from the works of authors in the twentieth and twenty-first centuries.

- Longtime educator Mary Ann Reilly writes a blog that offers numerous posts with excellent book lists—a full-throttle fire hose of book lists, really—here: http://maryannreilly.blogspot.com/search?q=book+list

chapter
TEN

Appendix

K-12 SELECTED LANGUAGE CCS TRACKER

	KINDERGARTEN							
L.K.1	Demonstrate command of the conventions of standard English grammar and usage when writing or speaking.							
L.K.1a	Print many upper- and lowercase letters.							
L.K.1b	Use frequently occurring nouns and verbs.							
L.K.1c	Form regular plural nouns orally by adding /s/ or /es/ (e.g., dog, dogs; wish, wishes).							
L.K.1d	Understand and use question words (interrogatives) (e.g., who, what, where, when, why, how).							

L.K.1e	Use the most frequently occurring prepositions (e.g., to, from, in, out, on, off, for, of, by, with).							
L.K.1f	Produce and expand complete sentences in shared language activities.							
L.K.2	**Demonstrate command of the conventions of standard English capitalization, punctuation, and spelling when writing.**							
L.K.2a	Capitalize the first word in a sentence and the pronoun I.							
L.K.2b	Recognize and name end punctuation.							
L.K.2c	Write a letter or letters for most consonant and short-vowel sounds (phonemes).							
L.K.2d	Spell simple words phonetically, drawing on knowledge of sound-letter relationships.							
	GRADE 1							
L.1.1	Demonstrate command of the conventions of standard English grammar and usage when writing or speaking.							
L.1.1a	Print all upper- and lowercase letters.							
L.1.1b	Use common, proper, and possessive nouns.							
L.1.1c	Use singular and plural nouns with matching verbs in basic sentences (e.g., He hops; We hop).							
L.1.1d	Use personal, possessive, and indefinite pronouns (e.g., I, me, my; they, them, their; anyone, everything).							
L.1.1e	Use verbs to convey a sense of past, present, and future (e.g., Yesterday I walked home; Today I walk home; Tomorrow I will walk home).							

L.1.1f	Use frequently occurring adjectives.						
L.1.1g	Use frequently occurring conjunctions (e.g., and, but, or, so, because).						
L.1.1h	Use determiners (e.g., articles, demonstratives).						
L.1.1i	Use frequently occurring prepositions (e.g., during, beyond, toward).						
L.1.1j	Produce and expand complete simple and compound declarative, interrogative, imperative, and exclamatory sentences in response to prompts.						
L.1.2	**Demonstrate command of the conventions of standard English capitalization, punctuation, and spelling when writing.**						
L.1.2a	Capitalize dates and names of people.						
L.1.2b	Use end punctuation for sentences.						
L.1.2c	Use commas in dates and to separate single words in a series.						
L.1.2d	Use conventional spelling for words with common spelling patterns and for frequently occurring irregular words.						
L.1.2e	Spell untaught words phonetically, drawing on phonemic awareness and spelling conventions.						
	GRADE 2						
L.2.1	**Demonstrate command of the conventions of standard English grammar and usage when writing or speaking.**						
L.2.1a	Use collective nouns (e.g., group).						
L.2.1b	Form and use frequently occurring irregular plural nouns (e.g., feet, children, teeth, mice, fish).						

L.2.1c	Use reflexive pronouns (e.g., myself, ourselves).							
L.2.1d	Form and use the past tense of frequently occurring irregular verbs (e.g., sat, hid, told).							
L.2.1e	Use adjectives and adverbs, and choose between them depending on what is to be modified.							
L.2.1f	Produce, expand, and rearrange complete simple and compound sentences (e.g., The boy watched the movie; The little boy watched the movie; The action movie was watched by the little boy).							
L.2.2	**Demonstrate command of the conventions of standard English capitalization, punctuation, and spelling when writing.**							
L.2.2a	Capitalize holidays, product names, and geographic names.							
L.2.2b	Use commas in greetings and closings of letters.							
L.2.2c	Use an apostrophe to form contractions and frequently occurring possessives.							
L.2.2d	Generalize learned spelling patterns when writing words (e.g., cage → badge; boy → boil).							
L.2.2e	Consult reference materials, including beginning dictionaries, as needed to check and correct spellings.							
L.2.3	**Use knowledge of language and its conventions when writing, speaking, reading, or listening.**							
L.2.3a	Compare formal and informal uses of English.							
	GRADE 3							
L.3.1	**Demonstrate command of the conventions of standard English grammar and usage when writing or speaking.**							

L.3.1a	Explain the function of nouns, pronouns, verbs, adjectives, and adverbs in general and their functions in particular sentences.						
L.3.1b	Form and use regular and irregular plural nouns.						
L.3.1c	Use abstract nouns (e.g., childhood).						
L.3.1d	Form and use regular and irregular verbs.						
L.3.1e	Form and use the simple (e.g., I walked; I walk; I will walk) verb tenses.						
L.3.1f	Ensure subject-verb and pronoun-antecedent agreement.						
L.3.1g	Form and use comparative and superlative adjectives and adverbs, and choose between them depending on what is to be modified.						
L.3.1h	Use coordinating and subordinating conjunctions.						
L.3.1i	Produce simple, compound, and complex sentences.						
L.3.2	**Demonstrate command of the conventions of standard English capitalization, punctuation, and spelling when writing.**						
L.3.2a	Capitalize appropriate words in titles.						
L.3.2b	Use commas in addresses.						
L.3.2c	Use commas and quotation marks in dialogue.						
L.3.2d	Form and use possessives.						
L.3.2e	Use conventional spelling for high-frequency and other studied words and for adding suffixes to base words (e.g., sitting, smiled, cries, happiness).						

L.3.2f	Use spelling patterns and generalizations (e.g., word families, position-based spellings, syllable patterns, ending rules, meaningful word parts) in writing words.							
L.3.2g	Consult reference materials, including beginning dictionaries, as needed to check and correct spellings.							
L.3.3	**Use knowledge of language and its conventions when writing, speaking, reading, or listening.**							
L.3.3a	Choose words and phrases for effect.							
L.3.3b	Recognize and observe differences between the conventions of spoken and written standard English.							
	GRADE 4							
L.4.1	**Demonstrate command of the conventions of standard English grammar and usage when writing or speaking.**							
L.4.1a	Use relative pronouns (who, whose, whom, which, that) and relative adverbs (where, when, why).							
L.4.1b	Form and use the progressive (e.g., I was walking; I am walking; I will be walking) verb tenses.							
L.4.1c	Use modal auxiliaries (e.g., can, may, must) to convey various conditions.							
L.4.1d	Order adjectives within sentences according to conventional patterns (e.g., a small red bag rather than a red small bag).							
L.4.1e	Form and use prepositional phrases.							
L.4.1f	Produce complete sentences, recognizing and correcting inappropriate fragments and run-ons.							

L.4.1g	Correctly use frequently confused words (e.g., to, too, two; there, their).							
L.4.2	**Demonstrate command of the conventions of standard English capitalization, punctuation, and spelling when writing.**							
L.4.2a	Use correct capitalization.							
L.4.2b	Use commas and quotation marks to mark direct speech and quotations from a text.							
L.4.2c	Use a comma before a coordinating conjunction in a compound sentence.							
L.4.2d	Spell grade-appropriate words correctly, consulting references as needed.							
L.4.3	**Use knowledge of language and its conventions when writing, speaking, reading, or listening.**							
L.4.3a	Choose words and phrases to convey ideas precisely.							
L.4.3b	Choose punctuation for effect.							
L.4.3c	Differentiate between contexts that call for formal English (e.g., presenting ideas) and situations where informal discourse is appropriate (e.g., small-group discussion).							
	GRADE 5							
L.5.1	**Demonstrate command of the conventions of standard English grammar and usage when writing or speaking.**							
L.5.1a	Explain the function of conjunctions, prepositions, and interjections in general and their function in particular sentences.							

L.5.1b	Form and use the perfect (e.g., I had walked; I have walked; I will have walked) verb tenses.						
L.5.1c	Use verb tense to convey various times, sequences, states, and conditions.						
L.5.1d	Recognize and correct inappropriate shifts in verb tense.						
L.5.1e	Use correlative conjunctions (e.g., either/or, neither/nor).						
L.5.2	**Demonstrate command of the conventions of standard English capitalization, punctuation, and spelling when writing.**						
L.5.2a	Use punctuation to separate items in a series.						
L.5.2b	Use a comma to separate an introductory element from the rest of the sentence.						
L.5.2c	Use a comma to set off the words yes and no (e.g., Yes, thank you), to set off a tag question from the rest of the sentence (e.g., It's true, isn't it?), and to indicate direct address (e.g., Is that you, Steve?).						
L.5.2d	Use underlining, quotation marks, or italics to indicate titles of works.						
L.5.2e	Spell grade-appropriate words correctly, consulting references as needed.						
L.5.3	**Use knowledge of language and its conventions when writing, speaking, reading, or listening.**						
L.5.3a	Expand, combine, and reduce sentences for meaning, reader/listener interest, and style.						
L.5.3b	Compare and contrast the varieties of English (e.g., dialects, registers) used in stories, dramas, or poems.						

	GRADE 6							
L.6.1	**Demonstrate command of the conventions of standard English grammar and usage when writing or speaking.**							
L.6.1a	Ensure that pronouns are in the proper case (subjective, objective, possessive).							
L.6.1b	Use intensive pronouns (e.g., myself, ourselves).							
L.6.1c	Recognize and correct inappropriate shifts in pronoun number and person.							
L.6.1d	Recognize and correct vague pronouns (i.e., ones with unclear or ambiguous antecedents).							
L.6.1e	Recognize variations from standard English in their own and others' writing and speaking, and identify and use strategies to improve expression in conventional language.							
L.6.2	**Demonstrate command of the conventions of standard English capitalization, punctuation, and spelling when writing.**							
L.6.2a	Use punctuation (commas, parentheses, dashes) to set off nonrestrictive/parenthetical elements.							
L.6.2b	Spell correctly.							
L.6.3	**Use knowledge of language and its conventions when writing, speaking, reading, or listening.**							
L.6.3a	Vary sentence patterns for meaning, reader/listener interest, and style.							
L.6.3b	Maintain consistency in style and tone.							
	GRADE 7							

L.7.1	**Demonstrate command of the conventions of standard English grammar and usage when writing or speaking.**							
L.7.1a	Explain the function of phrases and clauses in general and their function in specific sentences.							
L.7.1b	Choose among simple, compound, complex, and compound-complex sentences to signal differing relationships among ideas.							
L.7.1c	Place phrases and clauses within a sentence, recognizing and correcting misplaced and dangling modifiers.							
L.7.2	**Demonstrate command of the conventions of standard English capitalization, punctuation, and spelling when writing.**							
L.7.2a	Use a comma to separate coordinate adjectives (e.g., It was a fascinating, enjoyable movie but not He wore an old[,] green shirt).							
L.7.2b	Spell correctly.							
L.7.3	**Use knowledge of language and its conventions when writing, speaking, reading, or listening.**							
L.7.3a	Choose language that expresses ideas precisely and concisely, recognizing and eliminating wordiness and redundancy.							
	GRADE 8							
L.8.1	**Demonstrate command of the conventions of standard English grammar and usage when writing or speaking.**							
L.8.1a	Explain the function of verbals (gerunds, participles, infinitives) in general and their function in particular sentences.							
L.8.1b	Form and use verbs in the active and passive voice.							

L.8.1c	Form and use verbs in the indicative, imperative, interrogative, conditional, and subjunctive mood.						
L.8.1d	Recognize and correct inappropriate shifts in verb voice and mood.						
L.8.2	**Demonstrate command of the conventions of standard English capitalization, punctuation, and spelling when writing.**						
L.8.2a	Use punctuation (comma, ellipsis, dash) to indicate a pause or break.						
L.8.2b	Use an ellipsis to indicate an omission.						
L.8.2c	Spell correctly.						
L.8.3	**Use knowledge of language and its conventions when writing, speaking, reading, or listening.**						
L.8.3a	Use verbs in the active and passive voice and in the conditional and subjunctive mood to achieve particular effects (e.g., emphasizing the actor or the action; expressing uncertainty or describing a state contrary to fact).						
	GRADES 9-10						
L.9-10.1	**Demonstrate command of the conventions of standard English grammar and usage when writing or speaking.**						
L.9-10.1a	Use parallel structure.						
L.9-10.1b	Use various types of phrases (noun, verb, adjectival, adverbial, participial, prepositional, absolute) and clauses (independent, dependent; noun, relative, adverbial) to convey specific meanings and add variety and interest to writing or presentations.						

L.9-10.2	Demonstrate command of the conventions of standard English capitalization, punctuation, and spelling when writing.						
L.9-10.2a	Use a semicolon (and perhaps a conjunctive adverb) to link two or more closely related independent clauses.						
L.9-10.2b	Use a colon to introduce a list or quotation.						
L.9-10.2c	Spell correctly.						
L.9-10.3	Apply knowledge of language to understand how language functions in different contexts, to make effective choices for meaning or style, and to comprehend more fully when reading or listening.						
L.9-10.3a	Write and edit work so that it conforms to the guidelines in a style manual (e.g., MLA Handbook, Turabian's Manual for Writers) appropriate for the discipline and writing type.						
	GRADES 11-12						
L.11-12.1	Demonstrate command of the conventions of standard English grammar and usage when writing or speaking.						
L.11-12.1a	Apply the understanding that usage is a matter of convention, can change over time, and is sometimes contested.						
L.11-12.1b	Resolve issues of complex or contested usage, consulting references (e.g., Merriam-Webster's Dictionary of English Usage, Garner's Modern American Usage) as needed.						
L.11-12.2	Demonstrate command of the conventions of standard English capitalization, punctuation, and spelling when writing.						

L.11-12.2a	Observe hyphenation conventions.							
L.11-12.2b	Spell correctly.							
L.11-12.3	**Apply knowledge of language to understand how language functions in different contexts, to make effective choices for meaning or style, and to comprehend more fully when reading or listening.**							
L.11-12.3a	Vary syntax for effect, consulting references (e.g., Tufte's Artful Sentences) for guidance as needed; apply an understanding of syntax to the study of complex texts when reading.							

SAMPLE OVERVIEWS OF WEEKLY ELA ROUTINES

Before you write detailed lesson plans, it helps to create a 35,000-foot overview that captures your weekly routines. Over the course of the year, depending on the genre(s) you're focusing on, you might revise these routines.

Following are several sample overviews that map out ways to integrate whole-class vocabulary, reading, and grammar/writing work with different genres—shifting the focus of the work accordingly.[200] These generic overviews can obviously be modified based on the grade level(s) you teach, and they assume you have at least 45 minutes of ELA instruction per day. If you have more time, great. If you have less, you might need to adjust your plans. Or change your schedule.

Regarding Do Nows, the assumption is that students will spend 3-5 minutes (max) doing the work, then another 3-5 minutes going over it (so: 8-10 minutes total).

An Exit Ticket may take more than 5 minutes (e.g., a paragraph that students begin writing during the Class Focus time might require 10-15 minutes); in that case, the Exit Ticket row is more a reflection of what you intend to collect.

Regarding homework (HW), I recommend including independent reading (IR) on top of whatever else you require. It never hurts to remind students to read.

PS: Please note these are rough outlines for a five-day cycle. Day 1 doesn't have to be Monday. And if you're on a six-day cycle, simply add a column.

---

200 The "Sample Overviews of Weekly ELA Routines" can also be downloaded from the TLC "Using Grammar to Improve Writing" page found at https://www.literacycookbook.com/page.php?id=161.

Option 1: Poetry Analysis and Writing

	DAY 1	DAY 2	DAY 3	DAY 4	DAY 5
Do Now (8-10)	Intro 1st 4 new VOCAB words	Wordplay for 1st 4 VOCAB words	Intro 2nd 4 new VOCAB words	Wordplay for 2nd 4 VOCAB words	Quiz on all 8 VOCAB words
Class Focus (30)	CLOSE-READ a poem.	Intro GRAMMAR points relevant to yesterday's writing.	Show Call paragraphs. (5) GRAMMAR point→ Revision. (5) POETRY reading. (20)	CLOSE-READ a poem.	Show Call paragraphs. (5) Pairs/trios CLOSE READ a poem. (25)
Exit Ticket (5)	WRITE a paragraph analyzing the poem.	Use these GRAMMAR points to REVISE yesterday's writing.	Complete "Speed Dating with a Poem."	WRITE a paragraph analyzing the poem.	WRITE a paragraph analyzing the poem.
HW	Wordplay for 1st 4 vocab words; IR	Wordplay for 1st 4 vocab words; IR	Wordplay for 2nd 4 vocab words; Revise paragraph again.	Wordplay for all 8 vocab words; IR	Complete Exit Ticket if class time did not permit it.

Option 2: Narrative Reading and Writing

	DAY 1	DAY 2	DAY 3	DAY 4	DAY 5
Do Now (8-10)	Intro 1st 4 new VOCAB words	Wordplay for 1st 4 VOCAB words	Intro 2nd 4 new VOCAB words	Wordplay for 2nd 4 VOCAB words	Quiz on all 8 VOCAB words
Class Focus (30)	CLOSE-READ a story.	Intro GRAMMAR points relevant to narrative writing.	Show Call narrative writing. (5) GRAMMAR point→ Revision. (5) PARTNER READ a story. (20)	CLOSE-READ a narrative.	Show Call writing. REVISE yesterday's writing.
Exit Ticket (5)	WRITE: Practice some aspect of narrative writing OR write about today's story.	Use these GRAMMAR points to write a narrative.	Complete DDAT organizer re: character analysis.	WRITE: Practice some aspect of narrative writing OR write about today's story.	REVISE yesterday's writing.
HW	Wordplay for 1st 4 vocab words; IR	Wordplay for 1st 4 vocab words; IR	Wordplay for 2nd 4 vocab words; Revise yesterday's narrative.	Wordplay for all 8 vocab words; IR	Complete Exit Ticket if class time did not permit it.

Option 3: Novel Study

	DAY 1	DAY 2	DAY 3	DAY 4	DAY 5
Do Now (8-10)	Intro 1st 4 new VOCAB words	Wordplay for 1st 4 VOCAB words	Intro 2nd 4 new VOCAB words	Wordplay for 2nd 4 VOCAB words	Quiz on all 8 VOCAB words
Class Focus (30)	CLOSE-READ a section of the novel.	Intro GRAMMAR points relevant to yesterday's writing.	Show Call para-graphs. (5) GRAMMAR point→ Revision. (5) PARTNER READING of a chapter. (20)	CLOSE-READ a section of the novel.	Show Call para-graphs. (5) SOCRATIC SEMINARS about the novel. (25)
Exit Ticket (5)	WRITE a paragraph analyzing the section or character.	Use these GRAMMAR points to REVISE yesterday's writing.	Complete "What's Important" organizer for the chapter.	WRITE a paragraph analyzing the section or character.	QUICK-WRITE in response to issue(s) raised during SOCRATIC SEMINARS.
HW	Wordplay for 1st 4 vocab words; read more of the novel.˙	Wordplay for 1st 4 vocab words; read more of the novel.	Wordplay for 2nd 4 vocab words; revise para-graph again.	Wordplay for all 8 vocab words; read more of the novel.	Read a chapter and complete "What's Important" organizer for the chapter.

*See footnote[201]

---

201 For tools to support students reading novels, see TLC "Analyzing Literature" page found at https://www.literacycookbook.com/page.php?id=2.

Option 4: Nonfiction Reading and Writing

	DAY 1	DAY 2	DAY 3	DAY 4	DAY 5
Do Now (8-10)	Intro 1st 4 new VOCAB words	Wordplay for 1st 4 VOCAB words	Intro 2nd 4 new VOCAB words	Wordplay for 2nd 4 VOCAB words	Quiz on all 8 VOCAB words
Class Focus (30)	QUADRANT ANALYSIS* of an image on a topic we'll read about.	Intro GRAMMAR points relevant to yesterday's writing. (15) READ TEXT about the topic from yesterday. (15)	Show Call writing. (5) GRAMMAR point→ Revision. (5) PARTNER READ ANOTHER TEXT on related content. (20)	CLOSE-READ ANOTHER TEXT on related content.	Show Call paragraphs. (5) SOCRATIC SEMINARS about the readings from the week. (25)
Exit Ticket (5)	WRITE a sentence or paragraph that explains what message(s) the image is trying to convey.	Use these GRAMMAR points to REVISE OR EXPAND yesterday's writing.	QUICK-WRITE an argument about today's text.	WRITE a paragraph making an argument about today's text.	QUICK-WRITE in response to issue(s) raised during SOCRATIC SEMINARS.
HW	Wordplay for 1st 4 vocab words; IR	Wordplay for 1st 4 vocab words; IR	Wordplay for 2nd 4 vocab words; IR	Wordplay for all 8 vocab words; IR	Complete Exit Ticket if class time did not permit it.

*See footnote[202]

202 See TLC Blog post on Quadrant Analysis found at https://theliteracycookbook.wordpress.com/2013/02/06/approaches-to-the-common-core-quadrant-analysis-as-a-way-to-boost-comprehension/

SAMPLE WEEK OF LESSON PLANS: POETRY ANALYSIS AND PARAGRAPH WRITING

Following is a sample week of lesson plans focused on poetry analysis and paragraph writing.[203] While these plans tackle standards from grades 3, 5, and 6, you can use them in grades 3 and up with some modifications. (It's not illegal to address standards from higher grades!) Here are some Websites that should come in handy:

- **For elementary,** check out "28 Must-Share Poems for Elementary" posted by Stacey Tornio on *We Are Teachers*, March 25, 2016, found at
- https://www.weareteachers.com/28-must-share-poems-for-elementary-school/
- **For middle and high school,** check out "24 Must-Share Poems for Middle and High School" posted by Samantha Cleaver on *We Are Teachers*, November 17, 2015, found at
- https://www.weareteachers.com/24-must-share-poems-for-middle-school-and-high-school/
- **For additional resources on poetry and literary analysis,** check out the TLC "Analyzing Literature" page at https://www.literacycookbook.com/page.php?id=2

---

203 The "Sample Week of Lesson Plans: Poetry Analysis and Paragraph Writing" can also be downloaded from the TLC "Using Grammar to Improve Writing" page found at https://www.literacycookbook.com/page.php?id=161. The questioning-the-text approach outlined in these plans is found in Sarah Tantillo, *Literacy and the Common Core: Recipes for Action* (San Francisco: Jossey-Bass, 2014), 124-125.

MONDAY

OBJECTIVES: *SWBAT...*

- Use context clues in order to infer the meaning of vocabulary words.
- Analyze a poem using a questioning-the-text approach in order to explain what the poem means.

MATERIALS:	STANDARDS:
<ul><li>Do Now: "Vocabulary Hypothesis Sheet" for first 4 words (See sample following these plans.)</li><li>Poem 1 (See resource links above and select a poem of your choice.)</li><li>HW: Vocabulary wordplay handout (for first 4 words)</li></ul>	**Reading Anchor Standard #4:** *Interpret words and phrases as they are used in a text, including determining technical, connotative, and figurative meanings, and analyze how specific word choices shape meaning or tone.* **Writing Anchor Standard #9:** *Draw evidence from literary or informational texts to support analysis, reflection, and research.*

DO NOW (~ 4 mins. to do, 4 to discuss):

Students complete "hypothesis sheet" for 4 new vocabulary words.

Discuss their hypotheses and derive a student-friendly definition for each word.

Our goal today is to use a questioning-the-text strategy that will enable us to analyze a poem and really figure it out. You can use this strategy with ANY kind of text, and this week we will use it several times with poems.

Here's how it's going to work. In a moment, we're going to turn over the handout I've given you, and you will see a poem. I'm going to read this poem aloud, and as I do, **you should read along silently and write a "?" every time you have a question.**

[The goal is to ask questions that, if answered, would help them understand the text as fully as possible. **Before you start, give examples of the different kinds of questions you might expect.** The questions can be as concrete as "What does this word mean?" or as abstract as, "Why would someone behave that way?" Note: Students should *not* record whole questions at this point, only question marks, because as they go they may find their questions answered (and plus, we want them to read along, not get distracted by writing questions in full).]

Read the poem aloud.

1. **Students re-read the passage, this time writing their questions in full.** Be sure to give them ample time and circulate to see if any vocabulary gaps are preventing them from asking more profound questions. If students are struggling with a word essential to literal comprehension of the text, quickly explain that word. A little bit of vocabulary support can raise the level of critical thinking for *all* students. Tell students, "Make sure you have at least two 'How' or 'Why' questions." These questions will compel students to build arguments supported with evidence and explanation. Give students a minute or two for Turn-and-Talk to compare their questions.

2. **Solicit *all* of their questions and write them on the board.** Given that they have already recorded their own questions, you could say, "As I record our questions, write down any new ones that you want to add to your list, especially ones you think you might like to discuss," or (to save time), "We will keep this list posted for our next steps." If you notice any lingering questions about key vocabulary, clarify meanings and give students time to add or revise questions because understanding more vocabulary will boost their comprehension and may stimulate new lines of questioning. Then add any new questions to the list.

3. **Direct students to form pairs or trios and identify what they consider to be the three most important questions on the list, then discuss their responses for 2-3 minutes.** Note: Pairs are optimal, trios are OK, and groups of four should *definitely be avoided*. The goal is to engage *every* student in these discussions. Warn students that you will be cold-calling on them to report out on these conversations, so they should jot down a few notes. Also, it's fine not to discuss all three questions if they don't have time; we want them to think deeply, not rush through their discussions.

4. **Go through the poem from top to bottom to find out what they discussed.** One thing you and the students will surely notice is that our natural inclination when discussing questions is to answer them with *evidence from the text*, which is how we build arguments and write effective paragraphs and essays: That's a vital lesson in this exercise. You should also note connections that students made and see if they have any additional questions. Depending on the topic/genre of the text, you could take this in many different directions. It may lead to further reading, research, or writing.

INDEPENDENT PRACTICE – YOU DO (~ 3 mins.):

1. **Ask students to complete this sentence:** *In the poem "Name of Poem," the author tries to convey the message that* _____.
2. **Ask students to reflect (in writing) on the process they just went through:** *What was challenging about what we just did? What did you like about it? What did you learn about the value of* questioning the text? [They should arrive at the insight that good readers ask lots of questions and as a result derive deeper meaning from the texts they read.]
3. **Cold-call on students to share their responses.**

ASSESSMENT/EXIT TICKET (~ 10 mins.):

Turn your argument sentence (In the poem "Name of Poem," the author tries to convey the message that _____.) *into a paragraph with evidence and explanation.*

HOMEWORK:

- Complete vocabulary wordplay handout [e.g., sentence stems; for resources, see TLC "Building Robust Vocabulary" page found at https://www.literacy-cookbook.com/page.php?id=4.]
- Independent reading

NOTES ON DIFFERENTIATION: How will you extend and differentiate your teaching to reach every student in the classroom?

TBD

TUESDAY	
OBJECTIVES: SWBAT...	

- Use context clues in order to infer the meaning of vocabulary words.
- Use subordinating conjunctions and commas properly in order to write complex sentences.

MATERIALS:	STANDARDS:
<ul><li>Hand back paragraphs students wrote about poems yesterday.</li><li>Do Now: Vocabulary wordplay handout (for first 4 words)</li><li>HW: Vocabulary wordplay handout (for first 4 words)</li></ul>	**Reading Anchor Standard #4:** *Interpret words and phrases as they are used in a text, including determining technical, connotative, and figurative meanings, and analyze how specific word choices shape meaning or tone.* L 5.2.b L 5.2.d L 3.1.h

DO NOW (~ 4 mins. to do, 4 to discuss):

Students complete a vocabulary wordplay exercise. [See TLC "Building Robust Vocabulary" page found at https://www.literacycookbook.com/page.php?id=4.]

Discuss their responses to the Do Now and last night's homework.

INTRODUCTION – HOOK/PITCH➜I DO (~ 10 mins.):

When we wrote our paragraphs yesterday, we began with this phrasing:

In the poem "Name of Poem," the author tries to convey the message that _____.

*Teachable Moment: *We put the name of the poem in quotation marks because it's a part of a thing, whereas a book is a whole thing, so a book title would be underlined or italicized. [L 5.2.d]*

It's a small thing, but that comma is really important. Why does it matter? And how can we know when we need one?

Let's look at a couple of sentences. We'll read them out loud and try to figure out when we PAUSE, then see if we can figure out WHY we need a comma.

Show students a few sentences such as the following, but leave the commas out: **When you pause, you need a comma. When you stop, you probably need a period.**

Why does this comma matter? Because it shows us how the sentence works. You can take out the dependent clause (or the prepositional phrase, such as "In the beginning,"), and the sentence will still make sense. Why? Because what's left is the INDEPENDENT clause, which, as we know, is a complete sentence.

Let's break those sentences down to see their parts:

When you pause [dependent], you need a comma [independent].

When you stop [dependent], you probably need a period [independent].

We know how to connect independent clauses with FANBOYS (For, And, Nor, But, Or, Yet, So), so we can write compound sentences like, "I went to the store, but I forgot to buy milk." Today we're going to practice more COMPLEX sentences. To write a complex sentence, you need an AAAWWUBBIS, also known as a **subordinating conjunction.**

"AAAWWUBBIS" =As, Although, After, While, When, Unless, Because, Before, If, Since.

GUIDED PRACTICE – WE DO (~ 15 mins.):

Let's write a practice sentence about [a character in a recent novel] beginning with "Although." Jot a sentence about [that character] that begins with "Although." Actively monitor. Have them compare with a partner, then highlight a few good examples (using Show Call).

*Teachable Moment: *Notice that these sentences we just created are arguments! They could become topic sentences for some nifty paragraphs!*

Give students more sentence practice with other AAAWWUBBIS prompts, and keep having them share out.

Then show them your sample paragraph about a character in a recently read novel that includes several sentences that include AAAWWUBBIS conjunctions but have failed to insert commas properly.

[Create your own paragraph and insert it here.]

Let's read this together and figure out if the writer inserted commas where needed....

After students have worked through where the commas belong, give them directions for independent practice.

INDEPENDENT PRACTICE – YOU DO (~ 10 mins.):

Take your paragraph from yesterday and rewrite it to include 3 subordinating conjunctions. I will score the paragraph based on two things: 1) All sentences must be complete, and 2) All conjunctions must be used correctly, with proper punctuation.

Staple the revised version ON TOP OF the original.

ASSESSMENT/EXIT TICKET (N/A)

Collect independent practice as the Exit Ticket. Note: Select 2-3 excellent examples to share with the class tomorrow.

HOMEWORK:

- Complete vocabulary wordplay handout [e.g., sentence stems; for resources, see TLC "Building Robust Vocabulary" page found at https://www.literacy-cookbook.com/page.php?id=4.]
- Independent reading

NOTES ON DIFFERENTIATION: How will you extend and differentiate your teaching to reach every student in the classroom?

TBD

WEDNESDAY

OBJECTIVES: *SWBAT...*

- Use context clues in order to infer the meaning of vocabulary words.
- Identify key features of MLA citation format in order to apply it in our own writing.
- Evaluate characteristics of various poems in order to describe features we like or don't like when reading poetry.

MATERIALS:	STANDARDS:
<ul><li>Hand back paragraphs students wrote about poems yesterday.</li><li>Do Now: "Vocabulary Hypothesis Sheet" for second 4 words (See sample following these plans.)</li><li>"AAAWWUBBIS" anchor chart, posted</li><li>MLA citation handout (need to create this)</li><li>6 poems divided into 3 "mini-packets" of pairs A, B, and C with enough copies so that each student can start with one pair (See resource links above and select a poem of your choice.)</li><li>"Speed Dating with a Poem" handout (See sample following these plans.)</li><li>HW: Vocabulary wordplay handout (for second 4 words)</li></ul>	**Reading Anchor Standard #4:** *Interpret words and phrases as they are used in a text, including determining technical, connotative, and figurative meanings, and analyze how specific word choices shape meaning or tone.* L 5.2.b L 5.2.d L 3.1.h RL 6.1

DO NOW (~ 4 mins. to do, 4 to discuss):

Students complete "hypothesis sheet" for 4 new vocabulary words [This assumes you purposefully teach 8 per week, introducing the second 4 mid-week, with a quiz on Friday].

Discuss their hypotheses and derive a student-friendly definition for each word.

INTRODUCTION – HOOK/PITCH→I DO (~ 12 mins.):

Yesterday we wrote sentences and then paragraphs using subordinating conjunctions (see our "AAAWWUBBIS" anchor chart over there), and today I want to highlight some good work that you did, then we're going to kick things up a notch. Because we constantly want to improve our writing.

Use Show Call with several student exemplars to review the comma rule introduced yesterday (L 5.2.b)— inviting students to explain the rule and praising several who followed it.

[Depending on which grade(s) you teach, the next point might be review or a stretch because it deals with a 6th grade standard. You may not need to teach this next bit, but it won't hurt to review it.]

Now, these paragraphs are very solid, so we can build on them. We're going to turn our attention to citation—specifically, how to use MLA (Modern Language Association) format to cite sources. In academic writing, we always cite sources. Why do you think we need to do that? [Solicit responses such as 1) to avoid plagiarism, 2) to be able to find the text out of interest, 3) to give credit to the author.]

Let's look at a sentence in which someone cites a source....

[Spend about 5 minutes analyzing examples of parenthetical citations ON A HANDOUT so that students can infer the rules. Then discuss how to cite lines in a poem: In the first reference, you put "lines 3-5," for example, in parentheses. After that, you only put the numbers.]

GUIDED PRACTICE – WE DO (~ 10 mins.):

Let's apply MLA to one of these example paragraphs [or mine].

Invite students to help incorporate proper citation into a paragraph or two. (5 mins.)

For homework tonight, *in addition to your vocabulary practice, you're going to revise your paragraph one last time to include MLA citation for lines you've referenced. Again, staple the newest version on top. This time I will be grading it strictly for proper citation format.*

Distribute "Speed Dating with a Poem" handout.

Now we're going to dig into some more poetry with a little game called Speed Dating with a Poem. We're doing this because it's a quick way for you to develop a clearer sense of the kind of poetry you like and the kind that maybe you're not into. Not all poetry is the same, as you will see!

Everyone will start out with one of three mini-packets (A, B, or C). You will have three minutes to look over the two poems in your mini-packet, pick one you "want to know better" even if you don't love it, and complete the information for that poem in the row on the "Speed Dating with a Poem" handout.

[Distribute the three mini-packets (A, B, or C) systematically in the room.]

After 3 minutes, you will hand your mini-packet to the person on your left, then we will repeat the process. By the end, you'll have written something about 3 of the 6 poems.

Here we go!

INDEPENDENT PRACTICE – YOU DO (~10 mins.):

Lead students in 3 rounds of "Speed Dating with a Poem," timed at 3 minutes each.

If time permits, survey students about which poems they preferred and why; also discuss what they liked about this process and what was challenging about it.

Let them know we will dig into several of these poems further in the next two days.

ASSESSMENT/EXIT TICKET (~ 1 min.):

Collect the "Speed Dating with a Poem" handout.

HOMEWORK:

- Complete vocabulary wordplay handout [e.g., sentence stems; for resources, see TLC "Building Robust Vocabulary" page found at https://www.literacy-cookbook.com/page.php?id=4.]
- Revise your paragraph one last time to include MLA citation for lines you've referenced. Again, staple the newest version on top. This time I will be grading it strictly for proper citation format.

NOTES ON DIFFERENTIATION: How will you extend and differentiate your teaching to reach every student in the classroom?

TBD

THURSDAY

OBJECTIVES: *SWBAT...*

- Use context clues in order to infer the meaning of vocabulary words.
- Analyze a poem using a questioning-the-text approach in order to explain what the poem means.

MATERIALS:	STANDARDS:
<ul><li>Copies of the poem that most students liked yesterday</li><li>Do Now: Vocabulary wordplay handout (for second 4 words)</li><li>HW: Vocabulary wordplay handout (for all 8 words)</li></ul>	**Reading Anchor Standard #4:** *Interpret words and phrases as they are used in a text, including determining technical, connotative, and figurative meanings, and analyze how specific word choices shape meaning or tone.* **Writing Anchor Standard #9:** *Draw evidence from literary or informational texts to support analysis, reflection, and research.* L 5.2.b L 5.2.d L 3.1.h RL 6.1

DO NOW (~ 4 mins. to do, 4 to discuss):

Students complete a vocabulary wordplay exercise. [See TLC "Building Robust Vocabulary" page found at https://www.literacycookbook.com/page.php?id=4.]

Discuss their responses to the Do Now.

INTRODUCTION – HOOK/PITCH→I DO (~ 2 mins.):

Yesterday, during "Speed Dating with a Poem," most of you seemed to like one particular poem the best. So today we're going to dig into that one together, using the strategy we learned on Monday, questioning the text. As you know, we've been working on writing, too, so today, of course, we're going to end up writing about this poem. I can't wait to see what you come up with!

Hand out the poem.

GUIDED PRACTICE – WE DO (~ 20 mins.):

See Monday's lesson plan. Repeat the strategy.

INDEPENDENT PRACTICE – YOU DO (~ 4 mins.):

1. **Ask students to complete this sentence:** *In the poem "Name of Poem," the author tries to convey the message that _____.*
2. **Invite them to compare responses with a partner.**
3. **Cold-call on students to share their responses.**

ASSESSMENT/EXIT TICKET (~ 10 mins.):

Turn your argument sentence (In the poem "Name of Poem," the author tries to convey the message that _____.) *into a paragraph with evidence and explanation.*

HOMEWORK:

- Complete vocabulary wordplay handout for ALL 8 words to prepare for quiz tomorrow [e.g., sentence stems; for resources, see TLC "Building Robust Vocabulary" page found at https://www.literacycookbook.com/page.php?id=4.]
- Independent reading

NOTES ON DIFFERENTIATION: How will you extend and differentiate your teaching to reach every student in the classroom?

TBD

FRIDAY

OBJECTIVES: *SWBAT...*

- Use context clues in order to infer the meaning of vocabulary words.
- Analyze a poem using a questioning-the-text approach in order to explain what the poem means.

MATERIALS:	STANDARDS:
<ul><li>Vocabulary Quiz on 8 words.</li><li>Copies of 5 poems remaining from "Speed Dating with a Poem"</li></ul>	**Reading Anchor Standard #4:** *Interpret words and phrases as they are used in a text, including determining technical, connotative, and figurative meanings, and analyze how specific word choices shape meaning or tone.* **Writing Anchor Standard #9:** *Draw evidence from literary or informational texts to support analysis, reflection, and research.* L 5.2.b L 5.2.d L 3.1.h RL 6.1

DO NOW (~ 8 mins.):

Complete Vocabulary Quiz on 8 words.

INTRODUCTION – HOOK/PITCH→I DO (~10 mins.):

I want to begin with shout-outs to a couple of students who did an exemplary job on yesterday's poetry analysis. Let's take a look at what they wrote.

Use Show Call to highlight 2 exemplary paragraphs. Invite other students to explain what they like about particular sentences and how these students successfully applied things we learned this week such as comma rules and MLA citation format. (5 mins.)

OK, today we're going to dive into one more poem, except this time you get to choose which one you want to analyze, and you will work with just two other people to do this.

Remind students which of the remaining 5 poems they can choose from. Quickly survey students for their preferences and distribute copies of the poems, then arrange students into pairs or trios. (5 mins.)

GUIDED PRACTICE – WE DO (~27 mins.):

I'm going to make periodic announcements about what your team should be doing. First thing: Select someone to be the facilitator. This person will read the poem out loud, then solicit everyone's questions. Please note: This person should also write his/her own questions, too. You have the next 7 minutes to read your poem aloud and record individual questions. (7 mins.)

OK, now the facilitator should take the next 4 minutes to solicit everyone's questions. (4 mins.) Note: After the timer goes off, if they need more time, give them 1-2 more minutes.

Now as a whole team, you should select three questions to discuss. I will give everyone 90 seconds to do this. (90 sec.)

OK, now you all have 8 minutes to discuss your questions as a whole team. (8 mins.)

OK, now you all have 3 minutes to finish this sentence: In the poem "Name of Poem," the author tries to convey the message that _____. (3 mins.)

Since some of the groups will be analyzing the same poem, it may help to solicit responses from the entire class. (3 mins.)

INDEPENDENT PRACTICE – YOU DO (~ ? mins.):

If time permits, students can begin writing the rest of their paragraph. Otherwise, it can be finished for homework.

ASSESSMENT/EXIT TICKET (~ ? mins.):

See note above.

HOMEWORK:

- *Turn your argument sentence* (In the poem "Name of Poem," the author tries to convey the message that _____.) *into a paragraph with evidence and explanation.* Staple your poem with questions and notes underneath your paragraph.
- Independent reading

NOTES ON DIFFERENTIATION: How will you extend and differentiate your teaching to reach every student in the classroom?

TBD

Sample Vocabulary Hypothesis Sheet[204]

Vocabulary words: entwine, beckon, silhouette, fragment

DIRECTIONS: Use the context clues to infer the meanings of the bolded vocabulary words. <u>Underline any CLUE WORDS</u> that help you form your hypotheses.

VOCABULARY WORDS	CONTEXT	HYPOTHESIS
entwine	If you want to arm-wrestle, you will need to **entwine** your arm with the person you're arm-wrestling with.	
beckon	To **beckon** her dog to return to her, the woman called, "Come here, Snoopy!"	
silhouette	When you stand outside a lit window at night, sometimes you can see the **silhouette** of a person watching TV.	
fragment	When I asked him for a cracker, he gave me only a **fragment**, which was not enough to satisfy my appetite.	

---

204 For additional vocabulary resources to maintain, reinforce, and assess words, see the TLC "Building Robust Vocabulary" page found at https://www.literacycookbook.com/page.php?id=4. See also Sarah Tantillo, *The Literacy Cookbook: A Practical Guide to Effective Reading, Writing, Speaking, and Listening Instruction* (San Francisco: Jossey-Bass, 2012), 28-36.

Speed Dating with a Poem[205]

You have been invited to speed dating… with a poem! The rules are simple. You'll sit across from two poems and will have 3 minutes to go on a "date" with ONE of them. You need to get to know ONE POEM during this brief period. For each speed date round, you will complete the following chart:

TITLE OF POEM	First impression of the poem	Reaction after reading the poem (positive or negative)	Would you like to "get to know this poem"? Why?

---

205 A "landscape" version of this handout can be found on the TLC "Analyzing Literature" page at (https://www.literacycookbook.com/page.php?id=2).

BONUS CONTENT AND HOW TO ACCESS IT

The following documents are accessible for FREE on The Literacy Cookbook Website "Using Grammar to Improve Writing" page found at https://www.literacycookbook.com/page.php?id=161:

Chapter 1

- Essay Writing Rubric

Chapter 2

- Sample Overviews of Weekly ELA Routines
- Sample Week of Lesson Plans: Poetry Analysis and Paragraph Writing

Chapter 3

- Sample Paragraph Responses for *When I Was Puerto Rican*
- Paragraph Response Scoring Checklist
- K-12 Selected Language CCS Tracker
- Trajectory Analysis Charts for Language Standards
- Trajectory Analysis Charts for Writing Standards
- K-12 ELA Common Core Standards Tracker

Chapter 4

- 5Ws and H Organizer Model
- What Is Important Organizer
- What Is Important Organizer Model-*Animal Farm* Ch 2
- Argument vs. Evidence Step 1—*Stone Fox*
- Argument vs. Evidence Step 2 Answer Key—*Stone Fox*
- Argument vs. Evidence Step 2.5 Answer Key
- Combatting Learned Helplessness Tool

Chapter 6

- How to Infer Themes Organizer
- DDAT Organizer
- Order of Cumulative Adjectives Handout

HOW TO USE THE LITERACY COOKBOOK WEBSITE
www.literacycookbook.com

As noted in the previous section, all of the documents mentioned in this book can be found for FREE on The Literacy Cookbook Website "Using Grammar to Improve Writing" page found at https://www.literacy-cookbook.com/page.php?id=161. Note: You do not need to log in to download these documents; just click on the free links.

If you would like to see **even more resources** that may be useful to you, The Literacy Cookbook Website offers hundreds and hundreds of documents that you can download instantly. Nearly all of them are in Word format, so you can modify them easily.

This book comes with a one-time free 30-day trial subscription and 50 percent off annual membership for those who would like to extend their access. New materials are added to the Website constantly!

To begin your one-time free trial membership, go to the TLC "Join" page at https://www.literacycookbook.com/register.php Then sign up (it takes less than a minute!) and enter the following code: TLCFREE (Note: this code is case-sensitive). You will receive immediate e-mail confirmation with your username and password, which will then give you unlimited access to all of the documents in The Download Zone. At the end of your free trial, you will be prompted to extend your subscription to a full year at half-price. Simply click on the prompting link and sign up. You can pay by credit card in less than a minute. If you need to pay via purchase order or check, you'll see directions on how to do that, too.